RACE

Race offers a compelling introduction to the study of ideas related to race throughout history. Its breadth of coverage, both geographically and temporally, provides readers with an expansive, global understanding of the term from the classical period onwards. This concise guide offers an overview of:

- Intersections of Race and Gender
- Race and Social Theory
- Identity, Ethnicity, and Immigration
- Whiteness
- Legislative and Judicial Markings of Difference
- Race in South Africa, Israel, East Asia, Asian America
- Blackness in a Global Context
- Race in the History of Science
- Critical Race Theory

This clear and engaging study is essential reading for students of Literature, Culture, and Race.

Martin Orkin is a Professor at the University of Haifa in Israel, where he teaches in the departments of Theatre and English.

Alexa Alice Joubin is a Professor of English, Theatre, International Affairs, and East Asian Languages and Literatures at George Washington University, USA, where she co-founded the Digital Humanities Institute.

THE NEW CRITICAL IDIOM

SERIES EDITOR: JOHN DRAKAKIS, UNIVERSITY OF STIRLING

The New Critical Idiom is an invaluable series of introductory guides to today's critical terminology. Each book:

- provides a handy, explanatory guide to the use (and abuse) of the term;
- offers an original and distinctive overview by a leading literary and cultural critic;
- relates the term to the larger field of cultural representation.

With a strong emphasis on clarity, lively debate, and the widest possible breadth of examples, *The New Critical Idiom* is an indispensable approach to key topics in literary studies.

Epic by Paul Innes
Grotesque by Justin D Edwards and Rune Graulund
Fairy Tale by Andrew Teverson
Translation by Susan Bassnett
Gothic—second edition by Fred Botting
Narrative—second edition by Paul Cobley
Comedy—second edition by Andrew Stott
Genre—second edition by John Frow
Colonialism/Postcolonialism—third edition by Ania Loomba
Adaptation and Appropriation—second edition by Julie Sanders
The Aphorism and Other Short Forms by Ben Grant
Modernism—third edition by Peter Childs
Reception by Ika Willis
The Sublime—second edition by Philip Shaw
Satire by John T. Gilmore
Race by Martin Orkin with Alexa Alice Joubin

For more information about this series, please visit: www.routledge.com/literature/series/SE0155

RACE

Martin Orkin with Alexa Alice Joubin

Routledge
Taylor & Francis Group

LONDON AND NEW YORK

First published 2019
by Routledge
2 Park Square, Milton Park, Abingdon, Oxon OX14 4RN

and by Routledge
52 Vanderbilt Avenue, New York, NY 10017

Routledge is an imprint of the Taylor & Francis Group, an informa business

British Library Cataloguing-in-Publication Data
A catalogue record for this book is available from the British Library

Library of Congress Cataloging-in-Publication Data
Names: Orkin, Martin, author. | Joubin, Alexa Alice, 1973– author.
Title: Race / Martin Orkin ; with Alexa Alice Joubin.
Description: Abingdon, Oxon ; New York, NY : Routledge, 2019. | Series: The new critical idiom | Includes index.
Identifiers: LCCN 2018043019| ISBN 9781138904682 (hardback : alk. paper) | ISBN 9781138904699 (pbk. : alk. paper) | ISBN 9781317445302 (epub) | ISBN 9781317445296 (mobipocket)
Subjects: LCSH: Race and literature. | Race in literature. | Race discrimination in literature.
Classification: LCC PN56.R16 O75 2019 | DDC 809/.933552–dc23
LC record available at https://lccn.loc.gov/2018043019

ISBN: 978-1-138-90468-2 (hbk)
ISBN: 978-1-138-90469-9 (pbk)
ISBN: 978-1-315-69623-2 (ebk)

Typeset in Times New Roman
by Wearset Ltd, Boldon, Tyne and Wear

Contents

ACKNOWLEDGMENTS

We would like to thank our series editor John Drakakis for his intellectual generosity. His editorial acumen has played a key role in shaping this book. He has made us understand the meaning of professional friendship in deed rather than word. His support remains an inspiration to us.

The scholarly examples evidenced by Jonathan Dollimore, Patricia Parker, Terence Hawkes, Alan Sinfield, Martin Chanock, Ania Loomba, Rey Chow, and Kim Hall have helped us think through thorny questions. Lily Wong and Cord Whitaker have been both intellectually capacious and generous. Conversations with them, as well as reading their cutting-edge works on critical race studies, have been invaluable as this book took shape. Nava Abel has encouraged us to see line and color at whatever we look.

Martin Orkin would like to thank his wife for shouldering the burden of living with someone who must endure the burden of illness. Her strength and courage continually gives him hope. Professor Chloe Orkin's daily messages have kept Martin in good spirits. Moshiko Grif and the Ichilov Hospital Movement Disorders Unit, Sourasky Medical Center, taught Martin how the human body can resist the ravages of Parkinson's Disease.

The co-writing process would not have been possible were it not facilitated with love and care by Joan Orkin, Mickey Orkin, and Basile Joubin across oceans.

We would like to dedicate whatever value this book may have to all those who suffer from racial discrimination and persecution.

Martin Orkin and Alexa Alice Joubin

INTRODUCTION

Race as a concept is often defined in relation to marginalized identities that are seen by members of dominant cultures as other. The project to define or describe race is notoriously complex and slippery. Older attempts to fix race often re-emerge or persist even where they seem to have disappeared or to have been superseded by newer understandings. Formulations of race are also complicated by the apparent symbiotic relation, which projects to identify race appear to have, with racism. Where race is, racism seems in one way or another never far behind. Perhaps this is because the definition of race often entails an identification of difference. The definition itself is an assertion of identity. In such transactions, an impartial conceptualization of race too often appears beyond human capacity.

Moreover, chronology is itself a complicating factor in the study of race. Many of the existing volumes on race trace the changing meanings of the term. But even if later meanings for the term race were not available, for example, in the early modern period, processes structuring pernicious individual or group relations were already under way. Race is one of the markers of identity used to define these relationships. In an age of trade, travel, and incipient colonization, contact with other peoples, as Ania Loomba and Jonathan Burton have argued, "meant that notions of geographic difference were in dialogue with questions of religion, nationality, colour, conversion, women, sexuality, the human body, lineage, diet, and human nature."[1] The eventual outcomes of many such dialogues were not, as the history of colonization shows, always benign.

Will we gain a deeper understanding of the notion of race in our times by analyzing pre-enlightenment texts? There have been debates between "presentism" and "historicism," between the approach that involves reading the past directly from the present perspective that acknowledges the partisan perspective of the enquirer, and the approach to isolate and privilege historical usage of a particular concept such as race without connecting it to the perspective of the enquirer, although this latter position has undergone some revision in recent years. We argue that even though evidence of early modern racial hatred comes under different terminologies, it is still hatred. Reading histories of race enables us to develop a broader perspective involving the identification of the various ways in which similar issues operate by way of different discourses or guises. We should not, therefore, allow the importance of studying racial histories to disappear in thickets of semantic debate about appropriate usage of the words "race" or "white" or "black" or the terminology such as "racial" and "racialist."

Cultural locations past and present affect notions of race. The idea of race informs a multitude of practices, including issues of labor, migration, culture, and even recreation. For example, Daniela Flesler has shown that contemporary Spain, like other Western countries, has experienced a transition in migration patterns from being an exporter of emigrants to being, in the final decades of the twentieth century and beyond, a country for the reception of immigrants.[2] In the case of Spain, Moroccans constitute the second largest national group of resident foreigners. They are the least accepted of immigrant groups in Spain and they have been the main victims of collective violent attacks. Hatred of Moroccan workers, stereotyped as alien attackers or invaders, is complicated by their characterization as "Moors," resonating the "Arab and Berber Muslims [known as 'Moors'] who colonized the Iberian Peninsula in AD 711 and who were responsible for its Arabization and Islamicization in the Middle Ages."[3] Likewise, football (soccer) in the United Kingdom, Russia, and Europe remains frequently embroiled in episodes entailing charges of racism and a struggle for anti-racism.[4] Such incidents of racism in football often reflect, too, even now, Western colonialist ways of imagining race. In a recent study of the proclaimed policy of color-blind casting in certain contemporary British theatre companies, Jami Rogers concludes that "there is still a very real glass ceiling in Shakespeare production, which the multiple and flawed practices of non-traditional or color-blind casting reinforces, perhaps unwittingly."[5] In the USA, strands of cinema or rap music openly challenge and confront present-day North

American modes of racism.[6] In Israel and Palestine, Ashkenazi Israeli remain hostile towards Mizrachi Jews from North African countries, and the Druze communities in Israel have mixed experiences. Recent right-wing Israeli reception of Eritrean and Somali refugees and extremist hatred between Jews and Muslims further exacerbate the situation.[7]

This range of examples suggests that race may be enunciated in multiple, sometimes complex and conflicting ways within particular locations (and in particular texts). At the same time, the terms race and racism are now bearers of particular, ever evolving, denotations precisely as a result of the more extensive analysis and research that has taken place during this period compared with preceding centuries. Some of the ways in which we now think about racism and the word "race" are all relatively newly developed.[8]

Since the project to construct or articulate race has been a fluid and constantly changing endeavor, the introductory part of our book, "Fixing the fetters of race," begins by tracing early attempts to demarcate the origins of the concept of race. These include articulation, prior to the eighteenth century, of cultural notions of barbarism, or religious difference, or the construction of epidermal schemata that have been deployed to denote the physical characteristics of a race. We will then register the imaginings, in the eighteenth and nineteenth centuries, of the scientific and biological underpinnings of race. Further, we will trace state legislation in various regions that sought to enshrine in law in the nineteenth and twentieth centuries, and to naturalize certain constructed categories of race. Lastly, we will seek to register social and political movements, based upon racial hatred, such as fascism, or eruptions of genocide in the twentieth century, that all depend upon entrenched assumptions about race.

The second part of the book, "Recasting the fetters of race," will examine significant examples of the re-writing of the concept of race arising, first, from the impact of slavery, second, from the decisive impact of the phenomena of colonialism and post-colonialism, and, third, from more recent, varied demarcations of one particular manifestation of race: "whiteness."

The third part of the book, "Loosening the fetters of race," will chart newly expanded articulations of race in motion, and the particular consequences of the movement of peoples, thereby initiating a theoretical awareness of the phenomenon of exile that has intensified across the world during the past few decades. We look, first, in Britain, at emergence of what is referred to as the New Racism as well as the shifts in identity formation in the contexts of increasing demographic diversity. Second, and in the larger context of Europe, we examine issues related to immigration. Third, in the particular case of the USA, the importance of the civil rights movement is discussed with attention to the disappointment in the gains it seemed to promise and to the emergence of what is known as critical race theory and arguments that it has generated for ongoing political activism. Fourth, juxtaposed against such dominant theoretical re-thinking of race, we consider aspects of racial histories in East Asia and the USA; fifth, we examine aspects of the Palestine–Israel conflict, and, finally, we turn to aspects of Islam and to non-Islamic responses to its claims and practices. The very terms "race" and "racism" are sometimes in these analyses shown to be limited, and, on occasion, brought into question.

The tensions inherent in racism, as we have already suggested, still seem to emerge and infect many different geographical locations. While questions of race and its afflictions have informed past national, communal, or personal situations, they still persist in the present, sometimes in terrible and violent permutations. In some cases deadly eruptions of racism make it imperative that we maintain and develop a critical focus upon the multiple imagined ways in which issues of race inform and inflect human interaction. The urgent question, in a book concerned with "the new critical idiom" is: in view of the current burgeoning of complex models for reading race and racism, how are we to respond effectively to historically generated discourses of racism that are increasing in intensity in the present? Moreover, how are we now to think about assertions—when these appear in one way or another in any text—that aim to privilege exclusive and exclusionist forms of group identity and the hierarchies of superiority and inferiority that they seek to promulgate? How do we deconstruct the presence of language that generates violently antagonistic stereotypes and hostile responses to individual or group difference?

In considering the various manifestations of race, this book will especially engage with some of the ways in which both the conception of race and the recent analysis of racism may help us to understand past and present-day writings around race.[9] But it is important to emphasize that our aim is never to imply or privilege particular definitions. Articulating the multifaceted and often fluid conceptualizations of race will perhaps always be a task in process. It is our hope, however, that such understandings of the multiple ways in which race has been or is now read, may help to counterbalance the destructive virulence of racisms of all kinds.

Notes

1 Ania Loomba and Jonathan Burton, eds., *Race in Early Modern England: A Documentary Companion*, New York: Palgrave Macmillan, 2007, 3.
2 See Daniela Flesler, *The Return of the Moor: Spanish Responses to Contemporary Moroccan Immigration*, Indiana: Purdue University Press, 2008. We are indebted to her for the information that follows.
3 Flesler, *The Return of the Moor*, 3.
4 See, for example, Jon Garland and Michael Rowe, *Racism and Anti-Racism in Football*, Basingstoke, UK: Palgrave, 2001.
5 See Jami Rogers, "The Shakespearean Glass Ceiling: The State of Color-blind Casting in Contemporary British Theatre," *Shakespeare Bulletin*, 31:3, 2013, 428.
6 See, for example, films such as the controversial *American History X* (1998) dir. Tony Kaye, or popular films such as *Remember the Titans* (2000) dir. Boaz Yakin, starring Denzel Washington. See also a related genre in rap music, for instance.
7 Lisa Hajjar, *Courting Conflict: The Israeli Military Court System in the West Bank and Gaza*, Berkeley: University of California Press, 2005.
8 In the early modern period, race "connote[s] family, class or lineage" (Loomba and Burton, *Race*, 2) or is used "largely to explicate European history and nation formation" (Robert Miles, *Racism*, London: Routledge, 1989, 31). It is only in the late eighteenth century that "the sense of difference in European representations of the Other became interpreted as a difference of 'race', that is, as a primarily [pseudo] *biological* and *natural* difference which was inherent and unalterable" (Loomba and Burton, *Race*, 31). Furthermore the editors of a recent reader containing theories of race and racism note, the

> study of race and "race relations" as important social issues can be traced back to the early part of the twentieth century, at least in relation to the United States of America. It has to be said,

however, that the expansion of research and scholarship in this field is far more recent. It is really in the period since the 1960s, in the aftermath of the social transformations around questions of race that took place during that decade, that we have witnessed a noticeable growth of theorization of race and racism.

(Les Back and John Solomos, eds., *Theories of Race and Racism: A Reader*, Second Edition, London: Routledge, 2009, 5)

The intensification of cultural or literary studies dealing with race, too, largely follows—with some modifications—this trajectory.

9 Our focus on recent critical idiom in the study of race does not imply replacement of, or resolution of, such critical cruces raised by historicist reservation.

PART I

FIXING THE FETTERS OF RACE

1

MARKING BARBARIANS, MUSLIMS, JEWS, ETHIOPIANS, AFRICANS, MOORS, OR BLACKS

This chapter is concerned with early attempts to formulate notions of race. First, it considers classical Greek articulations of identity, read as difference from an Asian, mainly Persian, other. Second, it explores medieval European Christian readings of religious others. Third, it examines early modern European readings of others, based not only on religion but also on different skin pigmentation. Traditional attempts to fathom the beginnings of notions of race also involved attempts to present these phenomena as constitutive or originary. But this strategy has been replaced nowadays with the recognition that ideologies of race, wherever and whenever they occur, are complex and often overlap. This will be evident even in the account that follows, which isolates particular strands for the sake of clarity and for purely analytical purposes.

"Civilization" and "barbarism"

One of the ways in which notions of race have emerged is in early impositions of a binary division between, on the one hand, that which is known, or familiar, deriving from the same culture that is designated as "civilized," and, on the other hand, that which is not understood, or that is hostile deriving from a strange culture that is designated "barbaric." This hostility is often accompanied by both ignorance and intellectual laziness. Take China, for example. On the one hand, due to lack of contact with the outside world, the premodern Chinese court and intelligentsia designated peoples of many ethnicities and cultural origins "black," or *kunlun*. These included the Malayans and other South-East Asians. On the other hand, increased knowledge of cultural others only seemed to have broadened the lump-sum category of blackness for the Chinese consciousness. According to a study by Don J. Wyatt, from the seventh to the seventeenth centuries and through expanded maritime activity, the Chinese came into contact with slaves from Africa (modern-day Somalia, Kenya, Tanzania) who accompanied European expatriates to Asia. This only made the term black more capacious in China, as it now included even Bengali peoples of the Indian subcontinent.[1] Peoples who had not previously been regarded as "black" were now given the label "black." Such a designation, like the word "barbarian" in the West, involved relative description and is sometimes used arbitrarily.

Likewise, the Classical Greek identification of "Persians" is another early example of evolving notions of civilization and barbarism.[2] Etymologically, the word "barbarous" first meant "one who does not speak Greek." Edith Hall has argued influentially that, although there were in ancient Greece a number of Greek communities and ethnic loyalties, a simultaneous heightening of Pan-Hellenic consciousness was partly a result of continuing enmity against the Persians, "which buttressed first the Delian league … and subsequently the Athenium empire … [as a consequence the] image of an enemy extraneous to Hellas helped to foster a sense of community between the allied states."[3]

Hall traces in detail the process whereby the polarization of "Hellene," or Athenian empire, and "barbarian" emerges in fifth century tragedy, and she argues that the opposition between rational Greek and savage barbarian turned, primarily, on political difference:

> The members of the league, by the middle of the century redefined as the Athenian empire, were encouraged to think of themselves not just as the inhabitants of a particular island

> or state, but as Hellenes, as democrats and supporters of
> Athens ... The invention of the barbarian was a response to
> the need for an alliance against Persian expansionism and the
> imposition of pro-Persian tyrants.[4]

The emergence of the concept of the "barbarian" in fifth century
Greek tragedy also coincided with the need to consolidate Athenian
democracy against the specter and the threat of despotism. Not only
did the Persians favor despotic rule, but certain Greek cities were also
ruled by tyrants. The defeat of the Persians, whose tyrants had ruled
Asiatic Greek cities in their domain during the fifth century BC, was
"conceptualized at Athens ... as a triumphant affirmation ... over the
demon of tyranny."[5] Thus the need to foster "Athenian hegemony in
the Aegean"[6] involved not only the isolation of Persians but also other
Greek cities which had fallen under Persian influence. In addition,
other groups, such as the Egyptians, and, to the West, the Thracians,
were also "barbarized."[7] Hall also traces how "barbarians" were conceptualized, in the tragedies, not only in "aspects of civic life—politics, law, speech-making,"[8] but also in terms of domestic and familial
life. In this way theatrical representations of "otherness" reflected particular facets of the process whereby cultural and political differences
could be assimilated into a binary structure in which the key terms,
"civilization" and "barbarism," were defined differentially and incor-
porated into the Greek language.

Of the several points that may be further stressed in Hall's study is
her recognition that "the character traits imputed to other ethnic
groups are usually a simple projection of those considered undesirable
in the culture producing the stereotypes."[9] From the outset she argues
that "Greek writing about barbarians is usually an exercise in self definition, for the barbarian is often portrayed as the opposite of the ideal
Greek."[10] Thus, for example, the "cardinal Hellenic virtues as defined
in fourth-century philosophy ... normally included wisdom or intelligence ... manliness or courage ... discipline or restraint ... and
justice."[11] She observes that Plato lists the vices that are differentiated
from these virtues, such as stupidity, cowardice, abandonment, and
lawlessness. Barbarian types "are often made to manifest one or more
of these vices, thus helping the tragedian to define the nature of Greek
morality."[12] Again, Greek moderation was defined against "different

kinds of extremism, stupidity or excessive cunning, cowardice or bravado, primitivism or luxuriousness."[13]

Furthermore, such mechanisms of projection and self-definition resonate in the process of differentiation, which involved the obscuring of, for example, indigenous Greek violence and cruelty and its projection onto different, alien, or foreign groups. For instance, whereas the distribution of the propensity for violence in Homer's earlier poems is more even-handed and, for example, "desecration of corpses is by no means the prerogative of non-Greeks,"[14] in fifth century tragedy, the conflict with Persia is conceptualized as "a struggle of united and disciplined Greeks against alien violence."[15] "Barbarians"—not merely Persians, but Egyptians, Danaids (Greeks in an alien environment), and Thracians— were represented in tragedy as being wholly without restraint, "invested with an overbearing temper or wild *ethos* … [as well as, sometimes, a] failure to control … sexual desire."[16] Thus, in one of Euripides's tragedies, *Hecuba*, the depiction of an imaginary Thracian king, Polymestor:

> delineates the wild barbarian character at its most uncontrolled; he has crawled out of the tent on all fours, like a "mountain beast", and even threatens to eat the corpses of the women who have punished him (*Hecuba*, 1057–8, 1070–2) … [v]ocabulary suggestive of animal nature or appetites is often used in the characterization of barbarians.[17]

Of course it may be possible to argue that these observations are merely a form of cultural differentiation or xenophobia, rather than evidence of a more sophisticated racism that was to come centuries later. However, Edith Hall notes that: "The Greek term *barbarous*, by the fifth century, used both as a noun and as an adjective, was ironically oriental in origin, and formed by reduplicative onomatopoeia … simply an adjective representing incomprehensible speech."[18]

Similarly, Ali Rattansi notes that the term "barbarian" "simply denoted someone who did not speak Greek, someone who babbled, could only speak 'barbar.'"[19]

There is, at the very least, embedded in such linguistic demarcations a potentially demeaning (racist) inference in the strong implication that Greek is speech whereas other languages are nothing more than incoherent babbling. In the early modern period, this potential becomes more explicit in Shakespeare's *The Tempest*, when Miranda defines Caliban's acquisition of English as an acquisition of the power of speech itself, thus dismissing his own language as the gabbling of a "thing most brutish":

> Abhorred slave,
> Which any print of goodness will not take,
> Being capable of all ill! I pitied thee,
> Took pains to make thee speak, taught thee each hour
> One thing or another. When thou didst not, savage,
> Know thine own meaning, but wouldst gabble like
> A thing most brutish, I endowed thy purposes
> With words that made them known. But thy vile race—
> Though thou didst learn—had that in't which good natures
> Could not abide to be with; therefore wast thou
> Deservedly confined into this rock,
> Who hadst deserved more than a prison.[20]

The image of the "slave," which informs Miranda's address to Caliban points to a further set of ambiguities that resonates in the ancient world. Exclusion from language implies both silence and lack of agency, both of which are elided into more general imaginings of racialized subordinate groups just as exclusion from political process denies a voice to a significant and expanding group within the Athenian polis. As Hall observes,

> the economic basis of the Athenian empire was slavery, and most of the large number of slaves in fifth-century Athens were not Greek ... [thus providing] further stimulus for the generation of arguments which supported the belief that barbarians were generically inferior.[21]

She goes on to observe that "The democratization of the political system in Athens was made possible only by expanding the slave sector, and almost all Athenian slaves were 'barbarians'. 'Free' was becoming synonymous with Hellenic, 'servile' with 'barbarian.'"[22]

In the ancient world, as in ensuing centuries, slavery may well have been taken for granted, but the cruelty inherent in established systems of political order, reduces and renders equivocal all claims to what is implied in definitions of civilization and freedom. And it does so for Miranda's self-admiring comments to Caliban, in a play written and performed in the early seventeenth century. Moreover, to justify herself, she uncannily reiterates the charge, imagined in the ancient world, of inferiority. Caliban's is a "vile race" that has that "which good natures/Could not abide to be with." It is for this reason that she insists that he has "deservedly" been "confined ... more than [in] a prison." The binary of the familiar, read as "civilized," and the foreign, read here as "barbaric," surfaces repeatedly as a strand in attempts to define race often, as in this example, without any necessary connection to, or influence from, the ancient Greek example. Indeed Hall registers, even in the ancient period, Egyptian and Chinese versions of a similar binary.[23] This strategy of representation emerges also as a feature in the representation of different peoples, groups, and eventually nations, at later periods.

Two examples will serve here to illustrate the point. First, the use of the phrase "swart gevaar" ("black danger") that was common during the apartheid period in South Africa and, second, aspects of the behavior of certain groups of spectators, and, on occasion, players, at present-day football matches in parts of Europe and the United Kingdom. The Afrikaans phrase, "swart gevaar" was used by the apartheid government in South Africa primarily to classify skin pigmentation in ways which favored those whom it determined to be "white." This, incidentally, was designed to identify the numerical threat of the groups of disenfranchised people it categorized as "black." However, the phrase attracts an important secondary meaning. First, the word, "swart" ("black") is a generalization that actually applies to several groups of people, speaking different languages, and with differing histories. Indeed, there are now, in post-apartheid South Africa, 11 official languages. Moreover the negative implications associated with the word, "black," in some uses of the color, as "unclear," "inchoate," "menacing," is intensified by its collocation with the word, "gevaar" ("danger"), thereby reinforcing a particular series of wholly negative political meanings.

The phrase, "swart gevaar," became part of the political rhetoric used by the supporters of apartheid to justify white and, by implication, "civilized," minority rule, in the face of the imagined threat from an inchoate and violent, engulfing "barbarism." Furthermore, the phrase lay behind aspects of the apartheid misrepresentation of South African history. For example, the history of the Eastern Cape in Southern Africa during the eighteenth and nineteenth centuries included numerous frontier wars. Over time, these involved settlers, the British and the Dutch or Boers who spoke what would become Afrikaans, and the predominantly Xhosa groups, the Koi and the San. In a segregationist and then apartheid revision, what were a series of struggles amongst several groups over land and livestock became a white minority civilization battling against the dangers posed by a totalized, potentially overwhelming, "black" barbarism.

In the second example, elements of racist abuse in the very different context of present day British and European football games also manifest an occasional surfacing of the civilization versus barbarian binary. In accounting for what they define as white working-class male fan behavior at British matches, Ellis Cashmore and Jamie Cleland advance a number of possible explanations for the behavior of these spectators and, sometimes, even players.[24] These explanations include a "history of fictive kinship,"[25] a structured, normalized fictive "whiteness,"[26] or envy at the skill and wealth of targeted "black" players.[27] The manipulation of the binary during colonialism may also have affected its recurrence during European football matches. In the case of Britain, Cashmore and Cleland cite the experience in the early 1980s of Kenny Mower, a black player for Walsall Football Club in the English West Midlands:

> Mower was a local man and went to school in the area. Every time he stepped on the playing field, there was a swift, brutal reception from the crowd. Violent racist abuse echoed round the stadium when Mower appeared; each time he touched the ball, there was a harsh, discordant mixture of sounds: epithets, boos and animal-like grunts. Fans hurled bananas at him, as visitors to a zoo might feed chimpanzees.[28]

Cashmore and Cleland argue that, although media coverage of such racism fluctuated in subsequent decades amongst certain groups, racism has always been present on such occasions. More recently, factors such as struggling economies, or fears of immigration, may have further encouraged a rise in the press reporting of such behavior in Britain, Europe, and Eastern Europe. The racist behavior of sections of football crowds also involves hooliganism. This hooliganism itself is a manifestation of the animality which such spectators engage in but is also simultaneously displaced onto others. Also, in these cases, and because of the crucial difference of skin pigmentation, hostility may be further generated by an inadvertent counter-identification with an allegedly barbaric other onto whom the spectators' own insecurity is projected. In other words, envy at the success of the other (the player of color) generates an exaggerated compensatory expression of superiority in the spectator that seeks to re-establish a particular social hierarchy. The result is a series of contradictions that an ideology under considerable pressure from the changes in social relationships, is designed to efface.

The imagined differences between the civilized and the barbarous is one of a number of components in the more complex process of the fashioning of race. As Albert Memmi points out, in the second half of the twentieth century, the reading of racial "difference" is itself complicated.[29] He notes that the term has been used, in the course of time, both by conservatives and by progressives. Conservatives, for example, who wished, and still wish, to defend the colonial order, treated the colonized subject as inferior while simultaneously constructing themselves as superior. Progressives, on the other hand, arguing against the notion of difference as signifying inequality, have come down in favor of the concept of a single and equal human nature that transcends time and geographical or cultural location. But emphasizing that difference, in culture, religion, and appearance is inevitable and that "[t]o be is to be different,"[30] Memmi argues that "the real stakes against racism, which must also inform anti-racism, do not concern difference itself but the use of difference as a weapon against its victim, to the advantage of the victimizer."[31] In other words, the issue involves the uneven distribution of power, and the ways in which one group internalizes its own power and exercises it over another. On the matter of difference Memmi concludes: "Differences can exist or not exist. Differences are not in themselves good or bad. One is not racist or anti-racist in pointing out or denying differences, but one is racist in using them against someone to one's own advantage."[32]

Two relatively recent implicit uses of the binary of "civilization" and "barbarism" as a means of reading encounters, between the ancient Romans and other groups serve to reinforce the argument advanced here. The twentieth century poet W.B. Yeats's wonderful poem "Long-legged Fly,"[33] is deeply disturbing, as the first stanza indicates:

That civilization may not sink,
Its great battle lost,
Quiet the dog, tether the pony
To a distant post;
Our master Caesar is in the tent
Where the maps are spread,
His eyes fixed upon nothing,
A hand under his head.
Like a long-legged fly upon the stream
His mind moves upon silence.

The imagery in these lines suggests the beautiful fragility of acts of concentration, intellectual endeavor, and creative order, notwithstanding the fact that the poem goes on to reveal that such acts are masculine, military, and informed by leader-worship, Greco-Roman or classical, European and Western, and, ultimately, by implication, "white."

Against this may be set the example of Howard Brenton's very different reading of the Romans, in his play, *The Romans in Britain*, performed in London in 1980.[34] Brenton's vision concentrates on the ferociously brutal impact that the Romans and, by implication, other Western "civilizations," made upon the peoples and the cultures that they colonized. An envoy warns the local Celts:

There is a Roman Army and it is coming.
It is an army of red leather and brass.
It is a ship.
It is a whole thing. It is a monster. It has machines.
It is Roman.[35]

The inversion in these lines invests the adjective, "Roman," with a mechanized and barbarous violence that underpins the contradiction to the claims it associates with "civilization." It confirms the well-known axiom from Walter Benjamin that every document in civilization is also, at the same time, a document in barbarism ("Es ist niemals ein Dokument der Kultur, ohne zugleich ein solches der Barbarei zu sein").[36]

Marking religious difference: imagined monstrosity, ugliness, and sin

Civilization and barbarism lean heavily for their definitions upon relative physiological and behavioral differences. However, another early emerging marker of race turns on religious binaries. For example, race and ethnicity have been important elements in the development of contemporary U.S. Buddhism. Joseph Cheah has identified traces of Orientalism in the writings of the founding figures of Western Buddhism, such as Brian Houghton.[37] The commonly used terms "ethnic Buddhist" and "convert Buddhist" are problematic concepts. "Ethnic" Buddhist is a term that has been used to describe Buddhists in the USA who are of Asian descent, while "convert" Buddhist refers to Buddhists who are of European ancestry. The two groups have different interpretations of the teachings of Buddhism, with the religion serving as a connection between Asian-Americans and their immigrant parents or grandparents. In this case, their religious identity merges with their ethnic identity.

Another example of how race and religion intertwine is the medieval Christian Church. It imagined threats from Muslims and Jews, who were part of a larger group of those whom the Church considered to be pagan enemies. The totalizing use of terms such as "Muslims," "Islam," or "Jews" is paradoxically as stereotypically reductive, as is, in many respects, the use of the term "medieval European Christianity" itself. To take one of the categories cited above, eleventh century Islam manifested within itself an increasing diversity and complexity: for example there were Turks in the East, Berbers, with very different views from those in the West, and there was also the growth, against Sunnism, of Shi'sm, that came with the revival of the Persian empire and the replacement of the caliphate with the sultanate. Christian imaginings of non-Christian religious groups, however, were not always, for one reason or another, uniformly negative. Thus, what follows, therefore, can offer only a partial picture of the historically more significant medieval Christian fabrications of non-Christian group identities.

In several respects, the construction of the categories of "Muslim" and "Jew" reflects a similar set of assumptions. For example, racial identity is defined here throughout the medieval and early modern periods by climate, or by astrological or humoral factors. It is also believed to be evident in physiognomy, and in suggestions of monstrosity, animality, and abnormality. At the same time, such imagined characteristics carry with them a theological and metaphorical significance in that they denote in one way or another, fantasized demonic agency. Such imaginings about non-Christian group identities are sometimes interwoven with notions of barbarism or wildness. Moreover, Debra Strickland has recently shown that,

> [c]lassical ideas about the structure of the universe, the make-up of the human body, and the nature of the "barbarian" ... were transmitted to medieval Europe either directly or in Latin translations from Greek or Arabic that were widely circulated in the West from the twelfth century onward.[38]

Classical and medieval authorities also held that particular climates, astrological influences, and the specific composition of bodily "humours," involving the combination of different fluids within the human body had an impact on physical experience and character.[39] For them, "the implications of climatic, humoral and astrological theories all point to ideal human types in Western Europe, not in Africa, India, the Near East, or the Far North."[40] These latter geographical locations were, inevitably, considered to be the edges of civilization. Thus, Muslims living in the excessively hot Middle East were deemed cowardly as a result of the climate they inhabited. William of Malmesbury quotes Pope Urban II's call to crusade at the Council of Clermont in 1095, which contains a description of Muslims as

> The least valiant of men ... It is in fact well known that every nation born in Eastern clime is dried up by the great heat of the sun; they may have more good sense, but they have less blood in their veins, and that is why they flee from battle at close quarters: they know they have no blood to spare.[41]

Medieval Christian writers and artists, as in the pre-Christian ancient world before them, also used physiognomical explanations to identify "sinners," both *within* the community as well as, on occasion, *outside* it. A famous example of this can be found in the way that Chaucer describes one of the pilgrims traveling to Canterbury, in his *General Prologue to The Canterbury Tales*:

> A Somonour was ther with us in that place,
> That hadde a fyr-reed cherubynnes face,
> For saucefleem he was and lecherus as a sparwe,
> With scalled browes blake and piled berd.
> Of his visage children were aferd.
> Ther nas quyk-silver, lytarge, ne brymstoon,
> Boras, ceruce, ne oile of tarter noon;
> cNe oynement that wolde clense and byte,
> That hym myghte helpen of his whelkes white,
> Nor of the knobbes sittynge on his chekes.[42]

> [A Summoner was in our company at the Inn
> Whose face was as fiery as a cherubin's
> Because of its eruption of pimples. He had tiny eyes.
> He was as hot and lecherous as the libidinous sparrow
> And had scabby black brows and a scanty beard.
> Children were terrified of his face
> For there was no quick-silver nor protoxide of lead,
> Nor borax, nor white-lead, nor cream of tartar
> No ointment of any kind that might cleanse and burn away,
> Or relieve him, neither of the white pimply blotches
> Nor of the knobby deformities to be found on his cheeks.]

The Summoner, who sold written indulgences that were supposed to possess the power to absolve Christians from their sins, is portrayed by Chaucer as one of the most wicked and corrupt figures in the *Prologue*. To Chaucer's first audiences, the Summoner's physiognomic ugliness would have served as metaphor for his inner evil.

Such applications of physiognomic ugliness or deformity intersect, in turn, with the depiction, in the Middle Ages, of imagined monsters and demons: to conceive of the "monstrous," implies the existence of a self-fashioned category of the "normative." Indeed, the ancient Greek binary postulated the barbarian as sub-human and, therefore, in one way or another, abnormal, and so, too, exploitable. Against the "civilized" was set the non-Greek imagined "monstrous" or "supernatural." Thus, as Strickland suggests,

> if the combined implications of climatic, astrological and physiognomical theories are carried to extremes, the results are the Monstrous Races: imaginary groups of elusive, malformed, and misbehaving creatures located at the edges of the known world, vaguely defined as India, Ethiopia, and the Far North.[43]

Medieval Christians, like the Greeks, initiated "the process of appropriating and expanding the Monstrous Races tradition to serve new theological purposes."[44] Monsters were said to share many characteristics with barbarians and many of these characteristics such as "location outside the city, strange habitat, incomprehensible speech, odd diet, exotic or immodest dress, and abhorrent social customs"[45] were transferred to other non-Christian groups in the Middle Ages, including "monstrous" Muslims, Jews, and Ethiopians. Monstrosity "was the primary conceptual catch-all for any rival religious sect or ethnic group, whether from within (heretics) or without (Jews, Muslims, other non-Christians)."[46] Sometimes characterized as the Old Testament figure of the fratricide Cain, or other manifestations of the Christianizing mission, monsters were made, symbolically, into "signs of sin."[47] In this way they conveyed "Christian ideas about evil that also informed representation of the living enemies of Christendom."[48]

The use of the concept of monstrosity to characterize non-Christians was accelerated during the period of the Crusades (1192–1289?). Muslims in the Middle East were the main enemies of the crusaders. To those illustrations supplied by Debra Strickland of the depiction of Muslims as members of the Monstrous Races and targets either for conversion[49] or slaughter,[50] of the depiction of Saracens (a derogatory term for the Muslims of the Middle East) as monsters in the *chansons de geste*,[51] of references to Muslims as "a race of dogs"[52] may be added a typical example from Chaucer, taken from *The Man of Law's Tale*.[53]

The portrayal of the mother of the Sultan of Syria who is a member of what is elsewhere in the tale called "the Barbre nacioun,"[54] is steeped in suspicion of imagined monstrous Oriental degeneracy, exhibiting, too, occasional misogyny. She is described as the second "Semyrame,"[55] an Assyrian queen thought to have legalized incest. She plans the murder of her own son for considering conversion to Christianity even though the act is presented as superficial, and is prompted by mercantile motives as well as by his desire for the Christian Roman Emperor's daughter, and by the desire to gain power for herself.

Referred to in the text variously as a "welle of vices,"[56] a "serpent under femynynytee,/Lik to the serpent depe in helle ybounde,"[57] a "scorpioun,"[58] and a "wikked goost,"[59] the Sultana pretends to her son that she too will convert, "[r]epentynge hire she hethen was so longe."[60] But to her own followers she says

> ye knowen everichon,
> How that my sone in point is for to lete
> The hooly laws of our Alkaron,
> Yeven by Goddes message Makomete.
> But oon avowe to grete God I heete,
> The lyf shal rather out of my body sterte
> Or Makometes lawe out of myn herte.[61]

> [Every one of you knows that
> My son is about to abandon
> The holy laws of our Quran
> Given by Allah's Prophet, Muhammad.
> But one vow I promise to great Allah
> I would rather that my life would burst from my body
> Than tear the laws of Muhammad from my heart.]

From a medieval Christian viewpoint, this manifests monstrous intractability and evil stubbornness and appears to fly in the face of possible conversion to the "true" faith. As far as the Sultan is concerned, the early Christian universalizing and humanizing claims to accept all comers made some allowance for "arguments that those who do not become Christian (or even the correct kind of Christian) should be signified as only potentially human/Christian or less than fully human."[62] In this context, the Sultan's "readiness to convert establishes a power relationship in which Christianity is held as unnegotiable."[63] Moreover in this respect the tale suggests the "fragility of Islamic religious conviction for it can be traded away to satisfy the Sultan's own contingent personal desire."[64]

Parallel to such imaginings, the "Cluniac *summula* asserted that Muhammed 'lived a barbarian among barbarians and an idolater among idolaters.'"[65] Another passage, this time concerning the Turks, taken from "a chronicle of the Third Crusade probably written by an English crusader," emphasizes blackness "along with the other standard pejorative characteristics of physical deformity and idolatry"[66] all of which convey the imagined evil of Muslim enemies:

> Among [the Christians'] opponents was a fiendish race, forceful and relentless, deformed by nature and unlike other living beings, black in color, of enormous stature and inhuman savageness. Instead of helmets they wore red coverings on their heads, brandishing in their hands clubs bristling with iron teeth, whose shattering blows neither helmets nor mailshirts could resist. As a standard they carried a carved effigy of Muhammad. There was such an enormous crowd of this violent race.[67]

Associations of "fiendishness," "blackness," physical deformity, demonic weaponry, reflect, too, the Christian representation of Muslims as diabolical, Satan's children, people of the Devil.

Jews were also connected in one way or another to the Devil, in medieval Christian imaginings. In his book, *The Devil and the Jews*, Joshua Trachtenberg outlines, "how deeply ... conception of the intimate relations between Satan and the Jews was implicit in the medieval point of view."[68] The Jews were associated with the Antichrist, an imagined link which "goes back to the earliest Christian period, but it assumed really frightening proportions ... toward the end of the Middle Ages ... Jews were expected to form the spearhead of his legions."[69] They were, on occasion, also referred to as "dogs." Such assertions include remarks such as, "coition with a Jewess is precisely the same as if a man should copulate with a dog,"[70] or, the Jews are the "devil's dogs."[71] Moreover, they were depicted with monstrous physical and inhuman characteristics, including the possession of horns, sometimes possessing a tail, or cloven hooves for feet and associated with the goat, traditionally a symbol for lechery. They were supposed, as well, to have an unpleasant odor, the *foetor judaicus*, that derived from the claim that Jewish men menstruated, and to suffer from copious hemorrhages, "quinsy, scrofula … skin diseases."[72]

Chaucer's *The Prioress's Tale* recycles a typical medieval reiteration of a selection of "traditional" markings of the Jew, although commentators are not in agreement about the level of the Prioress's irony, or about what these details may tell us about her personal affectations.[73] The tale draws on a number of earlier versions of the allegation that Jews habitually indulged in the murder of Christians, and that they sought the blood of Christian children (the Blood Libel).[74] Indeed Chaucer has the Prioress allude at the end of her tale (l. 684) to just such an accusation, made against the Jews of Medieval Lincoln, even though the Jews had been expelled from England 100 or so years before Chaucer wrote. Trachtenberg describes the incident in the following way:

> The case of Hugh of Lincoln (1255), which achieved tremendous notoriety, produced a similar charge. A large number of Jews were in Lincoln at the time to attend the marriage of Belaset, daughter of Magister Benedict fil' Moses. The day after the wedding the body of a boy, who had been missing for over three weeks, was discovered in a cesspool into which he had probably fallen while at play. But a more dramatic explanation of his death immediately suggested itself. Matthew Paris, in describing the alleged murder, related how "the child was first fattened for ten days with white bread and milk, and then how almost all the Jews of England were invited to the crucifixion." The Jew Copin was forced to confess that the boy was crucified *in injuriam et contumeliam Jesu*. Nearly one hundred Jews were arrested, of whom nineteen, including Copin, were hanged without trial. The rest, after being convicted and sentenced, were ultimately released when, the intervention of the learned Franciscan teacher

Adam Marsh having proved fruitless, Richard of Cornwall, who held the Jewry of the Kingdom in mortgage, and was naturally anxious to protect his property interceded in their behalf.[75]

Chaucer's Prioress begins, significantly, by setting her version of the ritual murder allegation in the East:

Ther was in Asye, in a greet cite,
Amonges Cristene folk, a Jewerye,
Sustened by a lord of that contree
For foule usure and lucre of vileynye,
Hateful to Crist.[76]

[In a great city in Asia there was a Jewish community
Maintained by a lord of that country
Living among the Christian population
Practicers of the filthy lucre of usury
That is so hateful to Christ.]

Children, "ycomen of Cristen blood,"[77] study there, as "smale children do in hire childhede,"[78] at a "litel scole of Cristen folk."[79] A seven-year-old amongst them learns by heart a hymn to the Virgin Mary. He sings it, "as he cam to and fro,"[80] in the vicinity of the Jewish Quarter. This prompts the Prioress immediately to draw on the well-used imagined alliance between the Devil and the Jews, who plotted against the innocent Christian child:

Oure firste foo, the serpent Sathanas,
That hath in Jues herte his waspes nest,
Up swal, and seide, "O Hebrayk peple, allas!
Is this to yow a thing that is honest,
That swich a boy shal walken as hym lest
In youre despit, and synge of swich sentence,
Which is agayn youre laws reverence?"[81]

[The serpent Satan, our greatest enemy
Whose wasps' nest lodged in the Jewish heart

> Swelled up, saying "For shame, Oh Hebrew people,
> How can your reaction be respectable
> When such a child is left to walk wherever he pleases
> In contempt of you and to sing such hymns
> Which reject your sacred laws?"]

In the Middle Ages "[t]he superstitious crimes that so strongly influenced medieval thought were considered to be the actions of 'the Jews' and not of this or that Jew and the entire community suffered the penalty for them."[82] Thus, for the Prioress, "[f]ro thennes forth the Jues han conspired/This innocent out of this world to chace."[83] She also avers that the "cursed folk of Herodes"[84] are responsible for hiring an "homycide"[85] to murder the boy. Moreover, she goes on explicitly to charge that, "The blood out crieth on your cursed deed,"[86] evoking the inflammatory resonances, both of the blood ritual allegations, and allegations of the originary culpability of the Jews for the crucifixion of Christ.

As in the case of the Prioress's allusion to Little Hugh of Lincoln in her tale, medieval Christian artists also represented Jews by means of relatively contemporary iconographic references, especially in the matter of dress. Commenting on this blend of "the actual and the fantastic … [in] constructed views of living non-Christians [which, at the same time] were nearly entirely stereotyped and imaginary,"[87] Strickland notes that

> there is no evidence to substantiate the ultimately routine claims made throughout the Middle Ages and well beyond … It is this discrepancy between the real and the imaginary that has prompted modern scholars to interpret medieval portraits … as imaginary embodiments of everything medieval Christians dreaded and feared about themselves, their society, and their own religion.[88]

Among the complex manifestations of an embryonic racism in the medieval European Church, we may note the extent to which its anxieties included material as well as spiritual and theological insecurities both within the emergent feudal Europe and beyond. England did not become Christian until the seventh century; the Germanic tribes,

Saxony and Bohemia not until the ninth; Scandinavia and Poland not until the tenth; while Prussia and Hungary held out a century longer.[89] The Church had to contend with numerous heretical Christian sects[90] and to subject its own clergy to conformity to official doctrine.[91] It has been argued that one "major impetus for the Crusades was the successful capture of Toledo from the Moors in 1085."[92] But if the Crusades were launched in 1095 to end Muslim occupation of what European Christians considered to be their Holy Land, they were also about the Church's struggle within Europe,

> in essence, as much about the desire of the papacy to exert control over others within its domain as to launch attacks on people outside of it … as much against pagan European Lithuanians and to recapture lost territory in Spain, as they were an attempt to invade the heartland of Islam, by capturing Jerusalem.[93]

As Catherwood observes, the papacy also wanted "to gain greater power within Europe, especially over Christian rulers who wanted to diminish papal strength for internal political reasons" and they wanted "to conquer pagan kingdoms contiguous to Christian soil, in the case of the campaigns in the Baltic area and in Central Europe."[94]

Parallel to such internal anxieties the Church intensified its animosity to the Jews, especially during and after the Crusades, "to prove its superiority to the Judaism it sought to replace."[95] Several factors contrived to make the Jews a special target against which Christians could imagine themselves, including, among other things,

> the anti-Jewish tradition stemming from the Gospels themselves; the dogmatic enmity of the Church underscored by the religious and cultural nonconformity of the Jewish people within what was essentially a totalitarian civilization; economic rivalry and the sometimes superior, or at any rate strategic, economic position of Jews; the gradual evolution of a new social balance of power and the political struggle it entailed; the emergence of the national spirit … ignorance and misunderstanding of Judaism[96]

and, like the Muslims, their refusal to convert. Thus the First Crusade unleashed a wave of violence against European Jews on the crusaders' way to the Middle East.

The Church was also preoccupied throughout the Middle Ages by the presence of "Islam in lands within and in close proximity to Europe during the period from the mid-seventh century to the sixteenth century."[97] Since 632, the year of Muhammad's death, Muslims had conquered a great deal of land from "the Atlantic coast of Spain in Europe, across the whole of North Africa and the Middle East, through to Persia and the borders of the Indus, in what is now India."[98] Only in 732 were Muslim forces in France checked by Charles Martel's army, in a battle which took place between Tours and Poitiers. Muslims who had colonized the Iberian Peninsula, in AD 711, "were responsible for its Arabization and Islamization,"[99] although, eventually, the Christians regained control of much of Spain as a result of a series of victories in places such as Cordoba (1236), Seville (1248), and Granada (1492). But, throughout the period, trade also ensured that one "sustained point of contact between Europe and the Islamic world was the Mediterranean region."[100] However, by the fourteenth century, perceived threats from Muslims, were "increasingly thought to lie with the rise of the Ottoman Turks" and "the image of the wild Saracen was replaced by that of the wild Turk."[101] Miles's choice of the word "wild," here, points, at least incidentally, to the medieval imagined *topos* of the Wild Man or Wild Woman: "beings covered in hair and leaves, highly sexed and licentious, and prone to seduce the unwary."[102] This fantasy of beings beyond the boundaries of known civilization runs at least parallel to earlier Greco-Roman imaginings of the lawless "barbarian" and of monstrous behavior.

Nevertheless, despite their other internal aims, the Church's declared thrust during the First Crusade was against the Muslim inhabitants of the Middle East and resulted, amongst other acts of violence, in the bloody slaughter of Muslims during the battle for Jerusalem. Of course European Christians used theology to justify the attempts to regain the Holy Land from the Saracens, as Robert Miles has observed.[103] At the same time, Miles notes that "Islamic resistance to the European armies was interpreted as further evidence of an inherent tendency towards violence and cruelty [whereas] ... identical acts of war by Christians were seen as means by which God could be glorified."[104] Moreover, as Strickland observes, in creating such or other negative versions of non-Christian groups, Christian imaginings, like those of the ancient Greeks and Persians, served to define and to assert their own superior religious identities alongside "the virtue of Christ, the Virgin, angels, saints, and ordinary Christians."[105]

Let us now tease out some of the implications inherent in these accounts of Christian imaginings of enemy religious groups. Noticeable, for example, in the process of the representation of Jews as monsters or infidels or heretics and sorcerers, is the extent to which these imaginings are also embedded and institutionalized in other statutory, or cultural, processes and institutions such as the Spanish Inquisition, the use of legislation, the issuing of proclamations, state mechanisms, and the enforced wearing of distinguishing badges that were also used to identify Muslims and Jews. In addition, "cultural" practices such as book burnings, and violence sanctioned and sometimes led by clergymen,[106] helped to sustain the persecution of marginalized religious and racial groups.[107] In this way negative group identity formation is institutionally legitimized and culturally validated, facilitated, encouraged sometimes, silently, by means of a wide range of legally authorized or officially sanctioned activities.

Again, the construction of group identity sometimes masks or elides aspects of the "reality" of what is actually happening. Even in the Middle Ages, processes of group characterization sometimes emerge as complex, distinguished by crucial silences and elisions. The account of the alleged killing of Little Hugh of Lincoln, quoted above, for example, suggests that the intervention of Richard of Cornwall, apparently on the Jews' behalf, arose from vested self-interest. Furthermore, as Trachtenberg observes, "the writings and sermons of the militant leaders of the Church inevitably whipped up public opinion and led to wild attacks upon the Jews, which these same leaders often felt bound in all conscience to deprecate."[108] Thus, he continues, "the *Constitutio pro Judeis*, expressly forbidding violence against the Jews, was endorsed by successive popes ten times from its issuance in 1120 until 1250" but had little actual effect on outbreaks of anti-Jewish violence; indeed it received somewhat lukewarm support from Pope Innocent III, the same pope "who sponsored acutely oppressive legislation against the Jews."[109] Such action, combined with a paradoxical rhetoric of compassion deployed towards the Jews, is belied by the shockingly inhumane treatment that they received.

A different kind of equivocation is evident in the widespread European marking of the Jew as usurer. Historically, Jews were indeed confined to the practice of usury, but their predominance in Europe as monopolist usurers lasted, it is now commonly acknowledged, for a relatively brief period. Strickland notes that the Jews were expelled

> from England in 1290; from France in 1306, 1322, and 1394; from Spain in 1492; and from dozens of German principalities and towns during the early fifteenth century, and from southern Italy in 1541. By the fifteenth century, there were almost no Jews left in Western Europe.[110]

By the time of their expulsion from England, and as a result of anti-Jewish laws over taxation, and "the increase in lending at interest by commercially-minded Christians,"[111] the Jews were impoverished. Yet the anti-usurers presented usury as always an essentially Jewish practice. Indeed, as David Hawkes has argued, by the time of Renaissance England, there was a "deeply rooted," "conceptual fusion between Judaism and usury … in Christian biblical hermeneutics … Usurers are figurative rather than literal 'Jews,'" an "idea … commonplace in the overtly didactic anti-usury tradition."[112] Particularly noteworthy here, is the relative invisibility of the identification of *Christian* usurers in the early modern period, in subsequent markings of group identity.[113] A comment by Theodor W. Adorno and Max Horkheimer centuries later may resurrect this imagery of the stereotyped Jew: "[P]eople shout: Stop thief!—but point at the Jews … scapegoats not only for individual maneuvers and machinations, but in a broader sense, inasmuch as the economic injustice of the whole class is attributed to them."[114] Adorno and Horkheimer wrote in the context of what they understood to be bourgeois habits of concealment.

Finally, this section began by noting the limitations of generalized terms such as "Islam," "medieval European Christianity," and the "Jews." Tracing what he argues to be a hidden discourse of enmity, Gil Anidjar observes the ways in which medieval European Christians "developed an array of narratives, categories, and classifications that made it easier to collapse the distinction between the Jew and the

Arab."[115] But, in a move that implicitly advocates greater scrutiny of such appellations, he argues, also in favor of the emergence of a crucial distinction in the imaginings of the two. Suggestively and provocatively he recalls an observation by Aquinas:

> Thus, against the Jews we are able to argue by means of the Old Testament, while against heretics we are able to argue by means of the New Testament. But Mohammedans and the pagans accept neither the one nor the other.[116]

He then asserts that, for medieval Christian Europe, by the thirteenth century "The Jew is the theological (and internal) enemy whereas the Muslim is the political (and external) enemy."[117] Thus, it is the case, as we saw earlier, that Chaucer's *The Man of Law's Tale* appears to acknowledge the spiritual and religious dimensions of Islam in references, amongst others, to the "hooly laws of our Alkaron" and to "Makomete" as "Goddes message." But this is outweighed by presentation of the Islamic Syrian world as not only impenetrably different from the laws of Christianity, but also as "uncivilized" and "perfidious," filled with the imagined "violence and treachery of the Syrians … reinforcing religious-cultural suspicions and animosities,"[118] a world of "unregenerate barbarity."[119] Moreover, in so doing, the tale draws "rigid lines between geo-political spaces that successfully obscure what Christianity and Islam with their common Hellenistic and Hebraic roots [may have] shared."[120]

Marking skin pigmentation by color

Coloured
When I was born, I was black.
When I grew up, I was black.
When I get hot, I am black.
When I get cold, I am black.
When I am sick, I am black.
When I die, I am black.
When you were born, You were pink.
When you grew up, You were white.
When you get hot, You go red.

When you get cold, You go blue.
When you are sick, You go purple.
When you die, You go green.

AND YET YOU HAVE THE CHEEK TO CALL ME COLOURED!!!
(A poem published in 1998 by an anonymous
British schoolchild)[121]

Another strand in imagined construction of group characteristics turns on differences between skin pigmentation generalized by use of the crude binary opposition between, "black" and "white." The use of such colors to mark the appearance and group identity of human beings has a long history in both East and West.[122] The predominance of negative associations attached to the physical appearance of darker-skinned peoples has strengthened over time as part of a moral economy in which what is good is associated with the color white and what is black is associated with evil. But, within the framework of the history of social evolution, there are paradoxically also occasions when skin color can be associated with primordial innocence, although even here "innocence" can sometimes be used to imply "primitive" or unsophisticated, terms that distinguish the civilized from the naively uncivilized.

For example, the term "Ethiopians" is a "conflation of all [Africans] living in sub-Egyptian Africa."[123] It was used by ancient Greeks and Romans. The Greek word Aethiops meant, literally, "burnt-faced person." It is based on the climatic theoretical principle "that blackness was caused by excessive exposure to the sun."[124] For Greece and Rome, moreover, "[b]lack was associated with death and the underworld, the realm of the dead," so that, often "the colour ... took on ominous symbolism."[125] These labels have been used casually to imply negative qualities in canonical literature as well as in social discourses. In the final scene of reconciliation and a staged test of true love in Shakespeare's *Much Ado About Nothing* (1598–1599),[126] a repentant Claudio, who earlier wrongfully accuses his fiancée Hero of infidelity, tells Hero's father Leonato that he would, as an act of atonement, marry Leonato's mystery "brother's daughter" even if she "were an Ethiope."[127] The god of the underworld was depicted as black (*niger*). There is no light in the underworld, and its inhabitants are therefore black. In theatre, those from the underworld were some-times cast as Ethiopians and Egyptians. During antiquity, dark persons, objects, and animals were "considered bad omens."[128] The color "black" together with the color "white" served "as metaphorical representations of good and evil, life and death."[129] Blackness, associated with the underworld thus came to represent evil.[130]

Despite this, Classical writers did sometimes register, in the midst of such myth-making, a number of variant physical features prevalent in differently located African groups. The picture is also, in other ways, even more complex than this suggests. On the matter of the occlusion of Egyptian origins within representations of Greek history Martin Bernal argues that "Classical, Hellenistic and later pagan Greeks from the 5th century BC to the 5th century AD ... saw ... their ancestors [as] having been civilized by Egyptian and Phoenician colo-nization and the later influence of Greek study in Egypt."[131] Describ-ing "the ambivalent relationship between Christianity and the Jewish biblical tradition on the one hand and Egyptian religion and philo-sophy on the other," he notes, in a way that has a bearing on elements that will be discussed in the following chapter, that contrary to much current thinking, "there was no doubt ... that up to the 18th century, Egypt was seen as the fount of all 'Gentile' philosophy and learning, including that of the Greeks."[132] He notes further that "at the begin-ning of the 18th century the threat of Egyptian philosophy to Christi-anity became acute" and that "the development of Eurocentrism and racism, with the colonial expansion over the same period, led to the fallacy that only people who lived in temperate climates—that is, Europeans—could really think" and thus "the Ancient Egyptians who—though their colour was uncertain—lived in Africa, lost their position as philosophers."[133] Tracing how the Greek War of Independ-ence in the early decades of the nineteenth century might have con-tributed to a strong sense of a European Greece that stood against "traditional Islamic enemies from Asia and Africa,"[134] he observes that "with the rise of ... racism in the early 19th century, the ancient notion that Greece was a mixed culture that had been civilized by Africans and Semites became not only abominable but unscientific."[135]

Medieval Christians, who "arrived at their images of Ethiopians through a complex interweaving of Classical mythological tradition,

Christianized physiognomical theory, and biblical exegesis,"[136] developed what have become more recurrent stereotypes. Ethiopians in medieval art "exhibit a very consistent set of physiognomical features: dark skin, woolly or tightly coiled hair, large eyes, flat noses, and thick, everted lips."[137] Furthermore, early Christian sources established a connection between the devil, the underworld, and hell.[138] By the second century the devil ("the Black One") and demons in general "became identified with the black African, the Ethiopian"[139] and to a lesser extent with the mythologized figure of the Jew.[140] The "symbolic equation of black with spiritual darkness, [implied] the concomitant equivalence of white with spiritual enlightenment, as expressed in the Gospel verse ... 'God is light and in him there is no darkness.' "[141] It informed the biblical exegesis of episodes such as Noah's curse on Ham or God's curse on Cain, as it did, also, the developing medieval patristic and later literary traditions.[142] The Ethiopian was viewed in the Middle Ages, too, "not only as a barbarian but ... as a marvelous [monstrous] exotic, an inhabitant of the mythical land of Ethiopia."[143] Moreover, in occasional visual depictions, the attributes of the Wild Man serve to intensify the Ethiopian's "barbarity."[144]

As has often been remarked, in view of such biblical, iconographic, patristic, and literary traditions, it is no surprise that "from the earliest stages of European expansion into Africa and other parts of the globe,"[145] "corporal properties such as skin colour, hair and other phenotypical differences constructed an epidermal schema not only for anchoring difference but for placing different groups of types of humankind into distinct types."[146] Furthermore, Back and Solomos go on to argue that "[w]hen we see a full-blown anti-Black attitude in Christian England beginning with the voyages of discovery, it is reasonable to suppose that what was, by then, an almost 1,300-year-old exegetical tradition may have been a contributing cause" and "[w]hen, with the discovery of Africa, the Ethiopian was encountered in reality, scriptural metaphor was easily translated onto a live human being."[147]

Such processes are particularly clear in aspects of early modern English colonial and travel narratives. For example, in his book *Marvelous Possessions*, Stephen Greenblatt, argues that the early modern trajectory of such writing invites adaptation of Marx's notion of the reproduction and circulation of mimetic capital[148] that he defines as "the stock of images, along with the means of producing those images and circulating them according to prevailing market forces."[149] He registers the global reach of "the will and the ability to cross immense distances and, in the search for profit, to encounter and to represent radically unfamiliar human and natural objects."[150] He also notes, "the growing stockpile of representations, a set of images and image-making devices that are *accumulated*, 'banked' as it were, in books, archives, collections, cultural storehouses, until such time as these representations are called upon to generate new representations."[151] And he then goes on to observe

> that any given representation is not only the reflection or product of social relations but that it is itself a social relation, linked to the group understandings, status, hierarchies, resistances and conflicts that exist in other spheres of the culture in which it circulates.[152]

Such representations, he concludes, "are not only products but producers."[153] Mention of these aspects serves to foreground the power of influence of such mimetic capital. Greenblatt emphasizes, also, that because of their possession of such mimetic capital, "[w]ith a very few exceptions, Europeans felt powerfully superior to virtually all the peoples they encountered."[154]

The pioneering work of scholars such as Winthrop D. Jordan and Eldred Jones recognizes just such emergent early modern impressions of cultures that English and European explorers encountered in the so-called New World and in Africa as a result of trade, the voyages of discovery and attendant travel writing, or early attempts at settlement.[155] The English interaction with actual Africans began about the mid-sixteenth century. By 1601 there were enough "black" people in London for Queen Elizabeth to complain about their presence.[156] Side by side with tendencies towards stereotyping, Jordan's account of the impact of contact between the English and Native Americans or Africans argues that the process of imagining or "explaining" group difference, or the fixing of group identities, are complicated, but that it also points to an often contradictory or ambiguous series of different processes.

As in the case of the medieval term "Ethiopian," the term "Moor" was used, in the Renaissance, imprecisely, to refer to groups of

Africans from diverse locations, including those from North Africa, who were all thought of as "black." But, as Jordan suggests, at the same time, and "with curious inconsistency ... Englishmen recognized that Africans south of the Sahara were not at all the same people as the ... Moors."[157] Again, conflicting and sometimes illogical attempts were made to explain the cause of blackness.[158] Climatic features were proposed as part of the explanation of physical appearance, but differences between the equatorial inhabitants of Africa and the equatorial inhabitants of America remained problematic. Moreover, the appearance of those Africans who lived in Northern Europe did not change over time. Maternal features were also invoked as another imagined cause of the birth of dark-skinned children.

The English showed a muted response to the Christian call for conversion of the infidel in Africa as compared with their attitude in the Americas.[159] Africans were seen, from a universalist Christian perspective, as part of a common humanity. But African cultural practices and language were often interpreted as "savage" and "barbaric." However, yet again, if Anglo-European ethnocentrism habitually used such differences to articulate or infer their own "contrasting" identities, the English on other occasions discovered some similarities, claiming, for instance, that the "structures of African societies" were analogous to their own, complete with "kings, counselors, gentlemen, and the baser sort."[160] There was no discussion of whether the Africans' "non-physical characteristics were inborn and unalterable."[161] But, in addition to all these mixed responses, Jordan also argues elsewhere that early modern English Protestantism, with its emphasis on personal piety and intense self-scrutiny facilitated the English tendency to judge comparatively the behavior of the people they encountered in other lands.[162] Anxieties about social problems such as vagrancy, increasing masterlessness, or a growing spirit of avariciousness, were all sometimes displaced onto the strange peoples that English explorers met.

Moreover, the pernicious imagined collocation of the monstrous, the savage, the barbaric, the bestial or "ape"-like, and the libidinous or sexually "wild" with imagined versions of the African emerges in sixteenth and early seventeenth century English and European encounters.[163] Edward Topsell's *Historie of Foure-Footed Beastes* (1607), an attempt to produce a classificatory scheme of animals, reiterates and reinforces such associations. Jean Bodin, in another effort at "systematic" somatic classification (1566), argued, with the aid of humoral theory, that "southerners" were darker than the two other types of humans he demarcates. They were allegedly more inclined to be jealous, and subject to intense passion, and, therefore, they were predisposed to sinfulness.[164]

The unfolding processes of slavery and the slave trade, as well as subsequent mercantile and colonial projects, would harden some of these impressions, and lessen other fluidities in the response to what were then newly encountered experiences of native skin pigmentations.

In addition, from the last few decades of the twentieth century onward, research has advanced significantly into early modern cultural understanding of the categories of "blackness" and "whiteness." For example, Kim Hall has shown how "gendered representation of alien cultures through the submission of those cultures to the discipline of European cultural and rhetorical order" involves the dissemination of particular conceptualizations of race.[165] She probes ways in which representations of the binary of the words "fair" and "dark" and their variants or synonyms, within the English language and within various modes of writing, work to effect notions of white power and beauty against notions of black servitude.[166] Development of the "ideology of fairness," "a Eurocentric beauty culture," she argues, "had its strongest articulations in the Renaissance."[167] Furthermore, in analyzing how tropes of blackness serve (often implicitly) to heighten especially European male whiteness, she foregrounds, in the early modern period "the role of colour in organizing relations of power"[168] as well as the "need to interrogate whiteness as a social construct."[169] Moreover, the emphasis she gives to processes of effacement is further significant in suggesting how structurations and discussions of race may also entail simultaneous occlusions. For example, in both writer and reader, there may exist an *unstated* homology of valuation, as in an *implicitly fantasized* shared and inferred superior "whiteness," that is present in the negative representation of tropes of blackness. Indeed, as she puts it, these are some of the ways in which "whiteness [thus] masks itself."[170] Patricia Parker, who also probes the emerging dynamic antagonism between "blackness" and "whiteness," particularly in the contexts of gender and sexuality, writes in a series of brilliant essays that the image of the Moor (punned with, and sometimes spelled as "More") as a symbol of excess transgresses both civic and sexual decorum, leaving whiteness as the implicitly, validated norm.[171] She also traces the "early modern linking of fascination with the secrets of [sometimes 'transgressive'] feminine sexuality to a story out of 'Barbarie,' provided by the travel narrative of [the] converted Moor" Leo Africanus (*Geographical Historie of Africa*, 1526), in works such as Ambroise Paré's *Des Monstres et Prodiges* (1573) and Helkiah Crooke's *Microcosmographia: A Description of the Body of Man* (1616).[172] The link with such terms as "blackness" and "Moor/More" as well as "domestic European anxieties surrounding the secrets of female sexuality and its control"[173] entails a projection of the European "monstrous" and the "barbarous" "onto the [black] other and outside, imaged yet again as the opposite to the [inner or home—and 'white'] 'civil' or 'civilized.' "[174]

Meanwhile, Ania Loomba advances the case for "[s]ensitivity to race, class and gender in feminist criticism."[175] She maintains that "the processes by which women and black people are constructed as the 'others' of white patriarchal society are similar and connected, and [that] they reflect other sorts of exclusion such as that based on class."[176] Similar to Kim Hall and to Jonathan Dollimore and Alan Sinfield, Loomba registers also that there is always, in addition, a politics involved in the *act* of reading. The site of reading itself involves complex processes in which issues of race and gender marginalization intertwine in the case of particular readers, and in particular texts, with other larger cultural, and political factors, especially those of patriarchy, colonialism, imperialism, and post-colonialism.

Loomba also suggests that "blackness" may signify, to differing degrees, and stand as a metaphor for "impurity." Thus the concept of the "blue blood" of the nobility, translated from the Spanish *sangre azul*,

> was claimed by several aristocratic families who declared they had never been contaminated by Moorish or Jewish blood, and hence had fair skins through which their blue blood could be seen. Thus blue blood is closely related to the idea of racial impurity or *limpezia de sangre* which developed as the

> Inquisition sought to identify "pure" Christians as opposed to those who had been "contaminated" by mixing with Jews and Moors, or "New Christians" who were converted Moors and Jews.[177]

Color becomes, according to these claims, an index of what is "pure" or "impure" within the discourse of religion. It may also be aligned with the claim of the aristocracy to a superior "purity" that provides an index of hierarchical, social, and class relations. Moreover, as Loomba suggests, "[p]atriarchal domination and gender inequality provided a [further] model for establishing (and were themselves reinforced by) racial hierarchies and colonial domination."[178]

In what follows we would like to glance briefly at a well-known early modern example of the imagining of characteristics of individual or group identity by way of color coding. We will then proceed to examine briefly a few examples of how some of the hate-procedures that we have already noted above endure well into our own time.

It is true that, as we will see shortly, William Shakespeare's *Othello* may be read in multiple ways, but, it is also well known that some aspects of the play and its language disturbingly reflect and reiterate traditionally negative attitudes towards groups of people of color and who, mostly, come from places beyond England and Europe, such as Africa, the so-called Middle East or Asia. In Shakespeare's play this applies not only to the obviously hate-filled voices of Iago and Roderigo, but is part of a larger social discourse. Their manifestly offensive utterances startlingly reiterate what we have already identified as traditional fears of miscegenation, allegations of sexual excess, perversion, bestiality, and imaginings of "black barbarity." For instance, during Iago's revelation of the elopement of Desdemona and the Moor Othello to her Venetian father Brabantio, he cries, "Thieves, thieves, thieves!"[179] Iago's "Even now, now, very now, an old black ram/Is tupping your white ewe. Arise, arise!/Awake the snorting citizens with the bell,/Or else the devil will make a grandsire of you,"[180] and "you'll have your daughter covered with a Barbary horse, you'll have your nephews neigh to you, you'll have coursers for cousins and gennets for germans,"[181] and again, "I am one, sir, that comes to tell you your daughter and the Moor are now making the beast with two backs"[182] reinforces age-old odious stereotypes of the "barbarian" or "Turk." Roderigo, in a slightly toned down version of Iago's descriptions, refers to Othello as "thick-lips"[183] and tells Brabantio that his daughter has been transported "to the gross clasps of a lascivious Moor"[184] and that she "hath made a gross revolt,/Tying her duty, beauty, wit and fortunes/In an extravagant and wheeling stranger."[185]

Nor are such negative descriptions confined to these two voices in the play. Once his mind has been poisoned by Iago and Roderigo, Brabantio accuses Othello of witchcraft. Surprisingly, even Desdemona's comment, "I saw Othello's visage in his mind,"[186] implies a level of implicit color coding whose veracity is reinforced by proverbial and biblical utterances such as, "can the Ethiopian change his skin, or the leopard his spots?"[187] Desdemona recognizes here Othello's "essence," but she articulates the qualities for which she loves him by means of the Venetian urban culture of color coding in which she lives. In short, Othello's "blackness" is compensated for by his spiritual and intellectual qualities. A host of Elizabethan proverbs, too, regard dark skin as an ineradicable negative indicator, such as *To wash an Ethiop white* (*c*.1542), *No more like than black is to white* (*c*.1570), *Black will take no other hue* (1538), and *A whore is like a crow, the more she washes the blacker she is* (1611). In a similar vein, the Duke tries to console Brabantio, the angered patriarch, with the adage, "If virtue no delighted beauty lack,/Your son-in-law is far more fair than black."[188] Othello, himself a converted Muslim, sometimes evidences this kind of interpellation in comments that include the traditionally coded rebuke to his brawling soldiers: "Are we turned Turks, and to ourselves do that/Which Heaven hath forbid the Ottomites?/For Christian shame, put by this barbarous brawl!"[189] We will shortly proceed to explore further the sorts of cultural strategies that we see Shakespeare deploying here and elsewhere in his plays.

Early modern European representations of Muslims often reflect the ways in which religious stereotypes often run parallel to, and intersect with, European stereotypes, evident in imaginings of "blackness." Scholars including Nabil Matar and Daniel Vitkus argue that early modern English anxiety and awe at Islamic power and wealth in Africa, the Mediterranean, and the East are responsible for this fantasy. The expansion of the Ottoman empire, the perennial threat of

Muslim piracy, the capture of English explorers and their conversion to Islam, all contributed to demonization of various kinds:

> The "Turk" was cruel and tyrannical, deviant, and deceiving; the "Moor" was sexually overdriven and emotionally uncontrollable, vengeful, and religiously superstitious. The Muslim was all that an Englishman and Christian was not: he was the Other with whom there could be only holy war.[190]

Shakespeare's *Othello* draws in many ways on the extensive mimetic capital of Greco-Roman structurations of barbarism, and on medieval and early modern fears of religious and color difference.[191] As we indicated, the negative characterizations imagined for people with dark skin pigmentation by groups with lighter skin pigmentation, intensified during processes of colonization and the expansion of slavery. The dogged and widespread endurance well into the twentieth century of such imaginings are illustrated here by means of a few random examples that in their detail confirm the chilling power of longstanding modes of racial hatred. They also show how such hatred interlocks with, or facilitates, other modes of oppression. Moreover, they also confirm that readings of racism are themselves often mixed in their effects.

In the case of my first example from the remarkably courageous but pre-feminist work of Solomon T. Plaatje, the silence about one gender evokes a strongly masculinist and patriarchal ethos that exists in opposition to his identification of disturbing political aspects around the issues of race and pre-apartheid segregation. Plaatje, in his remarkable opposition to the South African Land Act of 1913, which deprived the majority "black" population of South Africa of the right of ownership of over 90 percent of South African land (reserved at the same time for the far smaller "white" minority groups), quotes from largely—relatively (if often simultaneously paternalistic)—oppositional voices from the Union Parliament's Hansard report of the 1913 debate preceding the vote:

> One hon. member read into it that it was the separation of the two races ... but it could not be done now ... they had been developing the country with the labour of these people

> ... [Another person] had the idea that ... the Bill was going to set up a sort of pale—that there was going to be a sort of kraal in which all the natives were to be driven, and they were to be left to develop on their own lines. To allow them to go on their own lines was merely to drive them back into barbarism; their own lines meant barbarous lines; their own lines were cruel lines. ... It reminded him of what an English writer said about a similar policy in Ireland, because when the English went to Ireland they regarded the native Irish in the same way some extreme people here regarded the natives of South Africa. They thought they would root them out. They treated them as dogs, and thought that they were dogs.[192]

Plaatje spells out in his book what may well be called the savage cruelty of this law, its effects, and the hypocrisies it reflects. He remarks dryly that it was in some quarters wished that the supporters of the Bill, "a majority of whom are never happier than when attesting the Christian character of their race"[193] might actually attend to the teachings of their religion, but that others "knew that the only dividing fence between the Transvaal natives and complete slavery"[194] might now be British intervention from London, since the local Governor, Lord Gladstone, had ignored their pleas and had already signed the Bill into law.

Plaatje understands the nature of the material struggle to gain the land and create a migrant labor force that underlies this persecutory demarcation of "blackness" and he predicts that "the Boers ... will make it a crime for a native to live in South Africa, unless he is a servant in the employ of a Boer ... from this it will be just one step to complete slavery."[195] He pointedly quotes more oppositional speeches against the Bill, made in Parliament:

> [t]here was a disposition in certain directions to repress the natives. He (the speaker) believed that there was a feeling that white men had some divine right to the labour of the black, that the black people were to be hewers of wood and drawers of water ... There were those who said that if the natives would not submit to dictation they should be wiped out.[196]

Perhaps most telling in this recognition of the exploitative labor, economic, and class intersections that underpin this demarcation of skin pigmentation is Plaatje's appeal, made at the beginning of his book, which is worth quoting at some length:

> When Sir John French appealed to the British people for more shells during Easter week, the Governor-General of South Africa addressing a fashionable crowd at the City Hall, Johannesburg, most of whom had never seen the mouth of a mine, congratulated them on the fact that "under the strain of war and rebellion the gold industry had been maintained at full pitch," and he added that "every ounce of gold was worth many shells to the Allies." But His Excellency had not a word of encouragement for the 200,000 subterranean heroes who by day and by night, for a mere pittance, lay down their limbs and their lives to the familiar "fall of rock" and who, at deep levels ranging from 1000 feet to 1000 yards in the bowels of the earth, sacrifice their lungs to the rock dust which develops miners' phthisis and pneumonia—poor reward, but a sacrifice that enables the world's richest gold mines, in the Johannesburg area alone, to maintain the credit of the Empire with a weekly output of £750,000 worth of raw gold. Surely the appeal of chattels who render service of such great value deserves the attention of the British people.[197]

More than 50 years later, members of the Black Consciousness movement in South Africa maintained that it was necessary to contest the psychological damage inflicted by what had become the apartheid system, but also to emphasize its particular marking of different human bodies. The activist Steve Biko declared that, "our situation is not a mistake on the part of whites but a deliberate act, and no amount of moral lecturing will persuade the white man to 'correct' the situation."[198] Pascal Gwala asserted that

> through the conscientisation process of Black Consciousness blacks begin to feel they are part of the human race; that their black heritage is rich with deeply human attributes; that they are not and never were—savage or barbaric outside the context of primitive culture.[199]

And Barney Pityana maintained that: "Many would prefer to be colour-blind; to them skin pigmentation is merely an accident of creation. To us it is something much more fundamental. It is a synonym for subjection, an identification for the disinherited."[200]

Against the negative stereotypes, such activists struggled to construct a more positive image of "blackness." As Steve Biko declared at the trial of his political organization in May 1976,

> [w]e try to get blacks in conscientisation to grapple realistically with their problems, to develop what one might call an awareness, a physical awareness of their situation, to be able to analyse it, and to provide answers for themselves. The purpose behind it really being to provide some kind of hope.[201]

Such programs inevitably entailed a more negative recasting of stereotypes of "whiteness."

The workings of the law and the making of race

Assumptions about race often inform the practice of government, issues of jurisprudence, and the making and practice of the law. Moreover, aspects of legislation or judicial practice themselves, under the guise of the implementation of a "universal" justice, either explicitly, or often silently, define or legitimate preferred racial categories. To recall Stephen Greenblatt's adaptation of the notion of mimetic capital, accumulating laws, or discriminatory modes of practice in turn often also significantly "generate" and legitimize distribution of such preferred categories, thereby intensifying their influence. On the issue of race, government, legislation, and the judicial system are sites of struggle.

In her examination of this problem in relation to her recent study of African-American fiction, Karla F.C. Holloway argues that "African America's literary history paralleled African Americans' own history of personhood, in which the first task was to prove we were fully human rather than the fractional persons the Constitution declared us to be."[202] Holloway acknowledges the ongoing struggle in the USA, despite apparently enlightened civil rights advances, in the battle to establish for African-Americans the "claim of natural origin and full personhood,"[203] but she also argues that, regrettably, "the evolution of legal text did not, however, fully and/or finally determine social act."[204] Thus, despite the civil rights amendments of the 1860s and the Civil Rights Act of 1964, the protest poster carried by striking sanitation workers in a protest march in 1968, *four years later*, and led by Martin Luther King, was still forced to proclaim "I *Am* a Man." Holloway maintains that

> [t]he link of events from the eras of enslavement, civil rights activism, and the politics of a black presidency illustrates how issues of personhood and race in America were persistently seen as legal questions that revealed a nearly intractable sociality.[205]

There is thus an implicit recognition in Holloway's study that articulating "personhood" is partly always a matter of intersection with existent laws or "legal" writing, which itself may, in turn, be said, at least partly, to "hail" or interpolate the human into being.[206] Holloway's study provides a powerful acknowledgement that the "legal" writing of the human into being remains substantially, and in the case of certain subaltern populations and ethnic or "race" minorities, especially, a site of ongoing struggle.

Holloway's contemporary study of minority literary articulations of personhood within current legal and rhetorical articulations of such personhood, is suggestive for a reading of Shakespeare's *The Merchant of Venice* (*c*.1598) and *Othello* (*c*.1604), and their relationship to modern debates about racism and the law. Both plays contain articulations of race that turn, in part, on the binaries of "civilization" and "barbarism," Christian and infidel, black and white. Such binary markings are shown to intersect with the process of the law in different ways.

For example, Amanda Bailey has recently drawn attention to some of *The Merchant of Venice*'s central judicial concerns by investigating how it "stages the moment of forfeiture as an occasion to explore what constitutes ownership and under what circumstances it may give rise to possession."[207] Bailey meticulously traces evidence of the play's preoccupation with bonds, fungible and non-fungible property, and questions of forfeiture. She maintains that "monetary and moral economies," are "much more important than moneylending"[208] in the play. For her, the second half of the trial "investigates under what conditions ownership may give rise to possession":[209]

> the trial confirms a tripartite view of the individual as composed of person, body and soul; each entity is claimed respectively by the law, the state, and God. In this way Christianity automatically repositions anyone who attempts to claim absolute ownership over another Christian as a partial owner.[210]

For his part, Shylock the Jew, has, at least, this to learn in the course of the play's trial scene. Bailey claims that the play's primary concern is with the justice of early modern property law, which, she insists, provides its "dynamic energy."[211]

In the context of the formulation of race, searches for "pure" human origins or, indeed, "pure" origins of any other kind, it is worth recalling a cautionary passage from Albert Memmi's book, *Racism*:

> Except in certain rare cases (royal incest, for instance), artificial human selection has never been accomplished ... the necessities of survival, or the exigencies of war, have generally consigned humanity to continual intermixing; in effect, far from being static, human groups have undergone continual modification ... Supposing that purity may have actually been the case somewhere, it is not the general case for humanity. In truth, with the exception of chemistry, the very idea of *purity* is *either a metaphor, a prayer, or a fantasy*, the necessity for which is produced only by a certain human desire for perfection ... The truth remains relatively simple: *pure races do not exist, but humans differ.*[212]

It is not so much what Bailey registers about the play's primary legal interest, as what her discussion occludes, that makes her reading of the law in this play in relation to the question of race, so problematic. Her reading of the play's legal priorities may also be set alongside the legal philosopher Ronald Dworkin's contemporary arguments against notions of positivist law in favor of a notion of interpretive law:

> Law is an interpretive concept. Judges should decide what the law is by interpreting the practice of other judges deciding what the law is ... law as integrity unites jurisprudence and adjudication ... Adjudication is different from legislation, not in some single, univocal way ... inclusive integrity enforces distinct judicial constraints of role. Integrity does not enforce itself: judgment is required. That judgment is structured by different dimensions of interpretation and different aspects of these ... The interpretive judgment must notice and take account of these several dimensions; if it does not, it is incompetent or in bad faith, ordinary politics in disguise. But it must also meld these dimensions into an overall opinion: about which interpretation, all things considered, makes the community's legal record the best it can be from the point of view of political morality. So legal judgments are pervasively contestable ... Law is not exhausted by any catalogue of rules or principles, each with its own dominion over some discrete theatre of behaviour.[213]

Such an interpretive view of law concedes that in all its senses, including racial ones, the integrity of prevailing law, according to any particular jurisprudential interpretation should, in the fashioning of particular judgments, always to be subject to current revision and re-adjudication. For one thing, the judicial "integrity" of early modern English, and, as she identifies it, Christian debt law, which Bailey claims to be "less violent,"[214] is nonetheless shown in the play to be, in its application, brutal enough, but, at the same time, to necessitate an "adjudicative" appeal from Portia for an exercise of mercy extraneous to the operational "integrity" of that law.[215] In the eventual historical abolition of debtors' prisons, the hardhearted cruelty of this system of debt law has, since Shakespeare's time, finally been admitted. That is, the legal "integrity" which initially accommodated and sustained such debtors' prisons progressively developed into the legal "integrity" of a system that forbade them.[216]

Bailey's insistence upon the focus on debt law in the play may also be set against the "dynamic energy" of the actual language of *The Merchant of Venice*, which is not so much punctuated by recognitions of an early modern forfeiture system but, instead, by darker hauntings or returns of a clearly still active tradition of hatred. These hauntings continually pull against Bailey's version of its allegedly primary judicial integrity. Thus, of the many other possible and long since recognized examples, may be listed Antonio's remark, "The devil can cite Scripture for his purpose."[217] Antonio's utterance draws together proverbial lore and popular legendary depictions of the devil in European mystery plays. As we have noted in the second section of this chapter, such utterances conflate "the interests of devil and Jew."[218] As Bailey notes, "Jerome and other early Church Fathers frequently complained that the Jewish teachers consciously and deliberately perverted the meaning of [the Scriptures]."[219] In the same scene Salarino repeats allegations of an association between Shylock and the devil,[220] while in the following scene, Salerio's "creature that did bear the shape of man"[221] is borne out by Trachtenberg's account of the several ways in which "the Middle Ages [proclaimed] its belief that the Jew was not quite human."[222] The image of the hard-hearted "creature" Jew as an image of inhumanity which is repeated throughout the trial scene is also enunciated by the Duke at the beginning:

> I am sorry for thee. Thou art come to answer
> A stony adversary, an inhumane wretch,
> Uncapable of pity, void and empty
> From any dram of mercy.[223]

This nakedly coincides with and reflects a persisting tradition, which, as we have seen, regards the Jew as unacceptably "impure." Yet again, if the trial scene shows the outwitting of the Jew's understanding of forfeit and ownership, it does so, ironically, by means of a Jewish perspective in that Portia invokes an identifiable Jewish belief in a God of Mercy. At the same time, however, the text infers, for its "Jew" a preference for the (Christian) fiction of an "Old Testament God of Justice,"[224] whose very activity of "revenge" Shylock had earlier claimed to be following: "If a Christian wrong a Jew, wat should his sufferance be by Christian example? Why, revenge!"[225]

Shakespeare's Jew responds to the Duke's appeal for mercy and to Portia's appeal, with the language of the medieval and early modern Jewish stereotype. Moreover, behind the frustration of this "Jew's" alleged desire for blood, hovers the shadow of the myth of the Christian blood libel.

Why does the problem posed by prevalence in the text of an embryonically anti-Semitic discourse remain invisible in Bailey's otherwise compelling analysis of the roots of the play's originary sense of justice? Such hatred, as a system of then currently held beliefs, replete with a jurisprudential history, is likely to have been taken for granted by most medieval and early modern Christians. But in a play that is concerned with the injustices of an early modern English debt system, this vigorous linguistic sideshow that repeatedly surfaces in the text requires attention.

Shakespeare's play was written centuries after Jews had been expelled from England, while in much of Europe they had long since been barred from moneylending. Shylock, in these reiterative foldings of one kind of language into another, thus emerges as a vehicle for the "Venetian" displacement and projection of the indifference of an already material, coldly exploitative system. From various pre- and post-holocaust perspectives, this proposes, in a manner of speaking, that a *linguistic* "doppelganger" of Jew hatred still uncannily and retrospectively haunts Shakespeare's text. Moreover, if this tradition of Jew hatred hints at, to use Dworkin's term, the "integrity" of a particular anti-Semitic kind, and if Bailey's concern is with the "law" then "the interpretive judgement must notice and take account of [the presence of such] ... dimensions." If "integrity does not enforce itself," and if "judgement is required," explication of the play's legal probing of the human body as owned or owed property has to take account of the very anti-Semitic language within which this probing is simultaneously embedded. The play is so intensely haunted with the refrain of Christian anti-Semitism and the "integral justice" that sustains it, but, also, and frequently in Shakespearean comedies, the critical voice of the other—in this case of Shylock—points towards a doubleness in the representation of the very "integrity" of the "Christian" notion of forfeiture. It suggests a displacement of the brutalities of early modern English debt law and imprisonment onto the alleged barbarity of an alien Jew. But on this aspect of the play's presentation of the Jew, Bailey displays a disturbing and uncanny silence.[226] The text's omnipresent linguistic "doublings" into race hatred is, by such repression, both rendered invisible but also left intact.

Arguably, this facilitates continuing circulation of that very hate language ostensibly treated as invisible. Indeed, the play itself, together with certain critical readings of it, also treats as invisible, other instances of, what Albert Memmi calls, "a refusal of the Other and an affirmation of the self through that refusal."[227] Available data about relations between early modern Venetian Jews and the Venetian state[228] and about aspects of Jewish theology,[229] contrast notably with the dramatic characters inhabiting, the representation of Judaism in, and the atmosphere informing, the Venetian space of Shakespeare's play.[230]

The sympathies for the Jew figure that nonetheless have been argued for, remain embedded within obstructionist legal discourses of race. The games with color in that other Venetian play, *Othello*, seem to challenge traditional stereotyping. The most destructive and dishonest voice in the play is that of the "white" European Iago whereas, for most of the first half of the play, the "black" Moor is shown to have a "free and open nature."[231] But the text is nevertheless further complicated, by the more negative representations of its central character, as we have briefly seen in the previous section. Moreover, well known doublenesses in the fluctuating seventeenth century English admiration for Venetian openness to strangers but suspicion of its alleged licentiousness might also mean that what there may even be in the way of enlightened "Venetian" tolerance in the two plays has its limits. Thus Portia reminds Shylock, in *The Merchant of Venice*, that there are punitive legal consequences "[i]f it be proved against an alien/That by direct, or indirect attempts/He seek the life of any citizen."[232] Othello and Shylock are at times shown to be sporadically haunted by verbal specters of a Venetian "purity" under threat from strangers, aliens, and outsiders. In *Othello*, Iago continually manipulates the fear of adulteration, sometimes conflating the myth of pure origin with medieval demonology. Peter Erickson traces what he calls levels of insulation against "extravagant and wheeling" strangers, to be found also in the Duke's language,[233] as well as in tellingly ominous associations attached to words such as "slavery,"[234] "Barbary,"[235] and "Mauritania."[236,237] As will be obvious, such boundaries to the tolerance of others, what Derrida identifies as conditional hospitality, inflect in particular ways, the differing kinds of Venetian or alien humanity imagined by Shakespeare. By the time Lodovico asks

> Is this the noble Moor, whom our full Senate
> Call all in all sufficient? Is this the nature
> Whom passion could not shake? Whose solid virtue
> The shot of accident nor dart of chance
> Could neither graze nor pierce?[238]

much of Othello's behavior, too has already begun to conform to traditional stereotypings of "blackness." It is of course true that the play is complicated by other concerns, amongst them the violence of masculinity and, often, its misogyny. Moreover, the interventions of Iago provoke interrogations of the behavior of "whiteness." But, in the present context of conceptualizations of race, the play's intertwining of Othello with various processes of the law is particularly significant.

It is true that the reliability and the unreliability of narrative as testimony, in what is ostensibly a forensic judicial procedure, emerges from a series of quasi-trial scenes in the play. In the first of these, Othello and Desdemona defend themselves against the charge of witchcraft. In the second and third quasi-trial sequences, Iago provides false testimony and false evidence against Desdemona and Cassio. In the final quasi-trial scene, Othello presents himself as prosecutor, judge, and executioner.[239] The legal procedures of testimony and judgment in these quasi-trial scenes prove to be, for the most part, dangerously dysfunctional. They also lead to what is at least implicitly a racialized conclusion.

At the end of the play, Othello identifies Iago's malignity as literal and non-mythical, when he says, "I look down towards his feet—but that's a fable."[240] But, compared to the telling case of the "white" Iago, Othello's version of judgment, in the play's presentation of his own suicide or self-execution, "names" explicitly, and in a way that he earlier refuses to do, his own malign action. At this very moment, the convert reminds the audience of his non-Christian past and continues

> And say besides that in Aleppo once,
> Where a malignant and a turbaned Turk
> Beat a Venetian and traduced the state,
> I took by th' throat the circumcisèd dog
> And smote him—thus.[241]

English anxiety about conversion in what was a recently Protestantized country nervous about its Catholic recusants, was further compounded by English fears of the alien, prompted by traditional differences between Christianity and Judaism as well as by new encounters, in trade, travel, and exploration, with Muslims and with blacks. In *The Merchant of Venice*, Shylock the Jew is partly dealt with, in the play's trial scene, by the judicial sentence of enforced conversion to Christianity. In contrast, Othello is an already converted Christian at the start of the play. Furthermore, whereas *The Merchant of Venice*, amidst various anxieties about conversion, at the very least appears to portray the use of the law as a means to *contain* difference by attempting, within the ethos of Christian universalism, to efface, or assimilate that difference, in *Othello*, legal procedures may be said, in the final analysis, to be shown more blatantly to be involved in the isolation, confirmation, and demonization of that claimed universalism. The fear that conversion may not erase the stereotyped and racialized "difference" within, overtly surfaces in Othello's actions as well as in his language at the play's end. The threat to Europe of the growing power of the Ottomans that informs these lines, and hinted at in events, has become familiar to us. Moreover, in these lines, and unlike the obscurities attached to the definition of Iago's violence, Othello's destructive behavior is given a clear identity and origin. Othello translates the violence he himself has perpetrated, into the "barbarism" of the "Turk" and of "blackness."[242]

In articulations of race, the use of the binary concepts of "civilization" and "barbarian," Christian and Muslim or Jew or heathen, and "light" and "dark" or "black" and "white" may often extend back to the ancient and medieval periods, but they may also be seen, over the centuries, to display a disturbingly tenacious staying power. Frequently turned to in situations of vulnerability, uncertainty, or encounters with the unknown, they reflect often processes of doubleness and self-doubt, projection and scapegoating. Moreover, as the laws and practices of the medieval papacy and the formation of institutions such as the Inquisition, or Plaatje's contestation of segregationist legislation in early twentieth century South Africa, or aspects of Shakespeare's two hate plays, *The Merchant of Venice* and *Othello* show, the imagining of race is often generated, reproduced, or circulated by processes of government and the law. Such processes may, in their fashioning of race, also sometimes operate silently, remain, deliberately or coincidentally, unacknowledged, if not actively repressed. Their lasting effects for all marginalized races are no less potent or sinister.

Notes

1 Don J. Wyatt, *The Blacks of Pre-modern China*, Philadelphia: University of Pennsylvania Press, 2009, 17–18.

2 Edith Hall, *Inventing the Barbarian Greek Self Definition through Tragedy*, Oxford: Oxford University Press, 2004 (1989).

3 Edith Hall, *Inventing the Barbarian*, 2.

4 Edith Hall, *Inventing the Barbarian*, 16.

5 Edith Hall, *Inventing the Barbarian*, 59.

6 Edith Hall, *Inventing the Barbarian*, 55.

7 Edith Hall, *Inventing the Barbarian*, 133–139.

8 Edith Hall, *Inventing the Barbarian*, 201.

9 Edith Hall, *Inventing the Barbarian*, 103.

10 Edith Hall, *Inventing the Barbarian*, 1.

11 Edith Hall, *Inventing the Barbarian*, 121.

12 Edith Hall, *Inventing the Barbarian*, 122.

13 Edith Hall, *Inventing the Barbarian*, 127.

14 Edith Hall, *Inventing the Barbarian*, 26.

15 Edith Hall, *Inventing the Barbarian*, 58.

16 Edith Hall, *Inventing the Barbarian*, 125–126.

17 Edith Hall, *Inventing the Barbarian*, 126.

18 Edith Hall, *Inventing the Barbarian*, 4. This contrasts with earlier, less critical references, during the archaic period, to other languages, groups, and cultures (see Hall, *Inventing the Barbarian*, 12–13; see also 19ff. 76–79, 117–121).

19 Ali Rattansi, *Racism: A Very Short Introduction*, Oxford: Oxford University Press, 2007, 14.

20 *The Tempest*, 1.2.350–1.2.361. All quotations from Shakespeare are taken from William Shakespeare, *The Riverside Shakespeare*, Second Edition, ed., G. Blakemore Evans, New York: Houghton Mifflin, 1996.

21 Edith Hall, *Inventing the Barbarian*, 2.

22 Edith Hall, *Inventing the Barbarian*, 101.

23 Edith Hall, *Inventing the Barbarian*, 60–62.

24 Ellis Cashmore and Jamie Cleland, *Football's Dark Side: Corruption, Homophobia, Violence and Racism in the Beautiful Game*, London: Palgrave Macmillan, 64–80.

25 Cashmore and Cleland, *Football's Dark Side*, 76.

26 Cashmore and Cleland, *Football's Dark Side*, 77.

27 Cashmore and Cleland, *Football's Dark Side*, 79.

28 Cashmore and Cleland, *Football's Dark Side*, 68.

29 Albert Memmi, *Racism*, Minneapolis: University of Minneapolis Press, 2000 (1982), 39–52.

30 Memmi, *Racism*, 49.

31 Memmi, *Racism*, 51.

32 Memmi, *Racism*, 52.

33 W.B. Yeats, *The Collected Poems of W. B. Yeats*, London: Macmillan, 1958, 381–382.

34 Howard Brenton, *The Romans in Britain*, London: Eyre Methuen, 1981.

35 Brenton, *The Romans in Britain*, 23–24.

36 Walter Benjamin, *Illuminations*, ed. Hannah Arendt, trans. Harry Zohn New York: Harcourt Brace Jovanovich, 1968, p. 256.

37 Joseph Cheah, "Buddhism, Race, and Ethnicity," in Michael Jerryson, ed., *The Oxford Handbook of Contemporary Buddhism*, Oxford: Oxford University Press, 2017, 650–661.

38 See Debra Higgs Strickland, *Saracens, Demons, & Jews: Making Monsters in Medieval Art*, Princeton: Princeton University Press, 2003, 29–30. She registers, also, a "medieval debt to Classical Greek scientific and pseudo scientific theories that explain the 'natural causes' for external physical form and its moral implications, as well as attitudes to barbarians" (17); see also "[i]nformation about the Monstrous Races first compiled by Classical authorities reached the Middle Ages through a number of different routes, the most important of which were the Alexander tradition and the writings of Pliny and Solinus" (41).

39 See Strickland, *Saracens, Demons, & Jews*, 29–39.

40 Strickland, *Saracens, Demons, & Jews*, 38.

41 Cited in Strickland, *Saracens, Demons, & Jews*, 177–178.

42 Geoffrey Chaucer, *General Prologue to The Canterbury Tales*, ed. F.N. Robinson, London: Oxford University Press, 1957, 23. All quotations from Chaucer's prologue and his tales come from this edition.

43 Strickland, *Saracens, Demons, & Jews*, 41.

44 Strickland, *Saracens, Demons, & Jews*, 48.

45 Strickland, *Saracens, Demons, & Jews*, 42.

46 Strickland, *Saracens, Demons, & Jews*, 8.
47 Strickland, *Saracens, Demons, & Jews*, 52.
48 Strickland, *Saracens, Demons, & Jews*, 59.
49 Strickland, *Saracens, Demons, & Jews*, 159, 161.
50 Strickland, *Saracens, Demons, & Jews*, 162, 163.
51 Strickland, *Saracens, Demons, & Jews*, 159.
52 Strickland, *Saracens, Demons, & Jews*, 159–160.
53 *The Man of Law's Tale*, in Robinson, ed., *General Prologue to The Canterbury Tales* (l. 281), 65.
54 *The Man of Law's Tale*, 65.
55 *The Man of Law's Tale*, 359.
56 *The Man of Law's Tale*, 323.
57 *The Man of Law's Tale*, 360–361.
58 *The Man of Law's Tale*, 404.
59 *The Man of Law's Tale*, 404.
60 *The Man of Law's Tale*, 378.
61 *The Man of Law's Tale*, 330–336.
62 Denise Kimber Buell, "Early Christian Universalism and Modern Racism," in Miriam Eliav-Feldon, Benjamin Isaac, and Joseph Ziegler, eds., *The Origins of Racism in the West*, Cambridge: Cambridge University Press, 2009, 129.
63 Brenda Deen Schildgen, *Pagans, Tartars, Moslems, and Jews in Chaucer's Canterbury Tales*, Gainesville: University of Florida Press, 2001, 55.
64 Schildgen, *Pagans, Tartars, Moslems, and Jews in Chaucer's Canterbury Tales*, 56.
65 Cited in Strickland, *Saracens, Demons & Jews*, 166.
66 Strickland, *Saracens, Demons & Jews*, 169.
67 Strickland, *Saracens, Demons & Jews*, 169.
68 Joshua Trachtenberg, *The Devil and the Jews: The Medieval Conception of the Jew and its Relation to Modern Anti-Semitism*, Philadelphia: Jewish Publication Society of America, 1983, 22: see also 18–31.
69 Trachtenberg, *The Devil and the Jews*, 39; see also 32–43.
70 See Trachtenberg, *The Devil and the Jews*, 187.
71 Trachtenberg, *The Devil and the Jews*, 193.
72 Trachtenberg, *The Devil and the Jews*, 50; see also 44–53, 163.
73 See Schildgen, *Pagans, Tartars, Moslems, and Jews in Chaucer's Canterbury Tales*, 93–108.
74 See, for example, Trachtenberg, *The Devil and the Jews*, 124–139, 140–155.
75 Trachtenberg, *The Devil and the Jews*, 131–132.
76 Chaucer, *The Riverside Chaucer*, ed. L.D. Benson, Third Edition, Oxford: Oxford University Press, 1987, 488–492. All other references from Chaucer are from this collection.

77 Chaucer, *The Riverside Chaucer*, 497.

78 Chaucer, *The Riverside Chaucer*, 501.

89 Chaucer, *The Riverside Chaucer*, 495.

80 Chaucer, *The Riverside Chaucer*, 552.

81 Chaucer, *The Riverside Chaucer*, 558–564.

82 Trachtenberg, *The Devil and the Jews*, 167.

83 Trachtenberg, *The Devil and the Jews*, 565–566.

84 Trachtenberg, *The Devil and the Jews*, 576.

85 Trachtenberg, *The Devil and the Jews*, 567.

86 Trachtenberg, *The Devil and the Jews*, 578.

87 Strickland, *Saracens, Demons, & Jews*, 95.

88 Strickland, *Saracens, Demons, & Jews*, 95.

89 Trachtenberg, *The Devil and the Jews*, 161.

90 Trachtenberg, *The Devil and the Jews*, 173.

91 Trachtenberg, *The Devil and the Jews*, 161–162.

92 Christopher Catherwood, *Making War in the Name of God*, New York: Citadel Press, 2008, 29.

93 Catherwood, *Making War in the Name of God*, 29.

94 Catherwood, *Making War in the Name of God*, 30–31.

95 Trachtenberg, *The Devil and the Jews*, 162; see also 162–169.

96 Trachtenberg, *The Devil and the Jews*, 11–12.

97 Robert Miles, *Racism*, London: Routledge, 1989, 18.

98 Catherwood, *Making War in the Name of God*, 14.

99 Daniela Flesler, *The Return of the Moor: Spanish Responses to Contemporary Moroccan Immigration*, Indiana: Purdue University Press, 2008, 3.

100 Miles, *Racism*, 18.

101 Miles, *Racism*, 18.

102 Rattansi, *Racism*, 17.

103 Miles, *Racism*, 19.

104 Miles, *Racism*, 19.

105 Strickland, *Saracens, Demons, & Jews*, 39.

106 See, for example, Trachtenberg, *The Devil and the Jews*, 166–169.

107 See, for example, Trachtenberg, *The Devil and the Jews*, 159–187.

108 Trachtenberg, *The Devil and the Jews*, 163.

109 Trachtenberg, *The Devil and the Jews*, 165–166.

110 Strickland, *Saracens, Demons, & Jews*, 105.

111 Schildgen, *Pagans, Tartars, Moslems, and Jews in Chaucer's Canterbury Tales*, 103.

112 David Hawkes, *The Culture of Usury in Renaissance England*, New York: Palgrave Macmillan, 2010, 68.

113 See, however, John Drakakis, ed., *The Merchant of Venice*, London: Methuen, 2010, "Introduction," 12–17.

114 Theodor W. Adorno and Max Horkheimer, *Dialectics of Enlightenment*, trans. John Cumming, London: Verso, 1972, p. 174.
115 Gil Anidjar, *The Jew, The Arab: A History of the Enemy*, Stanford: Stanford University Press, 2003, 35; see also 33–34.
116 Anidjar, *The Jew, The Arab*, 38.
117 Anidjar, *The Jew, The Arab*, 38.
118 Schildgen, *Pagans, Tartars, Moslems, and Jews in Chaucer's Canterbury Tales*, 63.
119 Schildgen, *Pagans, Tartars, Moslems, and Jews in Chaucer's Canterbury Tales*, 66.
120 Schildgen, *Pagans, Tartars, Moslems, and Jews in Chaucer's Canterbury Tales*, 68.
121 By an anonymous pupil, U5Z King Edward VI School, Handsworth, Birmingham, UK. To be found in *The Children's Book of Poems, Prayers and Meditations*, ed. Liz Attenborough, Dorset, UK: Element Books, 1998, 58. Versions of this poem, unacknowledged, circulate on the Internet.
122 Pei-Chia Lan, *Global Cinderellas: Migrant Domestics and Newly Rich Employers in Taiwan*, Durham: Duke University Press, 2003.
123 Strickland, *Saracens, Demons, & Jews*, 79.
124 Strickland, *Saracens, Demons, & Jews*, 83.
125 David Goldenberg, "Racism, Colour Symbolism, and Colour Prejudice," in Eliav-Feldon, Isaac, and Ziegler, eds., *The Origins of Racism in the West*, 93.
126 Shakespeare, *The Riverside Shakespeare*.
127 Shakespeare, *Much Ado About Nothing*, 5.4.
128 Strickland, *Saracens, Demons, & Jews*, 84.
129 Strickland, *Saracens, Demons, & Jews*, 94.
130 Strickland, *Saracens, Demons, & Jews*, 99.
131 Martin Bernal, *Black Athena: The Afroasiatic Roots of Classical Civilization*, London, Vintage Books, 1991, 440.
132 Bernal, *Black Athena*, 440.
133 Bernal, *Black Athena*, 440.
134 Bernal, *Black Athena*, 441.
135 Bernal, *Black Athena*, 441.
136 Strickland, *Saracens, Demons, & Jews*, 79.
137 Strickland, *Saracens, Demons, & Jews*, 79.
138 Goldenberg, "Racism, Colour Symbolism, and Colour Prejudice," 101–102.
139 Goldenberg, "Racism, Colour Symbolism, and Colour Prejudice," 101.
140 Jonathan Schorsch, *Jews and Blacks in the Early Modern World*, Cambridge: Cambridge University Press, 2004.

141 Strickland, *Saracens, Demons, & Jews*, 84.

142 See Strickland, *Saracens, Demons, & Jews*, 80–90.

143 Strickland, *Saracens, Demons, & Jews*, 89.

144 Strickland, *Saracens, Demons, & Jews*, 90.

145 Les Back and John Solomos, "Origins and Transformations," in Les Back and John Solomos, eds., *Theories of Race and Racism: A Reader*, London: Routledge, 2009, 33–34.

146 Back and Solomos, "Origins and Transformations," 34.

147 Goldenberg, "Racism, Colour Symbolism, and Colour Prejudice," 104.

148 Stephen Greenblatt, *Marvellous Possessions: The Wonder of the New World*, Oxford: Clarendon Press, 1991, 1–25.

149 Greenblatt, *Marvellous Possessions*, 6.

150 Greenblatt, *Marvellous Possessions*, 6.

151 Greenblatt, *Marvellous Possessions*, 6.

152 Greenblatt, *Marvellous Possessions*, 6.

153 Greenblatt, *Marvellous Possessions*, 6.

154 Greenblatt, *Marvellous Possessions*, 9.

155 See Winthrop D. Jordan, *The White Man's Burden: Historical Origins of Racism in the United States*, New York: Oxford University Press, 1974, and "First Impressions" in Les Back and John Solomos, eds., *Theories of Race and Racism*, 37–54; Eldred Jones, *Othello's Countrymen*, London: Oxford University Press, 1965 and *The Elizabethan Image of Africa*, Charlottesville: University of Virginia Press, 1971.

156 See text quoted in Ania Loomba and Jonathan Burton, eds., *Race in Early Modern England: A Documentary Companion*, New York: Palgrave Macmillan, 2007, 136.

157 See Jordan, "First Impressions," 39.

158 See Jordan, "First Impressions," 40–42.

159 See Jordan, "First Impressions," 42–44.

160 Jordan, "First Impressions," 45.

161 Jordan, "First Impressions," 45.

162 Jordan, *The White Man's Burden*, 22–24.

163 Jordan, *The White Man's Burden*, 46–50.

164 See Loomba and Burton, *Race in Early Modern England*, 3–4.

165 Kim F. Hall, *Things of Darkness: Economies of Race and Gender in Early Modern England*, Ithaca: Cornell University Press, 1995, 10.

166 Hall, *Things of Darkness*, 10–11.

167 Hall, *Things of Darkness*, 264.

168 Hall, *Things of Darkness*, 7.

169 Hall, *Things of Darkness*, 15.

170 Hall, *Things of Darkness*, 257.

171 Patricia Parker, "Fantasies of 'Race' and 'Gender': Africa, *Othello*, and Bringing to Light," in Margo Hendricks and Patricia Parker, eds.,

Women, "Race," & Writing in the Early Modern Period, London: Routledge, 1994, 84–100. See also, for example, Patricia Parker, "Black *Hamlet:* Battening on the Moor," *Shakespeare Studies*, 31, 2003, 127–164; Patricia Parker, "Barbers and Barbary: Early Modern Cultural Semantics," *Renaissance Drama*, 33, 2004, 199–242.

172 Parker, "Fantasies of 'Race' and 'Gender," 84–86. Ambroise Paré, *Des monstres et prodigies*, Malesherbes: Gallimard, 2015 (1573); Helkiah Crook, *Mikrokosmographia: A Description of the Body of Man*, Harvard University Library, 1616.

173 Parker, "Fantasies of 'Race' and 'Gender," 95.

174 Parker, "Fantasies of 'Race' and 'Gender," 99.

175 Ania Loomba, *Gender, Race, Renaissance Drama*, Manchester: Manchester University Press, 1989, 1.

176 Loomba, *Gender, Race, Renaissance Drama*, 2.

177 Ania Loomba, *Shakespeare, Race, and Colonialism*, Oxford: Oxford University Press, 2002, 6–7.

178 Loomba, *Shakespeare, Race, and Colonialism*, 7.

179 William Shakespeare, *Othello*, ed., Michael Neill, Oxford: Oxford University Press, 2006, 1.1.79. All quotations from *Othello* are taken from this version.

180 Shakespeare, *Othello*, 1.1.88–1.1.91.

181 Shakespeare, *Othello*, 1.1.110–1.1.113.

182 Shakespeare, *Othello*, 1.1.115–1.1.116.

183 Shakespeare, *Othello*, 1.1.66.

184 Shakespeare, *Othello*, 1.1.125.

185 Shakespeare, *Othello*, 1.1.132–1.1.135.

186 Shakespeare, *Othello*, 1.3.250.

187 Jeremiah 13:23.

188 Shakespeare, *Othello*, 1.3.646–1.3.647.

189 Shakespeare, *Othello*, 2.3.161–2.3.163.

190 Nabil Matar, *Turks, Moors, and Englishmen in the Age of Discovery*, New York: Columbia University Press, 1999, 13.

191 Daniel J. Vitkus ("Introduction," *Three Turk Plays from Early Modern England*, New York: Columbia University Press, 2000, 15) writes, "[w]hether imagined as a dark-skinned African Moor, or a robed and turbaned Turk, the external appearance of the Islamic Other was often read as a sign of spiritual darkness or barbaric ignorance."

192 Solomon T. Plaatje, *Native Life in South Africa*, Braamfontein: Ravan Press, 1982 (1916), 38–39.

193 Plaatje, *Native Life in South Africa*, 70.

194 Plaatje, *Native Life in South Africa*, 70.

195 Plaatje, *Native Life in South Africa*, 71.

196 Plaatje, *Native Life in South Africa*, 74–75.

197 Plaatje, *Native Life in South Africa*, 20.

198 Cited in Abebe Zegeye and Maurice Vambe, *Close to the Sources: Essays on Contemporary African Culture, Politics and Academy*, Pretoria: University of South Africa Press and Routledge, 2009, 99.

199 M. Pascal Gwala, "Towards a National Theatre," *South African Outlook*, CII,1227, 1973, 132–133.

200 Cited in Zegeye and Vambe, *Close to the Sources*, 99.

201 Steve Biko, *I Write What I Like: A Selection of his Writings*, ed. Aelred Stubbs C.R., Oxford: Heinemann, 1987, 114.

202 Karla F.C. Holloway, *Legal Fictions: Constituting Race, Composing Literature*, Durham and London: Duke University Press, 2014, Preface, x.

203 Holloway, *Legal Fictions*, Preface, x.

204 Holloway, *Legal Fictions*, Preface, x.

205 Holloway, *Legal Fictions*, Preface, xv.

206 Holloway does not cite Althusser, but the notion of interpellation seems helpful here. Cf. "Black folks and black literature were equally bound, and determined, by law" (Holloway, *Legal Fictions*, Preface, x).

207 Amanda Bailey, "Shylock and the Slaves: Owing and Owning in *The Merchant of Venice*," *Shakespeare Quarterly*, 62:1, 2011, 1–24.

208 Bailey, "Shylock and the Slaves," 3.

209 Bailey, "Shylock and the Slaves," 14.

210 Bailey, "Shylock and the Slaves," 17.

211 Bailey, "Shylock and the Slaves," 2.

212 Memmi, *Racism*, 6–7.

213 Ronald Dworkin, *Law's Empire*, Cambridge: Harvard University Press, 1986, 410–411, 413.

214 Bailey, "Shylock and the Slaves," 18.

215 It is true that Bailey briefly cites early modern dramatic reference to the brutality (injustice) of such early debt law, involving power over person, referred to, as well, in the final line of her essay, where she remarks that "[i]t was just such a formulation that allowed the insolvent to languish in prison" (24).

216 In this regard, Bailey appropriately concedes that Shylock's bond with its pound of flesh, is itself only an "amplification" (11), of the "proprietary logic" (11) of an already existent early modern English punitive system, since delegitimated. Nor is Shylock, it might be added, in any way originator of this forfeiture system. See Luke Wilson, "Monetary Compensation for Injuries to the Body A.D. 602–1697," in Linda Woodbridge, ed., *Money and the Age of Shakespeare: Essays in New Economic Criticism*, New York: Palgrave Macmillan, 2003, 30.

217 William Shakespeare, *The Merchant of Venice*, ed., John Drakakis, London: Arden Shakespeare, Bloomsbury, 2010, 1.3.94. All quotations from *The Merchant of Venice* are taken from this version.

218 Joshua Trachtenberg, *The Devil and the Jews: the Medieval Conception of the Jew and its Relation to Modern Anti-Semitism*, Philadelphia: The Jewish Publication Society, 1993 (1983), 25.

219 Bailey, "Shylock and the Slaves," 15.

220 Shakespeare, *The Merchant of Venice*, 3.1.30. Drakakis, ed., *The Merchant of Venice*, 282, fn. 28 records that Salanio's "it is the complexion of them all to leave the dam" (3.1.27–3.1.28) registers a proverbial echo of Tilley, D225, *The Devil and his Dam*, c.1547, in this line, "associating the Jew and his absent wife with Satan."

221 Shakespeare, *The Merchant of Venice*, 3.2.274.

222 Trachtenberg, *The Devil and the Jews*, 50.

223 Shakespeare, *The Merchant of Venice*, 4.1.2–4.1.5.

224 See Martin Orkin, "Rendering Shakespeare, War and Race in Present-Day Israel," *Shakespeare*, 6:1, 2010.

225 Shakespeare, *The Merchant of Venice*, 3.1.63–3.1.64.

226 Natasha Korda, "Dame Usury: Gender, Credit, and (Ac)counting in the Sonnets and *The Merchant of Venice*," *Shakespeare Quarterly*, 60:2, 2009, 129–153, also displays a disturbing silence about the implications of Portia's attitude to the Prince of Morocco. Indeed, in a related if slightly different instance of de-Judaizing the text, Emma Smith, who argues interestingly that the sympathetic Shylock, victim of anti-Semitism, originates in nineteenth century performance traditions, goes so far as to propose as well that Shylock is a primarily a figment of Shakespeare's concern for the plight of early modern French protestant immigrants in London. See Emma Smith, "Was Shylock Jewish?" *Shakespeare Quarterly*, 64:2, 2013, 188–219.

227 Memmi, *Racism*, 192.

228 See Robert C. Davis, "Introduction," in Robert C. Davis and Benjamin Ravid, eds., *The Jews of Early Modern Venice*, Baltimore: John Hopkins University Press, 2001, xi; Benjamin Ravid, *Studies on the Jews of Venice, 1382–1797*, Aldershot: Ashgate, 2003, 115, x, xi. Ravid's work is nowhere cited in Laura Tosi and Shaul Bassi, eds., *Visions of Venice in Shakespeare*, Farnham: Ashgate, 2011. See as well, William Shakespeare, *The Merchant of Venice*, ed. Leah S. Marcus, New York: WW Norton, 2006, 130; Jason P. Rosenblatt, *Renaissance England's Chief Rabbi: John Selden*, Oxford: Oxford University Press, 2006, 118, 167, 168. See too Joanna Weinberg, "Preaching in the Venetian Ghetto: The Sermons of Leon Modena," in David B. Ruderman, ed., *Preachers of the Italian Ghetto*, Berkeley: University of California Press, 1992; Seymour Feldman, *Philosophy in a Time of Crisis Don Isaac Abravanel:*

Defender of the Faith, London: Routledge, 2003; Lawee Eric Jay, "'Inheritance of the Fathers': Aspects of Isaac Abarbanel's stance towards tradition," Harvard University PhD, 1993; B. Netanyahu, *Don Isaac Abravanel: Statesman and Philosopher*, Philadelphia: Jewish Publication Society of America, 1958; Benjamin Ravid "*Contra-Judaeos* in Seventeenth-Century Italy: Two Responses to the *Discorso* of Simone Luzzatto by Melchiore Palontrotti and Guilio Mmorosini," in Ravid, *Studies on the Jews of Venice, 1382–1797*. Nathalie Zemon Davis, "Fame and Secrecy: Leon Modena's Life as an Early Modern Autobiography," in Mark R. Cohen, ed., *The Autobiography of a Seventeenth-Century Rabbi: Leon Modena's Life of Judah*, Princeton: Princeton University Press, 1988.

229 It is true that James Shapiro (*Shakespeare and the Jews*, New York: Columbia University Press, 1996) provides a great deal of information about early modern Jews in his exploration of how early modern England defined itself against Judaism, and Janet Adelman (*Blood Relations: Christian and Jew in The Merchant of Venice*, Chicago: Chicago University Press, 2008) gives a compelling account of how the Hebraists drew upon Judaism as an (imperfect) origin of Christianity. Tenets of Judaism which Shakespeare's play purports to represent or infer, remain, in recent criticism of the play, arguably under-investigated, or barely acknowledged. More investigation into the knowledges we have about early modern Judaism itself is desirable on matters including Jewish understanding of revenge, mercy, usury, even the story of Jacob and Laban, referred to in the play. In this connection see S.Y. Zevin, "Mishpat Shylock," in *In the Light of Jewish Law [Le"or Hahalacha]*, Tel Aviv: Abraham Zion, 1957.

230 Such "refusal[s] of the Other" make the ongoing popularity of performance of *The Merchant of Venice* particularly in the United Kingdom and Germany, not a little disturbing. See Zeno Ackermann, "Performing Oblivion/Enacting Remembrance: *The Merchant of Venice* in West Germany, 1945 to 1961," *Shakespeare Quarterly*, 62:3, 2011, 364–395; see *The Merchant of Venice*, ed., Charles Edelman, Cambridge: Cambridge University Press, 2002; Dror Abend-David, *"Scorned My Nation": A Comparison of Translations of The Merchant of Venice into German, Hebrew and Yiddish*, New York: Peter Lang, 2003; Andrew G. Bonnell, *Shylock in Germany: Antisemitism and the German Theatre from the Enlightenment to the Nazis*, New York: Tauris Academic Studies, 2008.

231 Shakespeare, *Othello*, 1.3.387.

232 Shakespeare, *The Merchant of Venice*, 4.1.345–4.1.347.

233 Peter Erickson, "Images of White Identity in *Othello*" in Philip C. Kolin, ed., *Othello: New Critical Essays*, New York: Routledge, 2002.

234 Shakespeare, *Othello*, 1.3.137.
235 Shakespeare, *Othello*, 4.3.24.
236 Shakespeare, *Othello*, 4.2.224.
237 Peter Erickson, "Race Words in *Othello*," in Rubin Espinosa and David Ruiter, eds., *Shakespeare and Immigration*, Farnham: Ashgate, 2014. Geraldo U. De Sousa (" 'My Hopes Abroad': The Global/Local Nexus in *The Merchant of Venice*," in Espinosa and Ruiter, eds., *Shakespeare and Immigration*, 44), argues that, in *The Merchant of Venice*, Portia is

> champion of the locals, ... she uses her role as judge to underscore Antonio's roots as a Venetian, offer a spiritual defence of Venetian values and traditions, and embrace Antonio's global financial interests ... she defines the boundary between Venetian and alien.

238 Shakespeare, *Othello*, 4.1.256–4.1.260.
239 Shakespeare, *Othello*, 5.2.1ff.
240 Shakespeare, *Othello*, 5.2.284.
241 Shakespeare, *Othello*, 5.2.351–5.2.355.
242 The British actor, Hugh Quarshie, argued, in 1999:

> If a black actor plays Othello does he not risk making racial stereotypes seem legitimate and even true? When a black actor plays a role written for a white actor in black make-up and for a predominantly white audience, does he not encourage the white way, or rather the wrong way, of looking at black men, namely that black men, or "Moors", are over-emotional, excitable and unstable, thereby vindicating Iago's statement, "These Moors are changeable in their wills"? ... *I fear that figure still occupies the same space in the imagination of modern theatre-goers as it does among Shakespeare's contemporaries.*
>
> (Cited in Loomba, *Shakespeare, Race, and Colonialism*, 110; emphasis added)

2

PSEUDO-SCIENTIFIC MARKINGS OF DIFFERENCE

The discourses of natural sciences began to inform the concept of race from the late seventeenth century onwards and as parts of the movement variously represented as the age of reason, the age of science, or the age of enlightenment. Like the search for the elusive Holy Grail, this was a doomed project. "Evidence" culled from observation of the natural world was always partial, subsequently disproved, or permeated at the same time with unscientifically "proven," traditional, and binary assumptions about race. But despite crucial weaknesses, the myth of a science of race continued to be asserted. Versions, always scientifically flawed, were nonetheless accepted and, for a number of reasons, regarded as authoritative.

"Scientific method"

Although many scholars still claim that there was no concept of race and, therefore, no racism before the emergence of "scientific" formulations of race, this assertion needs some modification. The "naturalized" assumptions about particular group identities were already underway in the ancient and medieval European worlds. Formulations of hatred, from early on in Western history, included proto-scientific attention to phenotypic markings as well as proto-national and cultural, or religious assumptions. For the Roman writer Juvenal, while "Greeks, Orientals, Egyptians ... are all hated for their foreign ways and their potential to corrupt Roman culture, [b]lacks ... are hated ... for ... their skin colour."[1] Anthropological theorizing about phenotypical and environmental difference is to be found in Hippocrates's *Airs, Waters, and Places*, and in Aristotle's *Politics*.[2] Medieval theories also drew on these works. In medieval terminology, views of peoples involved both environmental thought and humoral medicine. This view was part of natural philosophy. According to Peter Biller, this view was disseminated by translation of texts from Greek and Arabic.[3,4] They spread because of the study of these texts in the European universities, which had recently come into existence. Medieval encyclopedias "included a great deal of science,"[5] and in such writing, the "continuum from physical to mental or psychological characteristics"[6] is emphasized.

Bartholomew the Englishman, for example, records in his work that "Europe feeds people that are larger in body, stronger in their force, bolder in spirit, and more beautiful in form and appearance than the peoples that Africa and Asia feeds."[7] Albertus Magnus's fourteenth-century treatise *On the Nature of Places*, taking "existing materials on the black man," registers

blackened bodies, the whiteness of teeth, the particular colour of tongues and throats when open, the prominence of mouths and eyes, the porosity and dryness of bodies, coldness and timidity of hearts, fast aging because of defect of natural *virtus*, the abundance of specific humours, light bodies, fatuous minds, and dryness and heat as the cause of the curliness ... of their ... hair.[8]

Albertus also focuses on "the greater hotness of black women" and in his comments on the Jews, introduces a reading "rooted in humoral medicine" so that in his "attention to *both* the sexual heat of black women and the dominance of melancholia in Jewish bodies, Albertus was developing the scientific element in proto-racist thought."[9]

It may be true that such or other medieval "scientific" versions of difference had not yet discovered or developed a generally acknowledged articulation of "a stable or unalterable analytical category"[10] of difference. Nonetheless, as Zeigler points out, there were "domains in medieval society where proto-racist ideas and feelings could thrive." These attitudes were based on assumptions about inherent characteristics:[11]

> The clear signs in theological and legal sources of a growing suspicion from the twelfth century onwards of Jewish converts suggest that for many clerics Jewish identity was an immutable, physical characteristic which could not be effaced by baptism or eradicated by conversion ... late medieval romance ... is replete with instances in which conversion to Christianity is insufficient to cancel out differences of colour or race and with references to embodied representations of Islamic and Jewish racial otherness. Religious difference thus came to mean also a theory of biological essence which was indivisible from religion itself.[12]

The late seventeenth, eighteenth, and nineteenth centuries, particularly, saw the introduction of several methods of measurement and classification, or the introduction of hierarchies in the examination of differences between designated groups of people. Such projects inevitably sought also to conceptualize groups or types of humans as each having a "fixed biological character."[13] For example, in 1684, François Bernier, used the term "race," to define "a major division of humanity displaying a distinctive combination of physical traits transmitted through a line of descent,"[14] and he applied it to what he demarcated as four or five "types" of people. Brian Niro observes that the eighteenth century taxonomist Carolus Linnaeus, who named, ranked, and classified living organisms, included in his *Systema Naturae* (1735) human beings in his classification of animals and plants.[15] Although it did not itself establish a hierarchy, this kind of classification was, in some senses, a version of the Renaissance notion of the Great Chain of Being. This later version of "natural" order traced a hierarchy, which stretched from God to humans and, below them, animals and plants. Linnaeus also delineated four partly "geographically" based, although also partly humorally based, varieties of humans, under the heading *homo sapiens.*

In his effort to distinguish "the causal mechanisms that might inspire human variation," Georges-Louis Leclerc, Comte de Buffon the French Naturalist thinker (1707–1788), criticized Linnaeus's classifications as being too arbitrary.[16] In an early instance of what we would now call bio-geography, he explicitly foregrounded, instead, "geographic placement [and] environmental conditions."[17] In accordance with the prevailing religious orthodoxy that validated monogenesis, which held that according to the biblical narrative all humans were descendants of Adam and Eve, Buffon argued that the human species, originally emanating from one couple, subsequently spread over the whole earth, and were then crucially and severally affected by particular climatic and geographical location. However, emphasis on the environment remained problematic: the search was for causal mechanisms that might be responsible for the existence of difference but that were *not* subject to environmental or any other influence. In the course of his research, and in an effort to clarify precisely the data being "observed," Buffon also defined the word species as "a constant succession of similar individuals that can reproduce together."[18] Thus, the horse and the ass were not of the same species because "their issue, a mule, cannot procreate."[19] It was because of this, Buffon maintained, that humans, even when differentiated into particular groups, were still members of one species.

In his search for a "scientific" version of the "natural" order, Immanuel Kant was also keen to affirm monogenesis. But he sought especially to theorize differences in humans within this conceptual framework in a way that would fix "race as a permanent characteristic that is unfailingly inherited."[20] This would help Europeans to conceptualize and classify the peoples beyond Europe that they occasionally encountered, and, more often, read about in travel literature. The desire to explain the existence of dark-skinned peoples was an ongoing obsession. For example, Kant contemplated the physical basis for blackness, "appealing to iron particles in 1777 ... and to phlogiston in 1785."[21] But his concern with the "the color of Africans ... focused on the question of the adequacy of mechanistic explanations [based on factors such as environment] offered in isolation from teleology."[22] He argued that

> when certain individuals undergo accidental change leading
> to the altered character being taken up into the generative
> force ... and thereby becoming hereditary, this has to be
> judged as the development of a purposive predisposition
> already in the species for the sake of its preservation.[23]

For Kant, this imagined predisposition was to be found in innate
"seeds" in each of the four kinds of humans in his taxonomy, which,
once individually activated by largely climatic factors, engineered
particular, irreversible change.

Kant's concern with "the conception of scientific investigation" in
the pursuit of a "natural history" that goes beyond mere description of
"external and accidental conditions" and drawing on his notion of
preformed "seeds, prompted him" to assert:

> What is a *race*? The word certainly does not belong in a sys-
> tematic description of nature, so presumably the thing itself is
> nowhere to be found in nature. However, the *concept* which
> this expression designates is nevertheless well established in
> the reason of every observer of nature who supposes a con-
> junction of causes placed originally in the line of descent of
> the genus itself in order to account for a self-transmitted
> peculiarity that appears in different interbreeding animals but
> which does not lie in the concept of genus.[24]

This was a clear articulation, by an "observer of nature," of a theoretical, "scientific" cause for an individuating "self-transmitted peculiar-
ity," or pre-formed "seed," in the "genus" "human." For Kant, this
accounted for the phenomenon of human "difference" in "nature."

Isaac de la Peyrère challenged the notion of monogenesis as early
as 1655 and in spite of its religiously legitimated authority. In the first
half of the eighteenth century, Voltaire also supported the case for
polygenesis, although his use of the argument that the difference
between peoples confirms that their origins are to be found in more
than one couple, has been read by many as evidence of Voltaire's
own anti-Bible polemic. Henry Home, Lord Kames, in *Sketches of the
History of Man*, first published in 1774, also held that there were
originally distinct races. The inference to be derived from such

arguments was that "distinct 'races' of human beings had always existed" and that, further, "the hierarchy of inferiority and superiority was therefore natural, inevitable, unalterable."[25] An increasing secularization informed such arguments. By the mid-nineteenth century, as Robert Miles has shown, "as science occupied an increasingly ascendant position over theology ... this theory of polygenism was dominant."[26]

The nineteenth and twentieth century interest in measurement of the size of skulls, and then of brains, offers yet another example of pseudo-scientific development. These kinds of investigation were anticipated, in the late eighteenth century, by Johan Friedrich Blumenbach. He identified five groups or varieties of human beings, limiting himself, as well, to "exhaustive physical descriptions."[27] As part of this, he undertook "empirical research, such as the measurement of skulls" which "set the tone for nineteenth-century research in Germany not just for the science of race but the biological sciences generally."[28] In addition, phrenology came, in the nineteenth century, to occupy a further, international, field of "scientific" measurement. Originating in Germany, it was developed, amongst others, by George Combe in Scotland who worked with the North American, Samuel George Morton.[29] In the same period, the Swede, Anders Retzius, developed the cephalic index as one method of measuring the skull. These and other British, North American, and European investigators engaged with one another in projects concerned with classifications of the size of the brain, or of the skull as well as with the more traditional phenotypic interest in facial characteristics. But, as Robert Miles observes, just as "each attempt at classification broke down under the weight of logical inconsistency and empirical evidence, a new classification was formulated."[30]

The putatively "scientific" concept of empirical observation, that underlay these, and many other endeavors, conferred upon them an imagined objectivity which, subsequently in the nineteenth century and beyond, would help to authorize the "truth claims" of the "science" of race. Scientists, natural historians, and people in general took the implied objectivity of such "scientific" formulations of "race" more and more for granted, notwithstanding the obvious shortcomings of such enterprises. In debates about race such assumptions became, in the nineteenth century and beyond, commonplace. Despite the repeated inadequacy, varying, and ultimately mistaken aspect of the data deployed in particular instances, its deficiencies did not impact on commonly held assumptions that these were "objective" readings of race. This, despite the fact that Charles Darwin, for example, had explicitly stressed the ongoing obscurity of claims as to a scientifically verifiable existence of races:

> as far as we are enabled to judge (although always liable to error on this head) not one of the external differences between the races of man [sic] are of any direct or special service to him ... [w]e have thus far been baffled in all our attempts to account for differences between the races of man.[31]

Pseudo-sciences and racial nationalisms

In his notorious essay, "A Modest Proposal *for Preventing the Children of Poor People in Ireland, from being a Burden to their Parents or Country, and for making them Beneficial to the Public*," written in 1729, Jonathan Swift parodied both the new method of calculating from observable data and the inhumanity of slave traders:

> The Number of Souls in *Ireland* being usually reckoned one Million and a half; of these I calculate there may be about Two Hundred Thousand Couple whose Wives are Breeders; from which Number I subtract thirty thousand Couples, who are able to maintain their own Children; although I apprehend there cannot be so many, under *the present Distress of the Kingdom*; but this being granted, there will remain an Hundred and Seventy Thousand Breeders. I again subtract Fifty Thousand for those Women who miscarry, or whose Children die by Accident, of Disease, within the year. There only remain an Hundred and Twenty Thousand Children of poor Parents annually born: The Question, therefore is, How this Number shall be reared, and provided for?[32]

Swift's scathingly satiric answer to this question is that, since "a Boy or a Girl before twelve Years old, is no saleable Commodity," he has it on the assurance of "a very knowing *American* of my Acquaintance in London" that: "A young healthy Child, well nursed, is, at a Year old, a most delicious, nourishing, and wholesome food: whether *Stewed, Roasted, Baked,* or *Boiled;* and, I make no doubt, that it will equally serve in a *Fricasie,* or *Ragout.*"[33] He therefore "humbly" offers it "to *public Consideration*" that:

> of the Hundred and Twenty thousand Children, already computed, Twenty thousand may be reserved for Breed; whereof only one Fourth Part to be Males; which is more than we allow to *Sheep, black Cattle,* or *Swine*; and my Reason is, that these Children are seldom the Fruits of Marriage, *a Circumstance not much regarded by our Savages.*[34]

From a literary point of view, Swift's hostility to the new methods of observation and calculation, as well as that of other Augustans, came from a conservative, neo-classicist viewpoint about "human nature," imagined as fixed and unchanging. The Augustans despised the attention to what they saw as miniscule details, evident in the emerging crafts of journalism and fiction. For them this reflected, in turn, the new scientific emphasis on measurement, calculation, and empirical observation. In their estimation the new worship of reason and its focus on external minutiae ignored the "eternal truths" about humans. For the Augustans, the journalists, scientists, and the new novelists, such as Defoe, were the inhabitants of "Grub Street," with minds tantamount to ones focused on insects instead of the broader significance of humankind.

But although the satire in Swift's passages, above, comes from such a position, these passages nevertheless highlight in other telling ways the limits and potential deficiencies in the project of what Ali Rattansi calls, for the later nineteenth century, "scientific racism."[35] For instance, Swift's persona describes the Irish, about whose poverty he felt deeply, as if they are beasts or slaves to be counted and bred. The tone suggests the traditional contempt for the Irish displayed by the English, whose long history, since the sixteenth century, of attempted colonization and exploitation is well known. Thus the voice of the author of the essay continually emphasizes the inferiority of the Irish. The "breeding" of them, as in the case of animals, needs to be made more efficient. They are "savages," but left to their own devices they are a drain on resources. Rattansi notes that, as late as the nineteenth century, in Britain, "the arrival of the Irish [immigrants], fleeing famine and living in appalling conditions in the cities provoked … a widely held view that the Irish were ape-like and innately fond of living in filth, just like their pigs."[36] The almost compulsive calculations that Swift had earlier applied to the Irish population register, even before the nineteenth century, a disturbingly disjunctive gap between the suffering objects of these almost abstract series of computations and the putatively "objective" observer who applies them.

Of course, enlightenment natural historians or scientists were seeking more than an abstract or superficial methodology. However, their methodology, was still, at times, informed by more traditional assumptions about the determinants and the composition of race. None of these "traditional" conceptualizations was exposed to the very rigors of investigation that the scientists or natural historians were trying to introduce.[37] In Swift's parody, Irish inferiority appears as an uninvestigated "given." We noted above that Linnaeus differentiated his four types of humans not just on the basis of geographical placement and physical differences, but also on the basis of the medieval theory of the humors, and on stereotypes encountered in the travel literature of the period. Climate and geographical location, regarded by some as key in the formation of race since the ancient period, had remained a preconception in other theories. Most significant, as Bernasconi observes,

> insofar as color was regarded as the most striking characteristic differentiating the various types, and insofar as Whites considered themselves clearly superior to everyone else, then one obvious way of organizing these types hierarchically that occurred to Europeans was from white to black.[38]

Buffon believed that white was the original color. Kant's focus on color as the primary indicator of difference, and his interest in the reason for blackness, may have been in line with the eighteenth century, and earlier, fascination with this question. But his hierarchy of races also accords with "his own [empirically uninvestigated] esteem of his white, European, educated, male standard of living."[39] Elsewhere, Kant argued that

> [t]he inhabitant of the temperate parts of the world, above the central part, has a more beautiful body, works harder, is more jocular, more controlled in his passions, more intelligent than any other race of people in the world. That is why at all points in time these peoples have educated others and controlled them with weapons. The Romans, Greeks, the ancient Nordic peoples, Genghis Kahn, the Turks, Tamburlaine, the Europeans after Columbus's discoveries, they have all amazed the southern lands with their arts and weapons.[40]

We noted in Chapter 1 that the negative construction of blackness was already underway in the ancient as well as in the medieval Christian world. If Kant's remarks here show the extent to which his furtherance of "scientific" methodology in his writings about race was also mixed with non-scientific, older habits of thought, it also suggests, as we argued in Chapter 1, that the imagining of race itself comprises multiple kinds of formulations including, in addition to a pseudo-science, cultural, religious, and politically inflected conceptualizations.

Drawing on this tradition, the philosopher G.W.F. Hegel, too, maintained, in the first half of the nineteenth century, that "world history proper begins only with the Caucasians," with other races having a "provisional" or "structural" role, and Africans "no role at all."[41] An entry ascribed to him in the *Encyclopaedia of the Philosophical Sciences* asserts, on the one hand—as if the statement is scientific truth— that "the physical difference between all these races is shown mainly in the formation of the skull and the face." Such theories have since been discredited. Moreover, the "scientific" tone in the entry is coupled with a notably uninvestigated, much older, generalized set of fabrications:

> Negroes are to be regarded as a race of children ... Good-natured and harmless when at peace, they can become suddenly enraged and then commit the most frightening cruelties ... In their native country the most shocking despotism prevails. There they do not attain to the feeling of human

personality, their mentality is quite dormant, remaining sunk within itself and making no progress, and thus corresponding to the compact, differenceless mass of the African continent.[42]

In the nineteenth century the "scientific" account of the term race itself became, for an increasing number of people, a standard means of authentication. Rattansi notes that there "emerged a whole range of theories that explained all human variation on the basis of innate racial characteristics."[43] Thus, whereas Charles Darwin argued against the existence of racial individuation, Arthur Comte de Gobineau, the nineteenth century cultural philosopher, argued that "the racial question overshadows all other problems of history."[44]

Gobineau claimed that humans are "divided into unlike and unequal parts, or rather into a series of categories, arranged one above the other, according to differences of intellect."[45] He discerns three categories, a white race, a black race, and a yellow race. For him, the white races were superior and "the human groups to which the European nations and their descendants belong are the most beautiful."[46] Racial mixing, or what he called "blood crossing" in the main, was the result of dilution of the "purity" of the blood of the superior race; this was what Gobineau understood to be what happened in each instance of "miscegenation." In his view, "miscegenation" contributed to degeneration. For Gobineau, "degeneration" was an unavoidable, potentially festering accompaniment to processes of "civilization." He held that, "mankind [*sic*] lives in obedience to two laws, one of repulsion, the other of attraction,"[47] but that "the human race in all its branches has a secret repulsion from the crossing of blood."[48] Nonetheless, conquering civilizations tended always to mix with those they conquered so that from "the very first day when the conquest is accomplished and the fusion begins, there appears a noticeable change of quality in the blood of the masters."[49] Gobineau held that the law of attraction "brought about the spread of civilization … but … the weakening brought about by race-mixing ultimately caused the decline of that civilization."[50] "Miscegenation" therefore diluted, diminished, and polluted racial types.

In the nineteenth century, such notions of "pure" and "impure" blood, the measurement of skulls (phrenology), studies of criminology, even allegations about the inferiority of women, and their deviant (rampant) sexualities were common "scientific" preoccupations. Rattansi cites the notorious display of the anatomized genitals, and its "supposed peculiarities," of the Hottentot woman, Sarah Bartmann, who, during her lifetime "was exhibited to European audiences so they could gape at her steatopygia, or protruding buttocks." This affords, also, one example of how women's imagined "innately pathological sexuality"[51] was also connected to "blackness" as, indeed, had sometimes been the fantasy in the pre-pseudo-scientific period.

Gobineau's assumptions about the information he amassed remain consistently unproven throughout his essay, but at the same time he often dressed his material up in the conceptual framework of the new sciences. He offered his own opinions about various techniques of craniology. Indeed, he outlined in detail, and by means of frequent references to current scientific theories involving anthropological, geological, or climatic study. Thus:

> [t]he existing races constitute separate branches ... They differed from each other in the shape and proportion of the limbs, the structure of the skull, the internal conformation of the body, the nature of the capillary system, the colour of the skin and the like; and they never succeeded in losing their characteristic features except under the powerful influence of the crossing of blood.[52]

Notions of "purity" and "degeneration," also surfaced in earlier centuries, but they took hold as a particular set of fixations and obsessions as the nineteenth century unfolded. Race was conflated with blood, nation, and hierarchy. Within Europe, national characteristics were also conceptualized in an aggressively discriminatory and hierarchical manner because

> if on the one hand human societies are called equal, and on the other we find some of them frivolous, others serious; some avaricious, others thriftless; some passionately fond of fighting, others careful of their lives and energies—it stands to reason that these differing nations must have destinies which are also absolutely different and, in a word, unequal.[53]

Within Europe also, there are, according to Gobineau, ineradicable racial differences even within the "white" race:

> The different groups within the white race itself are as unequal in strength as they are in beauty, though the difference is less marked. The Italians are more beautiful than the Germans or the Swiss, the French or the Spanish. Similarly, the English show a higher type of physical beauty than the Slav nations. In strength of fist, the English are superior to all the other European races; while the French and Spanish have a greater power of resisting fatigue and privation.[54]

Notoriously, Gobineau's arguments and procedures also led him confidently to assert:

> The Germanic races, which in the fifth century transformed the Western mind ... were Aryans ... of the first seven civilizations, which are those of the Old World, six belong, at least in part, to the Aryan race ... almost the whole of the continent of Europe is inhabited at the present time by groups of which the basis is white ... There is no true civilization, among the European peoples, where the Aryan branch is not predominant ... In the above list no negro race is seen as the Initiator of a civilization ... Similarly, no spontaneous civilization is to be found among the yellow races; and when the Aryan blood is exhausted Stagnation supervenes.[55]

The Italian novelist and cultural theorist, Umberto Eco, in his novel *The Prague Cemetery* (2012) parodies the stereotypical, and fantastical, often bizarrely ludicrous, and wildly insulting excesses of these nineteenth century presentations of nation or race:

> My grandfather described [the Jews'] eyes that spy on you, so false as to turn you pale, those unctuous smiles, those hyena lips over bared teeth, those heavy, polluted, brutish looks, those restless creases between nose and lips, wrinkled by hatred ... those eyes ... roll feverishly ... indicating a diseased liver, corrupted by the secretions produced by eighteen

centuries of hatred ... When he smiles ... his swollen eyelids half close ... a sign of cunning, some say of lechery ... the Jew, as well as being as vain as a Spaniard, ignorant as a Croat, greedy as a Levantine, ungrateful as a Maltese, insolent as a gypsy, dirty as an Englishman, unctuous as a Kalmuck, imperious as a Prussian, and as slanderous as anyone from Asti, is adulterous through uncontrollable lust ... [t]he German lives in a state of perpetual intestinal embarrassment due to an excess of beer and those pork sausages on which he gorges himself ... [t]hey fill their mouths with their *Geist*, which means spirit, but it's the spirit of the ale, which stultifies them from their youth and explains why, beyond the Rhine, nothing interesting has ever been produced in art, except for a few paintings of repugnant faces, and poems of deadly tedium. Not to mention their music ... [t]heir abuse of beer makes them incapable of having the slightest notion of their vulgarity, and the height of their vulgarity is that they feel no shame at being German ... Since the time when that man Gobineau wrote about the inequality of the human races, it seems that if someone speaks ill of another race it is because he regards his own to be better. I have no bias. [*sic*] As soon as I became French ... I realized that my new compatriots were lazy, swindling, resentful, jealous, proud beyond all measure, to the point of thinking anyone who is not French is a savage ... They are proud to have a state they describe as powerful but they spend their time trying to bring it down: no one is good as the Frenchman at putting up barricades for whatever reason and every time the wind changes, often without knowing why, allowing himself to get carried into the streets by the worst kind of rabble ... the Italian is an untrustworthy, lying contemptible traitor, finds himself more at ease with a dagger than a sword, better with poison than medicine.[56]

There are several points to be made about this present-day parody. In addition to alleged Jewish phenotypic details, the pseudo-scientific observation claims that there is such a condition of degeneration as evidenced by the use of words such as "polluted," "feverishly," "diseased liver," "corrupted by the secretions," and "swollen eyelids."

Eco's passage also parodies the habit of confident "biological" assumptions regarding differing "national" character traits, common in the nineteenth century. For example, the German philosopher, poet, and critic, Johann Gottfried Herder (1744–1803) proposed the idea of *Volksgeist*, or national spirit. It has become the foundation for cultural nationalism. While a nation may be made up of several races, each nation has its unique culture, or a *Volksgeist*, which is expressed through its language and traditions. Commenting on this, Ali Rattansi observes that there was "a short distance between notions of *Volksgeist* and racial character."[57] Thus Eco's passage enumerates, with apparent unquestioned, often outrageously ludicrous, confidence, a string of "naturalized" traits about the Jews, the Germans, the French, and the Italians.

Over time, fixations about "racial traits," about "degeneration," and about nation-building intensified, engendering, for instance, the notion that the outsider was "a potential carrier of pollution who could infect the body politic and the nation's health."[58] Phenotypic and skull measurements were used increasingly, to assert a biologically based explanation for national trait differentiation between different peoples. These produced various and varying, hierarchical classifications of national or race trait-types. Again, despite Charles Darwin's clearly expressed doubts about race, Social Darwinists who claimed that society was organized in accordance with the principles of human evolution thought to have been developed by Darwin, proceeded to argue that "each race became human separately within the evolutionary process."[59] The "science" of eugenics, with its notions of selective breeding and the elimination of inferior races, was a further disturbing misapplication of Darwin's arguments. By the end of the nineteenth century, "the dominant view [remained] that racial purity was necessary for a race or a nation to maintain its strength and vitality."[60]

Investment in pseudo-scientific versions of race persisted throughout the twentieth century despite the persistence of measurements and classifications that were continually found to be inadequate, and that were repeatedly replaced by alternative measurements and classifications. Bernasconi and Lott cite the work of Franz Boas as an example, in the early twentieth century, of emerging reservations. Using the cephalic index, he argued that the mental characteristics of " 'branches of the same race' may be subject to the modifying influences of the environment."[61] He thus challenged "the idea of absolute stability of human types as a ground for belief that certain types have heredity superiority over others."[62] Using various other phenotypic criteria, he also found that "each category" of human race

> contained within it a range of variation that overlapped with the variation of any other category ... [thus] although it may be the case that two populations can be shown to have a different average height, it does not follow that any two individuals selected from these two populations will demonstrate the same difference ... group differences do not correspond to individual differences.[63]

The questioning of the idea of distinct races and racial hierarchies continued to be pursued in the 1930s by scientists including Aldous Huxley (1894–1963), the grandson of Thomas Huxley (1825–1895), who is known as "Darwin's bulldog," and Lancelot Hogben (1895–1975). Moreover, in the post-1950 period, as Ali Rattansi notes, other biologists and social scientists sought to explain that

> the implications of the distinction between *genetic* variation in human populations, *phenotypic* differences such as external appearance (skin colour, hair type, shape of nose), and *cultural* and behavioural characteristics as evident in belief systems, level of technological development or political organization

were increasingly significant.[64] Rattansi emphasizes that the "introduction of the distinction between *genotype* [the hereditary potential of an organism] and *phenotype* in 1911 eventually proved seminal."[65] He argues that in view of such investigations on health, sports, and IQ factors,[66] "the concept of race is now regarded by the majority of biologists as having no credible scientific foundation."[67]

The "biological" theory of race was also challenged by arguments that culture was "a more important factor than inherited physical characteristics,"[68] as well as the argument that, "from the standpoint of modern experimental genetics, the anthropological conception of race as a biological unit is not only erroneous but also meaningless and thus should be disregarded."[69] However, even though genetic science continues to be a changing process of investigation, its findings always remain vulnerable to discriminatory manipulation. For example, although some of the relevant websites of the African history of Rwanda colonial race classification, to which we will turn shortly, cite genetic studies that pay little or no attention to phenotypic data, they argue that the Tutsi and Hutu peoples are largely of the same Bantu extraction, even though they were classified for largely political reasons as distinct races[70] Mahmood Mamdani records that recent scientific studies of the Tutsi and the Hutu in Rwanda do not pay attention to phenotype, but "to genotype: blood factors, the presence of the sickle cell trait, and the prevalent ability among adults to digest lactose."[71] However, it can be argued that this more recently accumulated scientific data remains vulnerable to distortion. For example, in one investigation that challenges genetic data that claims that there is no difference between Tutsi and Hutu, the "genetically determined characteristic said to differentiate Rwandan Tutsi from Hutu,"[72] turns out to be the failure to digest lactose. To what use such genetic investigation may on occasion putatively be put, as we see from this example, remains dangerously open-ended.

At the same time, the pseudo-scientific notions of race that have prevailed throughout the twentieth century demonstrate a sinister and lethal resilience. At the end of the nineteenth century, and on the eve of the commencement of the official Belgian colonization of the Congo (1908), and then Rwanda (1919), Joseph Conrad, in his novel *Heart of Darkness* (1899) notes an instance of the kind of pseudo-scientific practice that was used to bolster processes of trade and colonization. Early in the tale, the narrator gives an account of how, during his interview for the position of company agent in the Congo, an

old doctor felt my pulse, evidently thinking of something else the while. "Good, good for there," he mumbled, and then with a certain eagerness asked me whether I would let him measure my head. Rather surprised, I said Yes, when he produced a thing like calipers and got the dimensions back and front and every way, taking notes carefully. He was an unshaven little man in a threadbare coat like a gaberdine, with his feet in slippers, and I thought him a harmless fool. "I always ask leave, in the interests of science, to measure the crania of those going out there," he said. "And when they come back, too?" I asked. "Oh, I never see them," he remarked; "and, moreover, the changes take place inside, you know." He smiled, as if at some quiet joke. "So you are going out there. Famous. Interesting, too." He gave me a searching glance, and made another note. "Ever any madness in your family?" he asked, in a matter-of-fact tone. I felt very annoyed. "Is that question in the interests of science, too?"[73]

After World War I, the Belgians took over a Rwanda that had already been colonized by the Germans, one of whose notorious methods of colonial control was phenotypic and cranial measurements designed to validate and intensify for political reasons the divisions between the Tutsis and the Hutus. Although, before colonial rule, there were particularities observable in each of the population groups, and within different individuals within each group, Tutsi and Hutu had been, nonetheless, "part of a single economic and cultural community."[74] They "spoke the same language, practiced the same religion, and lived on the same territory."[75] But despite this, the Belgian colonial power seized on whatever distinctions, including "scientific" ones, to emphasize and magnify alleged differences. They also used the so-called Hamitic hypothesis, which imagined a Caucasian race origin for the Tutsi, as a further means of authorizing and legitimizing their divisive practices. To facilitate colonial administration, they favored the Tutsi above the Hutu, in institutional, educational, and legislative ways, as a minority, "executive" elite. Furthermore, after the official census was taken in 1933–1934, the colonial government introduced identity cards that fixed in legal and administrative terms the "identification" of separate Tutsi and Hutu "races." While "scientific" data about race was, at the same time, only one, albeit powerfully malign, element, in a more complex economic and political process,[76] the Belgians, as Mamdani points out,[77] had taken existing sociopolitical distinctions and *racialized* them. The subsequent terrible struggles between the Tutsis and the Hutus, led in the last decade of the twentieth century—as it had done on occasion before—to genocide, that was the product of multiple causes. But this element of race demarcation, and the scientific data that partly lay behind it, is one fluctuating but also recurrent element in this terrible history. The severed shrunken heads that, in *Heart of Darkness*, surround Kurtz's hut, may well reflect the excessively destructive predilection of European colonialism. But they may, as well, be read here as also prophetically suggestive of the often putrid and rotting effects of a number of "scientific" explanations of race throughout the twentieth century.

Eighteenth century doubleness about imaginings of race

In François-Marie Voltaire's satire on enlightenment optimism, *Candide*, his young European hero travels through many parts of the world. While exploring the imaginary South American kingdom of Eldorado, Candide finds a "palace of sciences" in place of courts of law. There is a mile-long gallery filled entirely with instruments for the study of mathematics and astronomy.[78] This is noted immediately before he undertakes a speculative project with "the thought of owning more treasure than could be mustered by Asia, Europe and Africa combined."[79] But immediately on commencement of this hopeful journey he and his companion encounter mishaps, which dampen the likelihood of their hope of good fortune. As he and his companion approaches the town of Surinam,

> they came across a negro stretched out on the ground, with no more than half of his clothes left, which is to say a pair of blue canvas drawers; the poor man had no left leg and no right hand.
>
> "Good God!" said Candide to him in Dutch. "What are you doing there, my friend, in such a deplorable state?"
>
> "I am waiting for my master Monsieur Vanderdendur, the well-known merchant," answered the negro.
>
> "And was it Monsieur Vanderdendur who treated you like this?
>
> "Yes, Monsieur," said the negro, "it is the custom. Twice a year we are given a blue pair of canvas drawers, and this is our only clothing. When we work in the sugar-mills and get a finger caught in the machinery, they cut off the hand; but if we try to run away, they cut off a leg: I have found myself in

both situations. It is the price we pay for the sugar you eat in Europe ... dogs, monkeys and parrots are a thousand times less miserable than we are; the Dutch ... who converted me to their religion tell me every Sunday that we are all children of Adam, whites and blacks alike. I am no genealogist; but if these preachers are telling the truth, then we are all second cousins. In which case you must admit that no one could treat his relatives more horribly than this" ...

"This is one abomination" ... [cried Candide] ... "I am giving up on ... Optimism ... [which is] ... the mania for insisting that all is well when all is by no means well." And he wept as he looked down at his negro, and was still weeping as he entered Surinam.[80]

Voltaire satirizes enlightenment confidence by this and other such juxtapositions. His observation of the "palace" of eighteenth century scientific "achievement," swiftly followed by reference to the young men's expectation of easy acquisition of wealth, is set not only against reports of immediate incidental mishap, but also against the disturbing details recorded in the passage above. Benign notions of enlightenment, the age of science and of reason, are undone by the harrowing description of racist colonial heartlessness, exploitation, and slavery.

While Voltaire sympathizes with the black slave's suffering, attitudes towards difference that he reveals elsewhere serve to illustrate that there is often a complexity and a doubleness to be observed in the persistence of assumptions about race and the circulation of myths, half-truths, and distortions that sustain them. Indeed, even in what from our point of view might be considered an incidental and contentious account of the hostility of Voltaire and some of his contemporaries towards a writer such as Shakespeare, the critic Richard Wilson detects a startlingly ingrained and unquestioned, eighteenth century, racism; in his book on *Shakespeare in French Theory* (2006), Wilson observes that

what is, perhaps, most striking today about the construction [of Shakespeare] in pre-Revolutionary France is how consistently it mobilises racist discourse to marginalize the plays in exactly Voltaire's terms, as from a barbaric back of beyond ...

> [Voltaire dismissed] the Bard as a "barbaric mountebank"
> whose "monstrous farces" were nothing but an "enormous
> heap of "dung" ... Shakespeare's "abominable black book"
> [was] "base, boorish and barbarous" ... [The] Academicians ...
> insisted that "*Le More de Venise* could not decently figure on
> any French stage: Othello's skin and Iago's soul are both too
> black." In the France of *les lumières* Shakespeare was scorned
> as an "Attila", a "savage whose sparks shine in a horrible
> night," because his stage accommodated so many different
> races, conditions, and types. ... "Every one must feel," as one
> translator explained in 1785, "it was ... necessary to whiten
> Othello's swarthy face" ... thus Othello's race became meto-
> nymic of the excremental darkness of a dramatist who had
> blackened himself, according to Voltaire, by having "swum in
> the sewer."[81]

This apparent vacillation, in varying contexts, in Voltaire's attitude to
difference does not necessarily indicate deliberate hypocrisy. But at
the very least it suggests how particular constructions of race may
coexist with other contrary, sometimes unacknowledged, perhaps also
unrealized, assumptions. Such easy and unquestioned formulations
about the "barbarity" or inferiority of "blackness" also suggest the
profound extent to which entrenched binaries, as in the case of Kant
and Hegel as well as Voltaire, informed eighteenth century *and* later
thinking about difference. It seems likely that these unquestioning
assumptions were also bolstered by the apparent "authority" lent to
such discriminatory binaries, by the new "scientific" articulations of
"race."

A pseudo-scientific confidence in an unquestioned and ostensibly
objective account of what was already emerging as a structuring of
the dynamics of race also surfaces from time to time in Daniel
Defoe's novel *Robinson Crusoe* (1719). The tale is, in a manner of
speaking, what a recent editor, Thomas Keymer has described as a
response "to the calls of the Royal Society of scientists that voyagers
should contribute to knowledge through systematic observation and
description of natural history in all its branches."[82] It mingles the
description of details of practical seafaring appropriate to voyage narrative and detailed description of practical and domestic strategies of

personal survival, with religious and moral reflections, from Defoe's religious viewpoint as a dissenter that is "structured on the basis of a familiar Christian pattern of disobedience-punishment-repentance-deliverance."[83]

But the narrative is also interspersed with occasional, morally untroubled, references to enslavement and slavery, or by morally unassuming negative remarks about Muslims, or about the dark-skinned people that from time to time Crusoe thinks about or encounters during his voyages. For example, Crusoe's second voyage, aboard a slaver's ship, is referred to fleetingly as "a Vessel bound to the Coast of *Africa*; or, as our Sailors vulgarly call it, a Voyage to *Guinea*,"[84] and it establishes him, without further elaboration or qualification, as being himself a "*Guiney* [slave] Trader."[85] However, on his third voyage when he is captured by pirates and taken to "*Sallee*, a Port belonging to the *Moors* [Turks]," he is forced to contemplate the plight of the slave as he is himself now transformed "from a Merchant to a miserable Slave."[86] After two years with "no Fellow-Slave, no *Englishman, Irishman*, or *Scotsman*"[87] to speak to about escape, he describes how he conceives his own plan and how, in its execution, he tricks the "Moor," with whom he regularly works, apparently without conscience, eventually flinging him overboard and leaving him either to swim ashore, or more likely, to drown.[88] Crusoe also engineers his escape from Sallee in the company of a "Morisco" boy, a Muslim from Spain, of whom he equally cold-bloodedly remarks, "I could ha' been content to ha' taken this *Moor* with me, and ha' drowned the Boy, but there was no venturing to trust him [the Moor]."[89] Indeed, in his manipulation of the boy he proceeds to manifest the same untroubled sense of religious superiority:

> When [the Moor] was gone I turn'd to the Boy, who they call'd *Xury*, and said to him, *Xury*, if you will be faithful to me I'll make you a great Man, but if you will not stroak your Face to be true to me *that is, swear by* Mahomet *and his Father's Beard*, I must throw you into the Sea too; the Boy smil'd in my Face and spoke so innocently that I could not mistrust him; and swore to be faithful to me, and go all over the World with me.[90]

But later in the tale, when expedience requires, Crusoe sells the boy into slavery despite the loyalty the youngster has shown him, with a vague promise that a conditional distant future conversion to Christianity, might eventually lead to his "freedom." Crusoe's improvisations and manipulations imply an imagined religious, intellectual, and bodily superiority over his darker-skinned and Muslim compeers.

When he first meets his "man Friday," Crusoe provides a version of what Keymer describes as a "detailed physical description of native peoples [which] was a standard feature of contemporary travel writing driven in part by the expectations of the Royal Society":[91]

> He was a comely handsome Fellow, perfectly well made; with straight strong Limbs, not too large; tall and well shap'd, and as I reckon, about twenty six Years of Age. He had a very good Countenance, not a fierce and surly Aspect; but seem'd to have something very manly in his Face, and yet he had all the Sweetness and Softness of an *European* in his Countenance too, especially when he smil'd. His hair was long and black, not curl'd like Wool; his Forehead very high and large, and a great Vivacity and sparkling Sharpness in his Eyes. The Colour of his Skin was not quite black, but very tawny; and yet not of an ugly yellow nauseous tawny, as the *Brasilians* and *Virginians*, and other Natives of *America* are; but of a bright kind of a dun olive Colour, that had in it something very agreeable; tho' not very easy to describe. His Face was round and plump; his Nose small, not flat like the Negroes, a very good Mouth, thin Lips, and his fine Teeth well set, and white as Ivory.[92]

The phenotypic features Crusoe records are themselves also comparatively evaluated and hierarchically graded in terms of current imaginary structurations of the scale from white to black. The conventional markings of European phenotypes, and notions of beauty, in contrast to Native American and, finally, African stereotypes are here taken for granted as scientific facts. Repeated references to the coast of Africa, throughout the novel, are also, on the whole, overtly negative. For example, in his early escape from Sallee, Crusoe hopes to mislead putative pursuers:

> for who would ha' suppos'd we were saild on to the south-
> ward to the truly *Barbarian* Coast, where whole Nations of
> Negroes were sure to surround us with their Canoes, and
> destroy us; where we could ne'er once go on shoar but we
> should be devour'd by savage Beasts, or more merciless
> Savages of humane kind.[93]

Towards the end of the tale, when on his way through the French Alps
from Spain, Crusoe observes of the howling of wolves, that, "except
the Noise I once heard on the Shore of *Africa* … I never heard any
thing that filled me with so much Horror."[94] On one of his explora-
tions after discovering the human footprint, Crusoe discovers on the
infrequently visited other side of his island, "the Shore spread with
Skulls, Hands, Feet and other bones of humane Bodies … where it is
suppos'd the Savage Wretches had sat down to their inhumane Feast-
ings."[95] As Defoe's novel unfolds, the word "savages," and its variants, used on occasion to apply to African groups, repeatedly connotes
"cannibal," with its own various resonances of barbaric horror.

The relatively incidental presence of such assumptions or associations, in a novel more celebrated as a depiction of the pioneering
spirit that accompanied capitalist, imperialist, and colonialist enterprises, suggests also how such activities drew on, came to depend on,
or, indeed, intersected with versions of race as part of what was taken
to constitute the natural world that "science" was in the process of
"uncovering." Crusoe's fear of cannibals, for example, is interwoven
with detailed accounts of the measures he endlessly takes to defend
himself and his property together with his "castle" and his "country
estate," as he calls them. After the discovery of the footprint, he
writes that this

> made my Life much less comfortable than it was before; as
> may well be imagin'd by any who know what it is to live in
> the constant Snare of *the Fear of Man*; and this I must observe
> with Grief too, that the discomposure of my Mind had too
> great Impressions also upon the religious Part of my Thoughts,
> for the Dread and Terror of falling into the Hands of Savages
> and Cannibals, lay so upon my Spirits … I … pray'd to God as
> under great Affliction and Pressure of Mind, surrounded with

> Danger, and in Expectation every Night of being murther'd and devour'd before Morning.[96]

It is not unreasonable to conclude that such fear, together with the frequency of the association of the various inhabitants of the Caribbean or of Africa with unspeakable violence, had its own cumulative effects on Defoe's readers.

Interestingly also, his "Horror of the Degeneracy of Humane Nature"[97] prompts him, when reflecting on the behavior of the cannibals, to give "God thanks that had cast my first Lot in a Part of the World where I was distinguish'd from such dreadful Creatures as these."[98] In this remark the association of the word "savage," and on occasion elsewhere, the word "barbarians,"[99] with the barbaric inhumane is also clearly articulated as *not* English. Crusoe also remarks, earlier, in humorous vein, of his non-English "barbarous"[100] dress, "had any one in *England* been to meet such a Man as I was, it must either have frighted them, or raised a great deal of Laughter."[101] His moustache, he notes,

> I had trimm'd into a large Pair of *Mahometan* Whiskers, such as I had seen worn by some *Turks*, who I saw at *Sallee*; for the *Moors* did not wear such, tho' the *Turks* did; of these Muschatoes or Whiskers ... they were of a Length and Shape monstrous enough, and such as in *England* would have pass'd for frightful.[102]

More recent commentators on Defoe's novel appear to be divided about the possible gulf between the ironies that might emerge in the presentation of Crusoe alongside his own comments on his behavior on the one hand, and the distance that this might suggest between the character himself and the attitudes of his author on the other. For example, Crusoe is given, on occasion, almost Montaigne-like sentiments, when he struggles against the impulse to ambush and murder the "savages" whom he regards as trespassing on "his" island. For the sixteenth and early seventeenth century French writer Michel de Montaigne, in his essay "Of Cannibals" that was translated into English in the early seventeenth century, the Europeans are the ones who are corrupt and savage. Crusoe observes that for him to kill these "savages" "would justify the Conduct of the *Spaniards* in all their Barbarities practiced in *America*, and where they destroy'd Millions of these People, who however they were Idolaters and Barbarians … were yet, as to the *Spaniards*, very innocent People" and that

> the rooting of them out of the Country is spoken of with the utmost Abhorrence and Detestation, by even the *Spaniards* themselves at this Time; and by all other Christian Nations of *Europe* as a meer Butchery, a bloody and unnatural Piece of Cruelty, unjustifiable to God or Man.[103]

Defoe may well have been influenced here by the Spanish historian and Dominican friar Bartolomé de Las Casas's (*c*.1484–1566) critique of the Spanish conquest of the Americas, and by his own anti-Catholicism. It may also be argued, that Crusoe's subsequent incarceration on the island is a suitable punishment for his early experiences as a slaver and that there are links between his treatment of Xury and, later in the tale, Friday. But, as in the case of Voltaire, these or other expressions of empathy, or the cruelty in such treatment of various "different" groups, coexist with an apparently automatically untroubled demarcation of "race" that contributed to the racial distinction between superiority and inferiority. Friday's lot as Crusoe's servant, to go no further, is never brought into question in the novel.

But if, as has also been argued in the novel itself, Crusoe remains morally indifferent to slavery[104] as an eighteenth century exemplum of the enterprising spirit, informed by new scientific observation and pragmatism,[105] both he and the narrative of the novel itself remain disturbingly silent about such ready-to-hand incidental assumptions about the savagery, cannibalism, wildness, or spiritual irrelevance of the darker-skinned peoples or Muslims whom he encounters. Whatever the arguments may be, sometimes by way of academic reference to Defoe's sequels and other writings, the largely inferential, often glancing reiteration, of traditional sets of hate-binaries, or the uncritical recirculation of contemporary "scientific" assertions about difference throughout the narrative in *Robinson Crusoe*, all serve to make this text the bearer of more than, say, "a myth of economic individualism," or "a prophecy of imperial expansion."[106] If anything, the many translations, and the wide circulation of this text have contributed to the reinforcement of some of these dubious myths. Regrettably, many representations of the practices of slavery and the early moments of settlement and colonization, as well as incipient aggressive European nationalisms, all seem to take for granted the mirage of objectivity promised by the fluctuating "scientific" discourse of race. And, depressingly, the authority lent to traditional negative binaries in the formulation of race by unstable, periodically fluctuating, or proto-scientific measurement and investigation replete with its manifest faults and general unreliability, continues to be an ongoing phenomenon right up to and including the present. Indeed, it continues to inform current versions of nationalism, and the entire debate around immigration that have recently surfaced across the world.

Notes

1 David Goldenberg, "Racism, Colour Symbolism, and Colour Prejudice," in Miriam Eliav-Feldon, Benjamin Isaac, and Joseph Ziegler, eds., *The Origins of Racism in the West*, Cambridge: Cambridge University Press, 2009, 88.

2 See Benjamin H. Isaac, *The Invention of Racism in Ancient Antiquity*, Princeton and Oxford: Princeton University Press, 2004.

3 Peter Biller, "Proto-Racial Thought in Medieval Science," in Eliav-Feldon, Isaac, and Ziegler, eds., *The Origins of Racism in the West*, 158.

4 Biller, "Proto-Racial Thought in Medieval Science," 159, mentions

medical texts translated from Arabic to Latin, but also from Greek in the milieu of Monte Cassino (and Salerno) in the eleventh to early twelfth centuries; the translations done in Spain from Arabic in the second half of the twelfth century and the early thirteenth century; a miscellany of Greco-Latin translations in the Italian peninsula from the early twelfth to the mid-thirteenth centuries, and the large number of Greco-Latin translations carried out by William of Moerbeke in the third quarter of the thirteenth century.

5 Biller, "Proto-Racial Thought in Medieval Science," 169.

6 Biller, "Proto-Racial Thought in Medieval Science," 173.

7 Cited in Biller, "Proto-Racial Thought in Medieval Science," 171.

8 Cited in Biller, "Proto-Racial Thought in Medieval Science," 173.

9 Cited in Biller, "Proto-Racial Thought in Medieval Science," 174.

10 Joseph Ziegler, "Physiognomy, Science, and Proto-Racism 1200–1500,"

in Eliav-Feldon, Isaac, and Ziegler, eds., *The Origins of Racism in the West*, 199.

11 Ziegler, "Physiognomy, Science, and Proto-Racism 1200–1500," 198.

12 Ziegler, "Physiognomy, Science, and Proto-Racism 1200–1500," 198. Ziegler (199) notes also that

> Valentin Groebner has recently traced the path by which the notion of complexion, originally designating the balanced pro- portion of humours specific to each individual, came to be used as a term for a person's bodily appearance and skin colour. When *complexio* turned into complexion the investigation became visual, surfaced to the skin (mainly its colour), and increasingly became prominent in the description of classification marks of groups. *Complexio* established itself as a collective category. Having shifted from the invisible, internal blend of fluids in one's body to something identifiable on the skin, it became a congeni- tal and immutable category. He located this shift in the second half of the sixteenth century, when the concept of complexion became crucial for describing the different bodily and mental natures of inhabitants of Africa and the Americas.

13 Robert Miles, *Racism*, London: Routledge, 1989, 32.

14 Robert Bernasconi and Tommy L. Lott, eds., *The Idea of Race*, Indiana- polis: Hackett, 2000, viii.

15 See Brian Niro, *Race*, Basingstoke: Palgrave Macmillan, 2003, 64ff.

16 Niro, *Race*, 67.

17 Niro, *Race*, 66.

18 For this and much else of the information referred to in this section, I am particularly indebted to Robert Bernasconi, "Who Invented the Concept of Race? Kant's Role in the Enlightenment Construction of Race," in Robert Bernasconi, ed., *Race*, Oxford: Blackwell, 2001, 16.

19 Bernasconi, "Who Invented the Concept of Race?" 19.

20 Bernasconi, "Who Invented the Concept of Race?" 25.

21 Bernasconi, "Who Invented the Concept of Race?" 25.

22 Bernasconi, "Who Invented the Concept of Race?" 26.

23 Bernasconi, "Who Invented the Concept of Race?" 27.

24 Cited in Bernasconi, "Who Invented the Concept of Race?" 29.

25 Miles, *Racism*, 33.

26 Miles, *Racism*, 33.

27 Niro, *Race*, 69.

28 Bernasconi, "Who Invented the Concept of Race?" 18.

29 Miles, *Racism*, 34.

30 Miles, *Racism*, 35.
31 Charles Darwin, "On the Races of Man," from *The Descent of Man*, cited in Bernasconi and Lott, *The Idea of Race*, 77.
32 Jonathan Swift, "A Modest Proposal for Preventing the Children of poor People in Ireland, from being a Burden to their Parents or Country, and for making them Beneficial to the Public," in Carole Fabricant, ed., Jonathan Swift: A Modest Proposal and Other Writings, London: Penguin, 2009, 231.
33 Swift, "A Modest Proposal." 232.
34 Swift, "A Modest Proposal." 232.
35 Ali Rattansi, *Racism: A Very Short Introduction*, Oxford: Oxford University Press, 2007, 32.
36 Rattansi, *Racism*, 38.
37 Niro, *Race*, 99, notes Darwin's apparent mockery of, for example, fluctuating numbers in

> noting that humanity should be "classed as a single species or race, or as two (Virey), as three (Jasquinot), as four (Kant), five (Blumenbach), six (Buffon), seven (Hunter), eight (Agassiz), eleven (Pickering), fifteen (Bory St. Vincent), sixteen (Desmoulins), twenty-two (Morton), sixty (Crawford), or as sixty-three, according to Burke" (Darwin, *The Descent of Man*, Amherst: Prometheus, [1871] 1998, 181).

38 Bernasconi, "Who Invented the Concept of Race?" 24.
39 Niro, *Race*, 74.
40 Immanuel Kant, "On the Different Races of Man," "On Natural Characteristics, so far as They Depend upon the Distinct Feeling of the Beautiful and Sublime," and "On Countries that are Known and Unknown to Europeans," in *Race and the Enlightenment: A Reader*, ed. Emmanuel Chukwudi Eze, Oxford: Blackwell, 1997, 64. Cited in Niro, *Race*, 74–75.
41 Bernasconi and Lott, "Introduction," x.
42 G.W.F. Hegel, "Anthropology," from the *Encyclopaedia of the Philosophical Sciences*, cited in Bernasconi and Lott, *The Idea of Race*, 40–41.
43 Rattansi, *Racism*, 31.
44 Adrian Collins, "Introduction," in Comte Arthur de Gobineau, *The Inequality of the Human Races*, UK: Lightening Source, 2011 (1853–1855), 3. Quotations from Gobineau come from this edition.
45 Gobineau, *The Inequality of the Human Races*, 64.
46 Gobineau, *The Inequality of the Human Races*, 54.
47 Gobineau, *The Inequality of the Human Races*, 12.

48 Gobineau, *The Inequality of the Human Races*, 12.
49 Gobineau, *The Inequality of the Human Races*, 13.
50 Bernasconi and Lott, "Introduction," x.
51 Rattansi, *Racism*, 33.
52 Gobineau, *The Inequality of the Human Races*, 48.
53 Gobineau, *The Inequality of the Human Races*, 15.
54 Gobineau, *The Inequality of the Human Races*, 54.
55 Martin Bernal (*Black Athena: The Afroasiatic Roots of Classical Civili-zation*, London, Vintage Books, 1991, 32), observes that, in the nine-teenth century, the

>   paradigms of "race" and "progress" and their corollaries of "racial purity", and the notion that the only beneficial conquests were those of "master races" over subject ones, could not tolerate … legends of Egyptian colonization in Greece … [t]he Aryan Model … was encouraged by a number of factors: the discovery of the Indo-European language family with the Indo-Europeans or Aryans soon seen as a "race"; the plausible postulation of an original Indo-European homeland in central Asia; and the need to explain that Greek was fundamentally an Indo-European language … there was intense historical concern with the Germanic over-whelming of the Western Roman Empire in the 5th century AD, and the Aryan conquest in India in the second millennium BC. The application of the model of northern conquest to Greece was thus obvious and very attractive … Naturally the purer and more north-ern Hellenes were the conquerors, as befitted a master race. The Pre-Hellenic Aegean populations, for their part, were sometimes seen as marginally European, and always as Caucasian; in this way, even the natives were untainted by African and Semitic "blood".

56 Umberto Eco, *The Prague Cemetery*, London: Harvill Secker, 2011, 5–11.
57 Rattansi, *Racism*, 36.
58 Rattansi, *Racism*, 37.
59 Bernasconi and Lott, "Introduction," xi.
60 Bernasconi and Lott, "Introduction," xi.
61 Bernasconi and Lott, "Introduction," xiii.
62 Bernasconi and Lott, "Introduction," xiii.
63 Miles, *Racism*, 37.
64 Rattansi, *Racism*, 72.
65 Genetic concerns current to Rattansi's time of writing, also include *gene pool* and *cline* (73).

66 Rattansi, *Racism*, 72–85.

67 Rattansi, *Racism*, 75.

68 Bernasconi and Lott, "Introduction," xiii.

69 Bernasconi and Lott, "Introduction," xiv.

70 Mahmood Mamdani, *When Victims Become Killers: Colonialism, Nativism, and the Genocide in Rwanda*, Princeton: Princeton University Press, 2001,45.

71 Mamdani, *When Victims Become Killers*, 45.

72 Mamdani, *When Victims Become Killers*, 45.

73 Joseph Conrad, *Heart of Darkness*, Fifth Edition, Norton Critical Editions, ed. Paul B. Armstrong, New York: W.W. Norton, 2016 (1899).

74 Mamdani, *When Victims Become Killers*, 42.

75 Mamdani, *When Victims Become Killers*, 50.

76 In addition to Mamdani, see, for example, Jared Diamond, *Collapse: How Societies Choose to Fail or Survive*, London, Penguin Books, 2011, 313–328.

77 Mamdani, *When Victims Become Killers*, 99.

78 Francois-Marie Voltaire, *Candide, or Optimism*, trans. and ed. Theo Cuffe, London, Penguin Books, 2005, 48.

79 Voltaire, *Candide, or Optimism*, 51.

80 Voltaire, *Candide, or Optimism*, 51–52.

81 Richard Wilson, *Shakespeare in French Theory: King of Shadows*, London: Routledge, 2007, 242–243.

82 Thomas Keymer, "Introduction," in Daniel Defoe, *Robinson Crusoe*, ed. Thomas Keymer, London: Penguin Books, 2008, xix.

83 J. Paul Hunter, cited in Keymer, "Introduction," xxvii.

84 Defoe, *Robinson Crusoe*, 16.

85 Defoe, *Robinson Crusoe*, 17.

86 Defoe, *Robinson Crusoe*, 18.

87 Defoe, *Robinson Crusoe*, 18.

88 See, for example,

> Another Trick I try'd upon him, which he innocently came into also, his Name was *Ismael*, who they call *Muly* or *Moely*, so I call'd to him, *Moely* said I, our Patroon's Guns are on board the Boat, can you not get a little Powder and Shot, it may be we may kill some [bird] for ourselves ... Yes, *says he*, I'll bring some.
>
> (20)

Shortly after, Crusoe gives a further duplicitous suggestion to this fellow slave who, once more, "thinking no harm agreed." Then having distracted his victim he stept forward to where the *Moor* was, and making as if I stoopt for something behind him, I took him by Surprize with my Arm under his Twist, and tost him clear over-board into the Sea … he begg'd to be taken in [but after Crusoe refuses] … he … swam for the Shoar, and I make no doubt [*sic*] but he reacht it with Ease, for he was an Excellent Swimmer.

(21)

89 Defoe, *Robinson Crusoe*, 21.
90 Defoe, *Robinson Crusoe*, 21–22.
91 Keymer, ed., *Robinson Crusoe*, 295.
92 Defoe, *Robinson Crusoe*, 173.
93 Defoe, *Robinson Crusoe*, 22.
94 Defoe, *Robinson Crusoe*, 250.
95 Defoe, *Robinson Crusoe*, 13.
96 Defoe, *Robinson Crusoe*, 138.
97 Defoe, *Robinson Crusoe*, 139.
98 Defoe, *Robinson Crusoe*, 140.
99 Defoe, *Robinson Crusoe*, 146, 154.
100 Defoe, *Robinson Crusoe*, 127.
101 Defoe, *Robinson Crusoe*, 126.
102 Defoe, *Robinson Crusoe*, 127.
103 Defoe, *Robinson Crusoe*, 145.
104 Keymer shows that, on the matter of slavery at least, Defoe's apparent silence was not shared by some of his contemporaries. See Keymer, "Introduction," xxxvii.
105 Cf., for example,

> I must needs observe, that as Reason is the Substance and the Original of the Mathematicks, so by stating and squaring every thing by Reason, and by making the most rational Judgment of things, every Man may be in time Master of every mechanic Art.

(59)

106 Keymer, "Introduction," vii.

PART II

RECASTING THE FETTERS
OF RACE

3

LEGISLATIVE, GOVERNMENTAL, AND JUDICIAL MARKINGS OF DIFFERENCE

Legislative and judicial practice sometimes proves crucial in the institution and the circulation of negative imaginings of group identities, and hence of markers of race. Three examples serve to illustrate this point. As the first example of this, we may take the discriminatory concept of citizenship established during the period of the formulation of the Constitution in the United States of America. This became the source of an ongoing judicial, administrative, and civil struggle over the meaning of "personhood" whose effects continue to be felt up to the present time.

The United States' struggle over racial categorization in law is in some ways different from our second example, the Union of South Africa. After the South African war ended at the start of the twentieth century the new imperial government's restructuring of the Transvaal included "building on the principle of legal *continuity* with the former republic, [and] enforcing, with greater efficiency the discriminatory legal regime about which its propaganda had been so critical before 1899" (emphasis added).[1] Indeed, the shift in South Africa to the

"British 'rule of law' meant not greater liberty, but stricter enforcement of rules."[2] The South African example will suggest instances of juridically and legislatively supported racism that prevailed for much of the twentieth century.

In the case of our third example, the National Socialists Workers Party in Germany used traditional law, side by side with the escalating introduction of revolutionary, but discriminatory, legislation, designed to promote terror and obedience, from 1933–1945. This offers an extreme, and criminal, version of legislative, governmental, and judicial intent to demarcate and persecute certain groups. In each of these examples, the issue of "race" as a determinant of the definition of personhood was central, and in the third example led to an attempt to exterminate an entire race of people.

Self-evident "truths": race and the law in the United States

At the end of the eighteenth century, Benjamin Franklin, envisioning the future of America, asked, "Why should we ... darken its people? ... Why increase the Sons of Africa, by planting them in America, where we have so fair an opportunity, by excluding all blacks and tawneys, of increasing the lovely white and red?"[3]

The Constitution of the United States came into force in 1789 and a year later, an Act of Congress restricted the rights of citizenship to "whites." It is true that The Thirteenth Amendment (1865), The Fourteenth Amendment (1868), and The Fifteenth Amendment (1870) all sought to abolish crucial deprivations of the liberty and civil rights of former slaves, as part of the post-Civil War Reconstruction effort. However, various legal definitions of "citizenship" remained a sticking point. Existing legislation and the racial attitudes they generated continued to legitimize and sometimes to inflame processes of race discrimination or violence.

After the American Civil War (1861–1865), the Southern States were obliged to abolish anti-"miscegenation" legislation. However, they introduced "the so-called 'Black Codes,'" that "prohibited blacks from entry into industrial and skilled work, confining them to field labour and sharecropping."[4] Before the Civil War, even in the Northern States, African-Americans were "barred from hotels and places of entertainment, from skilled crafts and professional colleges ...

segregated on trains and in churches."[5] Deprived of the vote, they nevertheless had to pay taxes. A Supreme Court ruling in 1883 allowed segregation in a way that facilitated "segregated schooling and separate facilities in trains, buses, libraries, parks, swimming pools and other public amenities."[6] Legislation against inter-racial marriage, particularly in the Southern States, was still possible. Such laws were notoriously referred to as the " 'Jim Crow' system of segregation ... named after a 'blackface' character, played by whites, portraying blacks as lazy, idiotic, child-like, and happy."[7] Moreover, contrary to the notion of civil order which is embodied in the Constitution, illegal acts of racism flourished. In the nineteenth and twentieth centuries, lynchings, or the violence of secret white organizations such as the Ku Klux Klan, maintained a climate of fear and hatred. As the civil rights movement grew in the mid-twentieth century, racial discrimination worsened. For example, the present-day incidence of overwhelmingly black populations within the penal system; apparently indiscriminate shootings by police of African-Americans; and ongoing racist significations attached to the Confederate flag. All of these suggest that battles over equality of citizenship in the United States are not over.

The predicament of holding a vulnerable racially inflected type of citizenship is captured, amongst many others, by the North American writer, Alice Walker (1944–). She structures her most famous novel, *The Color Purple* (1982), in the form of letters written by Celie, the central character, the majority of which are addressed to "God." In the narrative that emerges, Celie records the heart-breaking events of her early life in the American South, subject to conditions of unavoidably extreme poverty and being deliberately deprived of education. These conditions are never remarked on directly, but are evident everywhere in the detail of the language. Raped at the age of eight by her father and then forced into marriage at "near twenty,"[8] she is shown to be vulnerable to sexual violence, wife-beating, and the dominating violence of patriarchy. Her predicament also reveals her to be subjected to the equally violent indifference of the North American social order. Her letters, for most of the novel unsigned, reflect her sense that she has no legal presence, no personhood, as far as the social, economic, and legislative structures within which she is located are concerned. Nevertheless, her letters bear witness to the events they describe. They are addressed to "God" because there is no system of justice within the country, to which she may turn which will both listen to and respond to her testimony:

> Dear God
> I spend my wedding day running from the oldest boy. He twelve. His mama died in his arms and he don't want to hear no nothing bout no new one. He pick up a rock and laid my head open. The blood run all down between my breasts. His daddy say Don't *do* that! But that's all he say. He got four children instead of three, two boys and two girls. The girls hair ain't been fresh. He say bad luck to cut a woman hair. So after I bandage my head best I can and cook dinner—they have a spring not a well, and a wood stove look like a truck—I start trying to untangle hair. They only six and eight and they cry. They scream. They cuse me of murder. By ten o' clock I'm done. They cry their selves to sleep. But I don't cry.[9]

The aspiration towards a less hate-ridden and exploitative social order, evident in efforts at Civil War Reconstruction legislation, or the civil rights movement continues, in the United States, to be mixed with more rebarbative and exclusionist tendencies, as Walker's novel shows. Existing race legislation or that restored or introduced into the statute books in the Southern states, together with aspects of judicial, civil, and administrative practice, continue to complicate such liberal impulses to legislate in favor of a freer social order. In his "Author's Introduction" to *Invisible Man* (1952), which he wrote in 1981 for a new edition of the novel, the North American writer, Ralph Ellison (1914–1994) registers this "persistence of racial violence and the unavailability of legal protection."[10] It is for such reasons also that Karla Holloway argues, "U.S. racial identity [remains] a constructed legal fiction":[11]

> Race still matters in twenty-first-century America in ways that reinforce two centuries of institutionalized harms ... [Moreover] legislative responses to differences that provoke social bias [has] developed ... a nation that is both practiced in and intensely dedicated to using race as a metric for voting patterns, education policies and outcomes, medical assessments,

predictors of social and economic success, housing choices, incarceration patterns, aspirational objectives, religion, and just about every means of stratification in both ... public and private lives.[12]

In the South, as Rattansi reminds us, blacks were also forbidden to "serve on a jury, or even appear as witnesses in court."[13]

Moreover, juridical formulations of property, contract, and evidence are, in the United States, informed by the multiple concepts of personhood that had been necessitated by the institution of slavery. The English legal tradition, for example, associated personhood with the notion of natural law and the concept of rights that had been initiated by the late seventeenth century philosopher, John Locke. As Holloway observes, the "right to property, or the right to enter into contract, or the right to bear witness" became also implicit to the Jeffersonian ideal of citizenship.[14] These rights were considered fundamental in the framing of the American Constitution and each was "specifically attached to citizenship that, for blacks, was first described [in the Constitution] as [only] three-fifths of all other *persons*."[15] The condition of humanity, and attendant notions of "normativity," accordingly negotiated, and in time re-negotiated, through the constitution of citizenship, meant that "the idea of rights codified national particularities that would [over time] sustain legally cognizable differences between human beings."[16] In the case of laws of evidence, and the right to give testimony, this attachment of rights to citizenship, created ongoing complications in juridical reading that sometimes, so far as African-American slaves were concerned, sanctioned a legalization of discrimination. Admissible evidence, for example, "binds narratives of property and contract."[17] It "stands [first] as the evident physicality of a claim in the person of the body who makes it, or [second] in the *materia* that allows property and contract to emerge as fundamental rights."[18] But were slaves persons or property? If the latter they could *stand as* evidence but could not *give* evidence. For, as Holloway argues, evidence might "depend on [concepts of] contractual obligations and those [in turn] could easily depend on [vested concepts of] ownership and standing."[19]

Such legal debates influenced the ways descendants of slaves were also perceived in procedures of law. In *The Color Purple*, that the character Sofia, who angrily refuses to act as servant to the white wife of the mayor, has no legal presence and, as a woman and property-less person, little or no legal validity, is evident from Celie's letters. This emerges in the way Sofia's trial and sentence of 12 years' imprisonment is given, in Celie's narrative of the event and its "judicial" aftermath, *no space at all*. She writes merely:

> Dear God
> They put Sofia to work in the prison laundry. All day long from five to eight she washing clothes. Dirty convict uniforms, nasty sheets and blankets piled way over her head. Us see her twice a month for half a hour. Her face yellow and sickly, her fingers look like fatty sausage.
>
> Everything nasty here, she say, even the air. Food bad enough to kill you with it. Roaches here, mice, flies, lice and even a snake or two. If you say anything they strip you, make you sleep on a cement floor without a light.
>
> How you manage? us ast.
>
> Every time they ast me to do something, Miss Celie, I act like I'm you. I jump right up and do just what they say...
>
> Twelve years a long time to be good though, she say.[20]

Just as the violence of the police treatment of her, inferred from her previous letter,[21] the working of the penal system itself emerges as expressly designed to humiliate and break any spirit of resistance of the kind that Sofia displays frequently elsewhere in the novel.

The predicaments of demotion and disempowerment, that such legislation, police action, and penal execution of the law promote, reflects the extent to which "the [North American] ideal of achieving a true political equality eludes us in reality,"[22] amidst "the snags and whirlpools that mark our nation's vacillating course forward and away from the democratic ideal."[23] Indeed, in *Invisible Man*, Ralph Ellison uses invisibility as a metaphor for the predicament of African-Americans. In the face of the still ongoing social, legal, and political process of the vitiation of rights and freedoms, North American rhetoric about a free United States society rings hollow. The narrator of Ellison's novel states at the outset:

I am an invisible man. No, I am not a spook like those who haunted Edgar Allan Poe; nor am I one of your Hollywood-movie ectoplasms. I am a man of substance, of flesh and bone, fiber and liquids—and I might even be said to possess a mind. I am invisible, understand, simply because people refuse to see me ... That invisibility to which I refer occurs because of a peculiar disposition of the eyes of those with whom I come into contact. A matter of the construction of their *inner* eyes, those eyes with which they look through their physical eyes upon reality ... You ache with the need to convince yourself that you do exist in the real world, that you're part of all the sound and anguish, and you strike out with your fists, you curse, and you swear to make them recognize you. And, alas, it's seldom successful.[24]

To attempt to win recognition from a "tall blonde" man with "blue eyes" the narrator has to step outside the law. Frustrated, he resorts to violence but even then, after assaulting him "it occurred to me that the man had not *seen* me, actually; that he, as far as he knew, was in the midst of a walking nightmare!"[25] With the vigorous irony that characterizes his tone throughout the book, the narrator describes how he has given up "the routine process of buying service [in this case, electricity] and paying their outrageous taxes."[26] To gain a modicum of independence for himself he is forced once more to go outside the law:

I live rent-free in a building rented strictly to whites, in a section of the basement ... shut off and forgotten ... I found a home—or a hole in the ground, as you will ... warm and full of light ... I love light ... Light confirms my reality, gives birth to my form ... Without light I am not only invisible, but formless as well.[27]

In his "battle with Monopolated Light & Power" he has secretly wired the electricity company's supply to his own light bulbs, again obliged to transgress the law, so that he can "feel my vital aliveness."[28]

South African common law and Coetzee's fiction

The development in the South African context of *common law* and of *customary law* provides a somewhat different example of another way in which the law may be sometimes crucial in fixing, authorizing, and re-circulating particular imaginings of race.

For our purposes, common law may be understood as a legal tradition which originated in England, and which today constitutes the prevalent legal system in many parts of the world. The essence of common law is the development of law by means of binding judicial precedent. Customary law, also a feature of a number of contemporary legal systems within the South African context, may be understood as the often so-called traditional common rule or practice that evolved in South Africa into "native" law, thus becoming a legislatively enforced part of the accepted and expected conduct within the subordinated South African majority. Significantly, these notions of law were instituted and developed in South Africa decades before the Afrikaner Nationalist party came to power in 1948 and before it embarked on its own version of segregation, which it called apartheid.

Legislation to enforce racial discrimination and segregation in nineteenth and early twentieth century South Africa was generated by numerous factors, of which, as we noted in Chapter 2, the imagined notion of a "swart gevaar" was a consequence. The Great Trek, when Afrikaners left the British-ruled Cape Colony, partly because of the emancipation of slaves in 1834, was another factor. It contributed to the formation of Afrikaner Republics, which discriminated unfairly against ex-slaves or their descendants, and against the indigenous populations inhabiting the South African interior. Furthermore, the South African War, between the Afrikaner Republics and the British empire, ended in 1902, and the Union of South Africa was formed in 1910. But the issues that had caused the war were not eliminated, as Martin Chanock has observed; indeed, they

> were not laid to rest, and continued to call into question the legitimacy of the new state for decades. In addition to Afrikaner republicanism the state had to face a powerful new challenge from the largely British South African white labour movement, and the elemental task of maintaining white rule

over the black majority. In the period after 1902 the country faced several major political revolts. In Natal a Zulu rebellion was defeated in 1906. In the Transvaal strikes by white workers led to violence which necessitated repression by military action in 1905–7, 1913–1914 and 1918, and which culminated in an attempt at revolution in 1922. In 1914 an Afrikaner republican revolt in the armed forces brought civil war to areas of the country.[29]

The project to make the new state succeed was profoundly affected, too, by "the expansion of European law and the making of a colonial legal culture[30] both before and after nominal independence in 1910."[31] As a component in the British empire, South Africa "was a part of a world-wide system of racial and racist rule, in which both Britain and other white Dominions endorsed racist law."[32]

It is true that the influence of British modes of legal organization, court procedure, the conduct of judges, together with the language and linguistic forms of statute and government, was, and continues to be, pervasive. This may explain "the existence of a legal system clearly based on the liberal forms of law at the heart of an oppressive and racist state."[33] But at the outset the new state had no traditions of local common law or customary law to turn to. The history of the fashioning of such legal procedures and the creation of notions of precedent upon which it began to draw, moreover, involved the "complete colonization of African time and place":

> The process of creating the new common law depended on a focused scholarly enterprise of retrieval and translation of Roman and Renaissance texts. Fidelity to these texts, as embodying the inherent rationality of law, situated this rationality physically, historically and imaginatively in Europe and, specifically, not in Africa. The arcaneness of the texts limited access and comprehension. Few white lawyers had access to them, or could have understood them in these years. A source of mystery to the white population, they were nonetheless emblematic, an assurance that the white law contained the core of historical rationality, not simply the commands of the advantaged.[34]

The creation in this way of what was known as Roman-Dutch law was "mirrored by the simultaneous creation of a [system of] customary law ... [a]ppropriated from Africans, who ceased to be either its authoritative source or transmitters ... impenetrable to nearly all white lawyers and judges as well."[35] Chanock maintains that it was this division that was the foundation of racist South African law:

> Different sets of rules were seen as appropriate for the bearers of a 2000-year old legal tradition, and for barbarians who were still infants in evolutionary development ... the white state underlined the importance it placed on legal differentiation by passing the 1927 Native Administration Act, which institutionalized, nation wide separate courts applying separate law ... African input into the development and exposition of the customary law administered by the state's courts remained small.[36]

There were thus two systems of common law, neither of which, though interrelated, was clearly understood by the populations to which they, respectively, applied. Chanock continues:

> Few identified them, even rhetorically, as the source of their inherent rights. The ideological posture of the English common law, that it was the source of rights of "free-born Englishmen," was absent in South Africa where the racialised state was the identifiable source of rights or repression.[37]

Within such complexities, and "within a state based on racial dominance," what Chanock describes as the emerging South African legal culture exhibited at the same time a limited "multi-vocality and dissonance."[38] It manifested the overriding authority of government. In the course of providing, in one narrative, an example of the relationship between courts and subordinated black people, Chanock foregrounds the primacy given to "reasons of state ... the maxim that the safety of the state was the supreme law."[39] Then from the perspective of another narrative that explores the relationship between state and judges, he observes that "the ambivalent position of the judges [was] accorded some respect, yet without final power."

This reflects also a "combination of a respect for legal niceties, and formalism, with the willingness to discard them"[40] in situations of confrontation. Turning to ways in which the judges' juridical findings "construe the 'authorities' which appear to dominate both them and the litigants,"[41] he emphasizes how the use of arcane legal languages, such as Latin or legal French or Middle English, "entirely external to the society ruled"[42] also ignored concepts of local African law within which the system of law was actually located. This, in turn, insisted on the court's version of its "authorities," and the precedents for its own power as, crucially, *not* African.[43] But his final example, taken from the legal career in Natal and the Transvaal, of M.K. Ghandi provides an instance of "a different voice, developed in the struggle of subordinated people against the law"[44] and offers evidence of how, "within the law (though at its very fringes) genuinely alternative voices were formulated and heard."[45] Ghandi himself remarked of the system of justice he encountered while leading the Satyagrahi campaign against government curtailment of Asian rights in South Africa: "A thing acquired by violence can be retained by violence alone."[46]

Although one notion of legalism holds that the law is about the *limitation* of power, Chanock also maintains that,

> in the processes of building a new colonial state, law could best be understood as a way of *creating* powers, of endowing officials with regulated ways of acting, a *weapon* in the hands of the state rather than a *defence against it.*[47]

The "creation of separate regimes of [common] law for whites and [customary law for] non-whites, both in common law and by racially discriminatory statutes" was not only the product but also "the [style] and [form] of law that survived into the 1980s."[48] In such processes, the relationship between force and law in what was thought to be a still fragile state, was often crucial. Indeed, Chanock observes that

> [t]he role of judicial institutions, and legal doctrine, in the face of political unrest and revolution, remained a feature of South African legal history throughout the history of the white-ruled state … [t]he view that the constitutional design of the Union

> entailed the supremacy of the government over the constitu-
> tion was to be affirmed in the struggle between the Appeal
> Court and the government in the 1950s ... In the confronta-
> tion [of liberatory struggle and oppression] where the over-
> whelming anxiety of those who controlled the legal
> institutions was to protect authority, there were no echoes in
> the law of the visions of justice presented to it, no traces of a
> common link or language between rule and justice.[49]

We may now turn from this particular example, of the use of the law
to legislate and so fix crucial notions of race, to a more recent medita-
tion on the practice of the legal mechanisms of the racist state. The
South African novelist and critic J.M. Coetzee (1940–), in his novel,
Waiting for the Barbarians (1980), provides just such an example in
his exploration of the equivocal implications of the link "between rule
and justice" within processes of the legal and administrative fixing
and recirculation of imaginings about colonization or "Empire," apartheid and race.[50]

The Afrikaner Nationalist Party came to power in South Africa in
1948, at once instituting a blatantly racist program of legislation, in
order to strengthen the control over, and the exploitation of, the labor
of the majority black peoples of South Africa. Throughout its rule, the
Nationalist government was quite openly determined to intensify the
processes of political, judicial, economic, and social separation that
the period of segregation, which preceded it, had generated.[51] While
Coetzee's novel is deliberately located in an unnamed place in order
to investigate the complexities in any situation of the effects and practices of racial and colonial government, justice, and administration, it
remains significant that he published his novel during the period of
apartheid in South Africa. Indeed he may have decided prudently to
offer a more generalized presentation of "Empire," of the kind that
exists in a novel that clearly influenced him, Dino Buzzati's *The
Tartar Steppe* (1952),[52] even if he had his own location partly in
mind. Perhaps he sought to avoid the immediate banning of the work,
as in the cases of other artists working within societies that have
severe censorship legislation.

The exposure of the activities of the security police, the "Third
Bureau" in the novel, is one of the ways in which Coetzee

interrogates the legality of the Empire as evidenced by this particular executive unit whose task it is to protect the state by ensuring conformity to its legislation. At the outset of the novel, the menacing Colonel Joll, has been sent from the imperial center to a provincial outpost of the Empire to investigate a suspected outbreak of barbarian resistance and to prepare for a campaign to subdue it. He is, we learn, one of the officials of "the Third Bureau of the Civil Guard ... seen for the first time on the frontier, guardians of the State, specialists in the obscurer motives of sedition, devotees of truth, doctors of interrogation."[53] His practice of what proves very quickly to be a violent form of investigation, arrest, torture, and incrimination emerges as single-minded, informed by a discourse of empire that requires of subjugated local populations enforced obedience and submission to colonial domination. His operation seizes on innocents who happen to stray across the path of his investigations and who have their actions instantly re-defined according to the often paranoid "logic" of colonialist discourse. Thus, frightened local inhabitants who hide from Colonel Joll's exploratory force are detained because they are hiding, and then, because they are detained, treated as potential insurrectionists.

The magistrate, who is the narrator of the novel, remarks to his readers, of those frightened people who have been arrested, that

> these river people are aboriginal, older even than the nomads. They live in settlements of two or three families along the banks of the river, fishing and trapping for most of the year ... Living in fear of everyone, skulking in the reeds, what can they possibly know of a great barbarian enterprise against the Empire?[54]

However, the Colonel, oblivious to the fact that he and his men do not even understand or speak the prisoners' language, sticks to procedure, asserting that "[p]risoners are prisoners."[55] We may recall Miranda's attitude to Caliban's language, which we noted in Chapter 2. The magistrate records that the next day the Colonel begins his interrogations of two particular prisoners, noting that, whereas once "I thought him lazy, little more than a bureaucrat with vicious tastes," now "I see how mistaken I was," for "[i]n his quest for the truth he is tireless."[56]

The Colonel, it is clear, seeks evidence to confirm his discursive ordering of the "reality" that he "sees," and imposes upon it only his own "truth," that is set against the Magistrate's far less incendiary explanation of the activities of the two prisoners. As the magistrate is forced to conclude elsewhere,

> One thought alone preoccupies the submerged mind of Empire: how not to end, how not to die, how to prolong its era. By day it pursues its enemies. It is cunning and ruthless, it sends its bloodhounds everywhere. By night it feeds on images of disaster: the sack of cities, the rape of populations, pyramids of bones, acres of desolation.[57]

In addition to this presentation of mechanisms of the colonial state which, in the name of order, administers torture, Coetzee investigates equivocality in the links between the rule of law and the practices of justice, by way of his narrator, who, crucially, is himself a magistrate. His narrative probes the degree to which bureaucratic individuals caught up in the implementation of colonial or state legislative and judicial processes demonstrate complex and contradictory complicities within projects of racial domination. We may note that the complexity of white guilt, in other novels explicitly within the apartheid system, recurs as a theme in Coetzee's fiction.

Although there is no direct one-to-one correspondence between *Waiting for the Barbarians* and segregationist or apartheid South Africa, we may set beside Coetzee's presentation of his magistrate, certain aspects of the role magistrates played within the history of South African racist government. In the period of South African history with which he deals, Chanock notes, for example, that prosecutors preferred to bring charges in magisterial courts, "where legalism was less punctilious."[58] He remarks also that "it was bad for a magistrate to get a reputation for being 'slow'":[59]

> Over two hundred cases were handled in a single court in Johannesburg on Monday mornings ... [a contemporary commentator] wrote that a Witwatersrand magistrate "was recently held up to public admiration by a Johannesburg newspaper for having dealt with a record of over 500 cases in

one day ... It is the European case which tends to be heard and the native case to be 'polished off.' "[60]

From the point of view of the executive government, "the primary role of the magistrates was, in these years, a mixture of the political and the administrative"[61] but, clearly, *not* the judicial. In the Transvaal, some magistrates were not acquainted "with even the elementary principles of law,"[62] others had no "experience of legal practice, or magistracy."[63] Moreover, more generally,

The "rule of law" remained embedded within the constant construction of self and difference. This offers an avenue to understanding the adherence to the niceties of procedural and substantive legalism in the context of racial oppression. From one perspective the judges and their law appear to have been part of this structure of domination. But the judicial selves of the Supreme Courts appear to have evaded this continuum which stretched from the actions of officials and police, through the courts of the justices of the peace and native commissioners, and the magistrates' courts, and then to the Supreme Courts. Instead, they placed themselves within another continuum. In a feat of self-imagining they saw themselves as brothers to Grotius and the Master of the Rolls rather than to the farm foreman and prison warder. They found their reality and their law by connecting themselves to Renaissance European jurists and to the judges of the House of Lords and the Court of Criminal Appeal ... This legal identity not only helped evasion of South African actualities, but constructed a philosophical, juristic, correct and formal self which could be opposed totally to the barbarian other. The process of the creation of self broke the continuum with the lower realms of the legal/administrative machinery.[64]

A study of the more recent history of apartheid South Africa, also argues that the safeguard system failed political detainees.[65] The magistrates enjoyed a great deal of power and were supposed to implement the safeguard system. In the particular instance of political detainees, the complaints and safeguard system, which they were supposed to implement, failed. This was because magistrates were public servants and "as a result their independence was significantly compromised"[66] or because "as employees of the state magistrates confronted the situation of dual loyalties, on the one hand to their employer and colleagues and on the other to the detainee whose well being they were charged with ensuring."[67] Mostly, magistrates "saw law and justice as synonymous";[68] often, they exhibited "a routinized and bureaucratic approach, a lack of engagement with, or easy disengagement from, their potential to protect and safeguard, and a trust in or association with the custodial authorities that undermined magisterial effectiveness."[69]

Coetzee's magistrate exhibits related complexities, in his account of, for example, his reactions to knowledge of the largely nonspecified torture of Colonel Joll's detainees. These detainees are within the magistrate's jurisdiction. He is, accordingly, partly responsible for their protection. This induces moral unease in him, and he even questions the Colonel's behavior. At the same time, he allows the unspeakable processes to continue until the Colonel decides to move elsewhere.

The magistrate's narrative also registers the physical pleasures he derives, from his eating, his exploitative womanizing, his love of hunting, his love of the farmlands, and his love of archaeology. Even as he is attracted to and repelled by a barbarian woman whose eyes have been severely damaged by torture, he tries to understand her and he develops a complicated relationship with her. But he also allows her to act as his servant. His exploration of her body may bespeak his need to see and know her, but his actions also reflect patriarchal and colonial habits of the violation of, eroticization of, and feminization of explored or occupied territory.

Yet again the magistrate is, on the other hand, increasingly troubled by the torture implemented by the judicial and administrative system of which he himself is a part. During the nights they spend together he attempts repeatedly to discover what was done to the almost sightless barbarian. She protests,

> You are always asking me that question, so I will now tell you. It was a fork, a kind of fork with only two teeth. There were little knobs in the teeth to make them blunt. They put it in the

coals until it was hot, then they touched you with it, to burn you. I saw the marks where they had burned people.[70]

The magistrate is "chilled" to hear of the Colonel's intent to burn his way to the "truth" by means of pain, to "mark" his victim with evidence of his own discursive truth.[71] Earlier the magistrate recounts how, when trying to investigate the archaeology of the place he lives in, he attempts to read correctly certain "slips" he has found amongst the ruins. However, unlike the Colonel, he recognizes that there are limits to his own discursive knowledge. He recognizes too, his inability to comprehend the barbarian woman whose body he literally explores in proto-colonial, patriarchal, and sexist manner in extended dream-like sessions. Thus, during a passing sexual liaison with someone else that he uses to dissipate the anxieties caused by the "barbarian" woman, he nevertheless continues to think of how the "body of the other one, closed, ponderous, sleeping in my bed in a faraway room, seems beyond comprehension … I cannot imagine whatever drew me to that alien body."[72] This leads him to a further disturbing question:

Is this how her torturers felt hunting their secret, whatever they thought it was? For the first time I feel a dry pity for them: how natural a mistake to believe that you can burn or tear or hack your way into the secret body of the other![73]

The magistrate's quest for understanding thus emerges, unlike the Colonel's discursive blindness, as somehow capable of registering the limitations of the discursive system and the customary and legal authorities of which he, in contradiction, has all his life served.

His doubleness also emerges in other ways. He recklessly tells a young officer that the barbarians "want their land back":

It is … contempt for the barbarians, contempt which is shown by the meanest ostler or peasant farmer, that I as a magistrate have had to contend with for twenty years. How do you eradicate contempt, especially when that contempt is founded on nothing more substantial than differences in table manners, variations in the structure of the eyelid?[74]

The magistrate is also, paradoxically, articulate about current attitudes to the law. When the novel opens the magistrate's office at the courthouse with its "shelves upon shelves of papers bundled together and tied with ribbon, the record of decades of humdrum administration, the small bookcases of legal texts, the cluttered desk,"[75] suggests bureaucratic comfort and indolence, a humdrum provincial legal routine of lethargy and delay. But when later in the novel he is arrested as a putative traitor, he is brought back to what was his own office, to be interrogated by another policeman from the Third Bureau. Coetzee's interest in the imbrication of the law in imperialist and racial governmental processes is hinted at again in the detail of the magistrate's description:

> The careful reorganization of my office from clutter and dustiness ... [is] meant to say something, not only that he is now in charge ... but that he knows how to comport himself in an office, knows even how to introduce a note of functional elegance ... Does he fear I will sneer unless he armours himself in a décor picked up, I have no doubt, from careful observation of the offices of his superiors in the Bureau?[76]

The "knowledge" of the law hinted at in words such as "elegance" and "décor" suggests a vacuous formalism. When he hears the mistakenly speculative depositions trumped up against him, the magistrate responds, "I will defend myself in a court of law."[77] But he then comments ironically on his own knowledge of such legal process, that "will use the law against me so far as it serves them, then they will turn to other methods ... [t]o people who do not operate under statute, legal process is simply one instrument among many."[78]

Later, the now demoted magistrate recalls

> I think of a young peasant who was once brought before me in the days when I had jurisdiction over the garrison. He had been committed to the army for three years by a magistrate in a far-off town for stealing chickens. After a month here he tried to desert ... I lectured him. "We are all subject to the law, which is greater than any of us. The magistrate who sent you here, I myself, you—we are all subject to the law ... you

feel that it is unjust, I know, that you should be punished for having the feelings of a good son ... But we live in a world of laws ... a world of the second-best. All we can do is to uphold the laws, all of us, without allowing the memory of justice to fade." After lecturing him I sentenced him.[79]

That the law may be used as an instrument amongst several to enforce submission, is perhaps an obvious inference. But the comfort and security, the safeties of complicity, which conformity to the law's sanctions offers is more disturbing. Thus, although the magistrate goes on to identify his unease at the complexities that lie behind his sentence, his doubleness about the law leads him back to the seductions of submission:

I toyed more than once with the idea of resigning my post, retiring from public life, buying a small market garden. But then, I thought, someone else will be appointed to bear the shame of office, and nothing will have changed. So I continued in my duties.[80]

While it is also true that in the course of the terrible events the magistrate seeks some form of redemption by stating "that in this farthest outpost of the Empire of light there existed one man who in his heart was not a barbarian,"[81] it is also true that the doubleness he earlier exemplifies, suggests a certain structural pattern, even an inevitability, in racist judicial and legislative practice. When the magistrate reflects on the multiple ambiguities informing his desire to understand the barbarian woman and so also possess her, as he himself says "engrave myself on her,"[82] he comes to a chilling apprehension of just such a structural doubleness:

For I was not, as I liked to think, the indulgent pleasure-loving opposite of the cold rigid Colonel. I was the lie that Empire tells itself when times are easy, the truth that Empire tells when the harsh winds blow. Two sides of Imperial rule, no more, no less.[83]

Gready and Kgalema note, partly as a result of interviews they conducted with magistrates of the apartheid era that

Alongside the fact that magistrates saw law and justice as synonymous, one of the themes that comes out of the interviews is the distinction made by magistrates between structural authority (law, government) and the individual, and a belief that it was possible for an individual to inhabit and serve the structures while remaining independent, to secure justice, for example, within an unjust legal and state machinery. This set of attitudes, it is argued in this report, needs to be seen as a retrospective device enabling magistrates to distance themselves from and even criticize the apartheid regime for which they worked, while maintaining their individual credibility.[84]

But against this, as a less evasive register of doubleness and complicity, may be set the narrative of Coetzee's magistrate:

But I temporized, I looked around this obscure frontier, this little backwater with its dusty summers and its cartloads of apricots and its long siestas and its shiftless garrison and the waterbirds flying in and flying out year after year to and from the dazzling waveless sheet of the lake, and I said to myself, "Be patient, one of these days he [Colonel Joll] will go away, one of these days quiet will return: then our siestas will grow longer and our swords rustier ... the line that marks the frontier on the maps of Empire will grow hazy and obscure till we are blessedly forgotten." Thus I seduced myself, taking one of the many wrong turnings I have taken on a road that looks true but has delivered me into the heart of a labyrinth.[85]

Legal constructions of race in pre-1939 and World War II Germany

The concept of community law that was developed in South African "native" law, during the segregation and apartheid decades, was designed to demarcate and limit the rights of the indigenous inhabitants of the country, imagined as "primitive" and "child-like." The period of fascism in Germany, heralded by the burning of the German Reichstag (parliament) in 1933 that lasted until the end of World War II, drew upon the concept of "community" in enunciations or applications of the law. But the German legal system put the notion of "community" to a very different purpose from that evident in the South African example we have just noted. The imagined concept of "community" in German law was designed to assert and protect the German community itself, imagined as an Aryan group, superior to other groups, including Jews, foreigners, Slavs, homosexuals, and travelers.

The term *community* or *national community* was already a preoccupation during the Weimar Republic. Initially, Hitler's National Socialist Workers Party first allowed areas of the law to function just as it had during the Weimar Republic. This reassured "the bourgeois economic elites and, above all … civil servants and judges" who were "largely nationalistic and anti-parliamentarian in their thinking, but … also had a strong dislike of open terror."[86] Therefore, with respect to civil and criminal law, the National Socialists preserved the "façade." According to Michael Stolleis's research, "statutory law [was] taken over en bloc and continued to be valid unless it was superseded by new legislation."[87] The early period of National Socialist rule can be understood as partly manifesting, in areas such as these, legislation of "islands of 'injustice' interspersed within a system that, on the whole, still functioned as 'law.' "[88]

But in the matter of constitutional law after January 30, 1933, Germany witnessed a transition from a parliamentary system (or what was left of it) to dictatorship. New legislation significantly assured creation of a "militarized and authoritarian centralized state with strident propaganda about a 'communal way of thinking.' "[89] Alongside the law "there were 'arbitrary measures' … and 'Führer's orders,' some of which were no longer even published … the application of ['normal'] law stood alongside arbitrary terror."[90] The law was used blatantly, as Stolleis has suggested, to authorize processes that involved persecution of groups of people imagined to be racially inferior:

> Closely linked with constitutional law were fundamental violations of the principle of equality through the *disenfranchisement of minorities*. This began when the regime revoked the citizenship of its opponents. Soon after came the first discriminatory and persecutory measures against German (later also

European) Jews, as well as against other political, religious or racial minorities. These measures intensified from a series of cunning and insidious acts of disenfranchisement and humiliation (confiscation of property, compulsory levies, "Aryanization" of businesses, forced adoption of the first names "Israel" and "Sarah" for Jews, wearing of the yellow star, and so forth) to a state-organized pogrom in 1938 (Kristalnacht) and the murder of millions in the extermination camps. Until the gruesome final phase, in which disguise seemed superfluous, *all discriminatory and disenfranchising measures were enacted within the forms of the law; they were published and commented on by jurists.*[91]

Stolleis goes on to observe that

the reasons hitherto given to explain at least the judiciary's role in the injustice—the anti-Semitism that pervaded bourgeois circles, the coming together of legal positivism and the "subservient German spirit" as well as the latent and common readiness of majorities to oppress minorities—shed only a partial light on the problem.[92]

However, from our perspective, the very use itself, in fascist Germany, of the law to authorize forms of discrimination and racism is particularly significant.[93]

Moreover, the Reich Minister and President of the Academy for German Law, said, in 1934, "We start from the law of the community, and this communal law is the real inner reversal of our legal point of view and our legal system."[94] National Socialist literature, we should note, had "affirmed time and again that the subordination of the individual to the (national) community was not an act of external compulsion; instead, individuals were following the reawakened call of the blood, which was urging them toward community."[95] Such a community was "'ordered' and 'charged' by blood; the element establishing community was 'blood not some abstraction.'"[96] Roland Freisler, a German Judge and lawyer, who was also State Secretary of the Reich Ministry of Justice and President of the People's Court, a mechanism established outside the constitution, gave, in 1938, chilling articulation to the "new legal" mesh of race, community, and fascist leadership that was officially and publicly imagined and pursued:

> We Germans march in columns. As soldiers we look forward. And there we see one person: our leader. Wherever he points we march. And wherever he points he always marches first, ahead of us. That is in keeping with our German nature. In the face of this all the "constitutional law" of the past has blown away like chaff in the wind.
>
> The separation of powers; supervision of the leadership by the led; protection of personal rights by courts; a state based on the rule of law, which nobody wanted less than the organs of justice themselves, that is to say, the review of true acts of leadership to determine whether they are in full compliance with the law; constraints on the vanguard and limitations on their instruments of leadership; the rule of numbers over will, of anonymous numbers, that is, of irresponsibility.
>
> All this—once carefully hedged about in constitutions with legal guarantees—has now been swept away.[97]

The communal, in such a reading, asserts, in the business of racial, political, or juridical legislation a new system of law that is determinedly lawless.

T.S. Eliot, Enid Bagnold, racial "purity," and eugenics

We may append to this chapter two examples taken from right-wing British culture in the 1930s. The two historical cases demonstrate notions of racial purity and national homogeneity. While not in themselves evidence of legal, judicial, or governmental formulation, they inadvertently coincide with German racialized legislation and government-encouraged race movements.

The first example, a notorious passage by the North American born, and subsequently naturalized, British poet T.S. Eliot (1888–1965), is taken from *After Strange Gods*. The book was published in Britain in 1934 and immediately reprinted in the same year. The author, for whatever personal reasons, subsequently refused permission for any further reprinting of the volume. In this text Eliot declares:

> What we can do is to use our minds, remembering that a tradition without intelligence is not worth having, to discover what is the best life for us not as a political abstraction, but as a particular people in a particular place; what in the past is worth preserving and what should be rejected; and what conditions, within our power to bring about, would foster the society that we desire. Stability is obviously necessary. You are hardly likely to develop tradition except where the bulk of the population is relatively so well off where it is that it has no incentive or pressure to move about. The population should be homogeneous; where two or more cultures exist in the same place they are likely to be fiercely self-conscious or both to become adulterate. What is still more important is unity of religious background, and reasons of race and religion combine to make any large number of free-thinking Jews undesirable. There must be a proper balance between urban and rural, industrial and agricultural development. And a spirit of excessive tolerance is to be deprecated.[98]

T.S. Eliot was arguably expressing right-wing commonplaces of the time when he called for the fashioning and protection of a stable, settled middle class, that would be homogeneous, not adulterated by foreign elements, free from Jews, and not excessively tolerant towards difference.

Intolerance, moreover, was in the air in Britain during the 1930s and in the aftermath of the Great Depression of 1929. In October 1932 Oswald Mosley had founded the British Union of Fascists. In May 1935 he addressed a telegram to Julius Streicher, declaring "the power of Jewish corruption must be destroyed in all countries before peace and justice can be achieved in Europe."[99] Mosley ended in prison during World War II, and the movement dissipated and lost its steam. This otherwise obscure history became the source of inspiration for the 1995 film adaptation of Shakespeare's *Richard III*, directed by Richard Loncraine and starring Ian McKellen. The film transposes the history of the War of Roses to 1930s Britain in an imaginary context where the royal family had fascist leanings. It imagines an alternative history where Oswald Mosley's British Union of Fascists thrives. British anti-Semitism in the 1930s was "deep and broad":[100] The "Right Club," the Imperial Fascist League, the British Protestant League, the Militant Christian Patriots, were all "race-conscious Britons"[101]—as the Nordic League had it, including themselves. Amongst other diverse and often crack-pot goals, they wanted, like Eliot, to prevent the "weakening of England's racial 'stock,'"[102] though not always in his deliberately mannered way, But, equally significant, all these movements proved, in the long run, to be failures:

> The absence of ideas favourable to fascism, the consequent absence of any sustainable fascist tradition in [Britain], the paucity of fascism's intellectual appeal, the limited number of fascist fellow-travellers among intellectuals, the complete electoral failure of the BUF [it never won a seat in parliament], the strength of the Conservative party, the very positioning of Britain against fascism in World War II, the utter marginality of fascists in the political culture, has meant that it makes no sense to speak of an English anti-Semitism that is fascist in nature.[103]

At the same time, Eliot implicitly argued for a British racial superiority and exclusiveness when he made provision for a bubble of homogeneity within which his adopted "particular people in a particular place" that might remain "purely" located within their non-adulterated tradition. This racial superiority needed constant monitoring.

A second example is the work of the British writer Enid Bagnold (1889–1981). Her work explicitly expressed sympathy for contemporary German preoccupations about race, and their attempts to educate, encourage, or legislate a non-heterogeneous, "pure" nationhood into being. Scholar Anna Sebba notes that Bagnold "was deeply interested in events in Europe" (xiv) while writing *The Squire* (1938),[104] and that she drew her inspiration from contemporary German examples. Bagnold is the author of *National Velvet* (1935), which was made into a popular film in 1944, and starred Elizabeth Taylor and Mickey Rooney. As a significant feminist text, depictions of an upper-middle class household largely in the control of women in *The Squire*, its descriptions of the heroism and strength of women in childbirth, and in the role of maternity generally, is, perhaps, why the novel was republished, first by Virago Press in 1987, and then by Persephone Books in 2013. Bagnold wrote about Germany in some private notes at this time:

> the various European countries [are] squabbling children in a nursery with France, the neurotic child, wanting its own way: into this nursery comes the newborn baby, Nazi Germany. Not unusually the birth was difficult and ugly but "I love to see things born ... We are afraid of Hitlerism. We see in it retrogression. I see in Nazism Birth and all the horrors and beauties of birth."[105]

It is true that the influential Social Darwinist Herbert Spencer (1820–1893) and Francis Galton (1822–1911), whose work on intelligence led to eugenics and the notion of selective breeding designed to produce humans of a superior class and race, were both British.[106] Moreover eugenics attracted the interest even of members of the political left in Britain, such as the organization of left-wing thinkers known as the Fabians that included social economists Sidney (1859–1947) and Beatrice (1858–1943) Webb and playwright and political commentator George Bernard Shaw. Anne Sebba, in 1987, noted that Bagnold's own midwife, Ethel Raynham Smith "was driven by the conviction that, if the conditions of birth were correct, it would be possible to create a healthier race."[107] On the right, Oswald Mosley and his followers declared, "after Britain, we put the interests of the Empire [and in] a conflict of interest, whatever is best for the British people must prevail."[108] Commenting on the role of eugenics in British fascism, the historian Thomas Linehan observes

> British fascism bequeathed from Social Darwinism the notion of evolutionary development and ascent to more advanced modes of biological existence ... interwar fascists believed that fascism stood for a more advanced mode of political arrangement that would elevate society to a higher stage of socioeconomic development. As a Mosleyite optimistically asserted,

fascism was "the next step in civilization" ... for Social-Darwinists, the nation was a biological organism ... The Social-Darwinist [Benjamin] Kidd ... promoted an instrumentalist model of the state [which] represented a ... vulgarization of Darwin's theories, in that the conscious intervention of an external force would now replace the random operations of "natural selection" ... The national socialist Karl Pearson also revered the state. However he would introduce sinister racial concepts into the equation. The state's role was to enhance the nation's racial character ... This ... had its roots in Pearson's views on the importance of heredity in determining individual characteristics and conduct. These views were influenced by Francis Galton's eugenicist fantasies on genetic health care ... As late as 1947 [Mosley] wrote that "to evolve a higher type has become a practical aim. Once again we postulate that the prime necessity of our age is to accelerate evolution. This generation must play the midwife to Destiny in hastening a new birth".[109]

Bagnold's "belief that in any revolution blood would be shed initially but then a healthy child would emerge"[110] leads her, repeatedly in *The Squire*, to extol the cause of eugenics as crucial in the making of an imperial race, a superior ruling class, and a healthy "England." In one of the several passages in the novel when its characters discuss childbirth and childcare, the midwife says:

"I believe that all is done in these first few weeks. It is not my job to look beyond these days, for this present is my work. But if you ask me to look, and to speak of what I can't really know, I should say that as your baby is now so he will be in old age, that the perfection of his introduction to life will reassert itself again and again in all his crises ... The book of instinct has long, long been closed," said the midwife.

"But what do we get instead?" said the squire. "The science-guided baby! Labelled, its tears and stools in bottles, its measurements on a chart, its food weighed like a prescription!"

"Better than muddle," said the midwife.[111]

On another occasion the midwife declares

> How seldom I can care for a mother and her baby in the peace I want for my work, away from the household and its surroundings! My clinic would be a palisaded place, far in the country. There the mother should travel beforehand, passing through the isolation of a journey, leaving husband and family with their preoccupations in the world. There, in a camp, like an athlete in training she should do her work for the newborn out of sight of life. No legends, no nonsense. The highest medical efficiency. Pre-natal observations carried out.[112]

The "squire" in the novel is the wife of the squire of Manor House, who is absent for the entire novel, attending to his interests in "Bombay," and on his way back home, and, at the end in Marseilles. Apart from giving birth to their child, the wife/squire runs the House and its stables together with the large staff of household servants. She cares for her four children, pondering, during the course of the novel the meaning of their lives, that of the newborn child, and the significance of her own life. The squire broods incessantly "[f]rom what pockets of heredity came these children,"[113] realizing that "there was something in which she now acquiesced, a calm, a stoic pleasure in *procession* ... 'now I am a pipe through which the generations pass.'"[114] Her five children "did not know yet that they were part of her flesh, her past her heredity, her mother and her father."[115] She also imagines her need to protect her children as elemental, informed by what she describes as the uncomplicated processes of nature:

> "Where's Jay?" she wondered ... This she would do at odd moments in the flight of the day, as a bird looks under its breast on the nest to count once more its clutch of eggs. "Where's Jay? Where's Henry? Lucy? Boniface?"[116]

Philippa Levine writes that, during the period of colonialism, "the stress on heredity was crucial":[117]

> It was fitness and betterment—especially racial betterment—that lay at the heart of eugenic thinking, a philosophy and

practice that combined an earlier optimism in science as progress with a later nineteenth-century pessimism around degeneration. The existence of the latter helped push the prospect of the former into the limelight, most especially in an era of high and even hysterical imperialism. And the years between the Berlin Congress in the 1880s and World War I were among the most intense and aggressive eras of colonial rivalry and tension. The culmination of scientific growth and imperial expansion ... created a receptive climate for culturing eugenic ideas ... science in Britain enjoyed considerable "cultural and institutional security" in the later years of the nineteenth century, at a point when the British empire seemed unassailable in its pre-eminence. Making the case for eugenics late in his life, Galton saw eugenic practice as enabling the "race" to "be better fitted to fulfil our vast imperial opportunities." It was a clear statement of intent, of destiny and of desire, and only five years later it was echoed in the words of the ardent eugenicist Caleb Saleeby (1878–1940) who proclaimed that eugenics was the path to rebuilding "the living foundations of empire".[118]

For Bagnold, her focus on lineage intimates a particular kind of childrearing and a maternal pride that emerges from the inferences of class, race, and empire whose notions are also quietly set in the novel. British colonial history affords well-known examples of the kind of legislative and juridical, as well as cultural and social constructions, of race which the British overtly practiced. As the example of South Africa above demonstrates, local populations were conceived of as inferior and degenerative, justifying British control. Moreover, race, gender, and class were also conflated with the definition of the industrial workers in the nineteenth century. Here working class subjects were imagined as an inferior "breed" or "race." Working women, in the Victorian period, were held to be "examples of racial regression."[119] Local populations, in colonies such as India, were effeminized and, in the case of women, sexualized. Episodes of resistance produced even "more repressive and inferiorizing mode[s] of rule in the colonies."[120] The very idea of empire

became part of a widespread culture of racism. As trade within the empire grew by leaps and bounds, so advertising, in particular, disseminated even more widely images of blacks as uncivilized, inferior, but smiling, happy and grateful in their subservience. The empire was charged with "the white man's burden" of bringing Christianity and civilized habits ... to God's "coloured" peoples.[121]

No such details appear in Bagnold's novel, however. But a sense of empire and class is established both at its very beginning and throughout:

From the village green where the Manor House stood, well-kept, white-painted, the sea was hidden by the turn of the street. The house's front, pierced with windows, blinked as the sun sank, and on the step of the open front door stood the butler, Pratt, come out to breathe the evening air...

"Quite a trip," he thought, his mind on his master gone on his annual three months' visit to Bombay. The Unborn for whom the house waited in restless suspension and slightly growing indiscipline would be a big baby by his return ... Pratt went to his lady (now the squire, the Begum of this masterless house).[122]

The Manor House on the village green, with its butler come out to breathe the evening air, represents a traditional upper-middle class hierarchy. The loyal servant whose "wrappings of inherited servitude"[123] the squire alludes to later in the novel, the other servants she describes, the applicant for a position in her household whom she dismisses with the thought that she is "a born lavatory attendant, if ever there was one,"[124] the children of the village itself, all have demonstrably and implicitly different destinies, as the squire conceives them, compared with her own carefully bred children.

Pratt's unease at his master's annual absence in Bombay, also hints at the imperial purchase of the Manor House family, the business of empire fleetingly anticipated in the language of the novel's opening, by the image of the sea "hidden by the turn of the street." Occasionally this dimension will be quietly reiterated in the novel in several references: one to "the row of Indian fly-switches attached by their ivory handles to a carved rack studded with brass,"[125] or another, "the great cloth last brought from India, with beetles' green wings embroidered into the pattern with gold threads,"[126] or a third,

> Under a glass dome on a side table stood a model in brass and iron of an old smooth-bore field gun and limber, sixteen inches long. It had been handmade by a native Head Armourer of the Arungabad Division of the Nizam's army of 1838.[127]

The squire lives among such accumulated signs of her husband's participation in imperial power and acquisition. Towards the end, the narrative records that he, the Bombay merchant, is now on the sea, heading for Marseilles, and that his "room doors were set wide open, his Indian rugs hung sunning on wall and branch."[128] Pratt's irony, in thinking in the opening passage of the novel, of the squire, in his master's absence as his "Begum," a woman of high rank in India or Pakistan, is yet another reminder of an "appropriate" colonial, albeit subaltern, hierarchy. At another point in the novel Bagnold writes, with mischievous irony, of the squire "[s]itting, when [her son] had gone, solid like Queen Victoria on a dais."[129]

In such contexts, Bagnold's apparently incidental use of the colors "black" and "white" also emerges as telling. The apparently inconsequential reference at the start of the book, to the Manor House as "white-painted" heralds innumerable uses of the color "white" subsequently deployed in the novel to convey, for example the new baby's peace, "going red with anger in her arms" but "white with digesting sleep."[130] The day begins, "white before the sun rose."[131] The squire's newborn baby's face "which had been flushed was now snow-white."[132] She thinks of the yet pristine unknowability amongst her other children, of her baby's future "new note, white and voiceless, ready to be inserted."[133] She mentions her son Henry's "whitish hair,"[134] and asks her daughter to cut "white roses from the top rosebed"[135] for the lunch table. She calls for another son Jay whose "fair head"[136] thrusts out an answer.

These apparently haphazard but frequent uses of the word "white" and related variants, in an always positive sense, are matched by the conventional use of the word "black" and its variants. Thus, for Pratt, "sometimes life was too black."[137] The squire thinks of the struggles of giving birth as the "pressure of black violence."[138] Her friend

Caroline, thinking she has been criticized, asks the squire, "Are you blackening me?"[139] Henry, in argument, looks "black."[140] Bagnold's writing here seems less incidental and innocuous when set in the context of the squire's brooding about her origins and her children's futures, her obvious love of the settled routines of her particular class and race. After dealing as she often does in the novel with her servants, she thinks wryly, on one occasion: "Ah this old feudal nonsense in a toppling world! Nonsense and a trouble but it had to go on. No other way of living if you wanted to walk to your grave cloaked in the English life."[141]

When a little later the squire thinks of Europe, the kind of English life she has in mind becomes again apparent:

> Europe and the future, sickness, accident, dispersal and age rode like gaunt ships upon the breakers. But now she was allowed by time, by chance, her peace, her idleness. Nursing her baby she had a right to her quiet. She stared and saw nothing, not the flat planes of grass, not the lightless walls. The little glass of sherry cast her loose from her garden seat ... Under father Sun at midday, under the wild phenomenon of the moon at night she saw herself crouched with her litter, a pyramid of birth, a pheasant over its young under the Great Hawk's eye.[142]

The squire's imagined "right" to a settled homogeneous stability, occurs also in a world in which, behind the maternal strengths of her sense of her particular family's right to tradition, class, healthy procreative methods, lies an empire, but without even a reference to the ordinary lives of the subordinate darker-skinned millions it controlled. Only at the novel's end, there appears a relatively indirect allusion:

> Night closed more deeply down and lights were put out. Outside the black sky opened wider and showed by its signals its immensities. The squire's village, her white house, black windows [reflecting the blackness of the *outside*], rolled with the rest of the world among the wheels and geometrical terrors of heaven.[143]

The North American example with which this chapter began suggests how, in order to perpetuate racism, race may be rendered invisible. The examples of Eliot and Bagnold suggest how the objects of hatred may be rendered imperceptible and invisible. They also suggest how racist notions of superiority may be downplayed or hidden, by the very practitioners themselves of negative constructions of race.

Notes

1 Martin Chanock, *The Making of South African Legal Culture 1902–1936: Fear, Favour and Prejudice*, Cambridge: Cambridge University Press, 2001, 16–17.
2 Chanock, *The Making of South African Legal Culture*, 16–17.
3 Cited in David Goldenberg, "Racism, Colour Symbolism, and Colour Prejudice," in Miriam Eliav-Feldon, Benjamin Isaac, and Joseph Ziegler, eds., *The Origins of Racism in the West*, Cambridge: Cambridge University Press, 2009, 89.
4 Ali Rattansi, *Racism: A Very Short Introduction*, Oxford: Oxford University Press, 2007, 44.
5 Rattansi, *Racism*, 44.
6 Rattansi, *Racism*,44.
7 Rattansi, *Racism*, 44.
8 Alice Walker, *The Color Purple*, New York: Harcourt, 2003, 8. All quotations are from this edition.
9 Walker, *The Color Purple*, 12.
10 Ralph Ellison, "Author's Introduction," in Ralph Ellison, *Invisible Man*, with an Introduction by John Callahan, London: Penguin Books, 2001, xxxiii. All quotations are from this edition.
11 Karla F.C. Holloway, *Legal Fictions: Constituting Race, Composing Literature*, Durham and London: Duke University Press, 2014, 5.
12 Holloway, *Legal Fictions*, 1–2.
13 Rattansi, *Racism*, 44.
14 Holloway, *Legal Fictions*, 15.
15 Holloway, *Legal Fictions*, 15.
16 Holloway, *Legal Fictions*, 15.
17 Holloway, *Legal Fictions*, 19.
18 Holloway, *Legal Fictions*, 19.
19 Holloway, *Legal Fictions*, 21.
20 Walker, *The Color Purple*, 90–91.
21 Walker, *The Color Purple*, 86–89.
22 Ellison, "Author's Introduction," xxxviii.

23 Ellison, "Author's Introduction," xxxix.

24 Ellison, *Invisible Man*, 3–4.

25 Ellison, *Invisible Man*, 4.

26 Ellison, *Invisible Man*, 5.

27 Ellison, *Invisible Man*, 5–7. To make this point I have partly eviscerated the imaginative richness of the original.

28 Ellison, *Invisible Man*, 7.

29 Chanock, *The Making of South African Legal Culture*, 3.

30 See Chanock, *The Making of South African Legal Culture*, 23ff:

> A legal culture consists of a set of assumptions, a way of doing things, a repertoire of language, of legal forms and institutional practices ... a legal culture is made up of an interrelated set of discourses about law: some professional, some administrative, some popular.

31 Chanock, *The Making of South African Legal Culture*, 30.

32 Chanock, *The Making of South African Legal Culture*, 31.

33 Chanock, *The Making of South African Legal Culture*, 20.

34 Chanock, *The Making of South African Legal Culture*, 33.

35 Chanock, *The Making of South African Legal Culture*, 34.

36 Chanock, *The Making of South African Legal Culture*, 34.

37 Chanock, *The Making of South African Legal Culture*, 35.

38 Chanock, *The Making of South African Legal Culture 1902–1936*, 4. Chanock notes,

> There were also limits to multi-vocality. It is significant that there were no women's voices in any of the sites in which law was talked about: no women lawyers, no women politicians, no women "experts." An alliance of patriarchies relegated African women to the bottom of the social structure, and simultaneously elevated and demeaned white women. They became not invisible but inaudible, to state, polity and law.
>
> (26)

39 Chanock, *The Making of South African Legal Culture*, 10.

40 Chanock, *The Making of South African Legal Culture*, 10.

41 Chanock, *The Making of South African Legal Culture*, 16.

42 Chanock, *The Making of South African Legal Culture*, 15.

43 Chanock (*The Making of South African Legal Culture*, 28) notes, too, that in most histories of South African law, "[w]here African law has been dealt with at all, it has been separated from the history of mainstream law, as if South African common law developed in Europe, or at least in isolation from African law."

44 Chanock, *The Making of South African Legal Culture*, 16.

45 Chanock, *The Making of South African Legal Culture*, 16.

46 Chanock, *The Making of South African Legal Culture*, 19.

47 Chanock, *The Making of South African Legal Culture*, 22, emphasis added.

48 Chanock, *The Making of South African Legal Culture*, 27. The split can also be explored in terms of South Africa's constitutional history. See Chanock, *The Making of South African Legal Culture*, 36–42, which emphasizes the bifurcated nature of the South African state. There were two constitutional orders—one democratic and one authoritarian. Only the white democracy was protected.

49 Chanock, *The Making of South African Legal Culture*, 11.

50 J.M. Coetzee, *Waiting for the Barbarians*, London: Vintage, 2000. All quotations are from this edition.

51 Chanock, *The Making of South African Legal Culture*, notes, to take a few random examples, on South African criminology that, in a search "for an understanding of legalism in a colonial society in which racial differences are central to criminal justice," it is necessary to stress that in the early twentieth century, "South African discourses on crime were not focused on the immediate political and economic problems of a new and insecure independence in which a white minority ruled a black majority" (61). This period saw

> a huge leap in the numbers imprisoned and sentenced. Very nearly all were black men, prosecuted under taxation, pass, and masters and servants laws ... The labour of a dispossessed peasantry was being mobilized by mining, industry and an increasingly capitalist agriculture; many were being proletarianised and urbanized under the harshest conditions. The criminalization of huge numbers in these processes of labour coercion and the control of movement and residence was not, however, the primary matter seen and debated when the problems of crime and its control were discussed ... debates about crime drew upon ... the [at that time, racist] common sense of the Western scientific and legal worlds.
>
> (62)

The "briefest acquaintance with such discourse shows its remove from reality" producing "a criminal law which served to describe and constitute otherness of a subject population" (63). "Western criminology, itself deeply concerned with the construction of otherness, was in South Africa (and also in the USA) easily turned to the construction of racial separateness" (64). All the South African commentators, "hostile or sympathetic to the plight of Africans, employed a basic binary imagery revolving around categories such as innocence/corruption; savage/civilized; authority/lawlessness; purity/impurity" (72). Thus for instance the "answer to the violence of black urban crime was not primarily seen to be the policing of black communities, or the basic improvement in living standards, but to lie in the segregation of [so thought] crimogenic blacks from whites" (73). The "essential nature of blacks, whether cultural or psychological," and bolstered by allegedly scientific views, "rather than sociological or economic considerations ... explained their criminal acts" (81). In the matter of penology, "white and black in South Africa were subject to different kinds of social control, and criminalized as a result of different, but interlocking agenda" (97). On the matter of land, again, Chanock provides a "history of the ['legal'] dividing of the land of South Africa along racial lines" (361–400).

52 Dino Buzzati, *The Tartar Steppe*, Edinburgh: Canongate, 2007.

53 Coetzee, *Waiting for the Barbarians*, 9.

54 Coetzee, *Waiting for the Barbarians*, 19.

55 Coetzee, *Waiting for the Barbarians*, 23.

56 Coetzee, *Waiting for the Barbarians*, 23.

57 Coetzee, *Waiting for the Barbarians*, 146.

58 Chanock, *The Making of South African Legal Culture*, 116.

59 Chanock, *The Making of South African Legal Culture*, 116.

60 Chanock, *The Making of South African Legal Culture*, 116.

61 Chanock, *The Making of South African Legal Culture*, 118.

62 Chanock, *The Making of South African Legal Culture*, 118.

63 Chanock, *The Making of South African Legal Culture*, 118.

64 Chanock, *The Making of South African Legal Culture*, 130.

65 Paul Gready and Lazrus Kgalema, "Magistrates Under Apartheid: A Case Study of Professional Ethics and the Politicization of Justice," Research report written for the Centre for the study of Violence and Reconciliation, August 2000, 1.

66 Gready and Kgalema, "Magistrates Under Apartheid," 1.

67 Gready and Kgalema, "Magistrates Under Apartheid," 1.

68 Gready and Kgalema, "Magistrates Under Apartheid," 2.

69 Gready and Kgalema, "Magistrates Under Apartheid," 2.

70 Coetzee, *Waiting for the Barbarians*, 44.

71 Later, in a further sequence demonstrating the Colonel's barbarism, the word ENEMY is written on the backs of prisoners who are then lashed until ironically the word, on each bleeding back, disappears. Cf. Chanock (*The Making of South African Legal Culture*, 129–130),

the accused had been given two years and twenty-four lashes for the theft of two sheep. In reviewing the sentence Innes CJ noted that twenty-four out of twenty-seven district surgeons in the Transvaal had recently expressed the view in the light of their experience that only fifteen lashes could be administered without the risk of severe injury. "I am assuming that the lashes were

> inflicted on natives," Innes remarked; "in the case of Europeans
> and Asiatics the danger is greater still."

72 Coetzee, *Waiting for the Barbarians*, 45.
73 Coetzee, *Waiting for the Barbarians*, 46.
74 Coetzee, *Waiting for the Barbarians*, 54–55.
75 Coetzee, *Waiting for the Barbarians*, 25.
76 Coetzee, *Waiting for the Barbarians*, 90.
77 Coetzee, *Waiting for the Barbarians*, 91.
78 Coetzee, *Waiting for the Barbarians*, 92.
79 Coetzee, *Waiting for the Barbarians*, 152.
80 Coetzee, *Waiting for the Barbarians*, 152–153.
81 Coetzee, *Waiting for the Barbarians*, 114.
82 Coetzee, *Waiting for the Barbarians*, 148.
83 Coetzee, *Waiting for the Barbarians*, 148–149.
84 Gready and Kgalema, "Magistrates Under Apartheid," 2–3.
85 Coetzee, *Waiting for the Barbarians*, 149.
86 Michael Stolleis, *The Law under the Swastika*, trans. Thomas Dunlap,
   Chicago: University of Chicago Press, 1998, 7.
87 Stolleis, *The Law under the Swastika*, 7–8.
88 Stolleis, *The Law under the Swastika*, 8.
89 Stolleis, *The Law under the Swastika*, 13.
90 Stolleis, *The Law under the Swastika*, 13.
91 Stolleis, *The Law under the Swastika*, 14, emphasis added.
92 Stolleis, *The Law under the Swastika*, 14. In Europe,

> in the last decades of the nineteenth century and the first half of
> the twentieth, the traditional legends which had swirled about
> the Jews in the past were revived as foils for racial mysticism and
> as instruments of political mobilization.
>
> > (George L. Mosse, "The Jews: Myth and Counter-Myth," in
> > Les Back and John Solomos, *Theories of Race and Racism:
> > A Reader*, Second Edition, London: Routledge, 2009, 260)

Such legends, "whether the blood libel or that of the wandering
Jew," rootless and subversive, "offered explanation and coherence in
a world of industrialization, instability, and bewildering social change,
just as they had earlier been used as explanation for famines, sickness
and all manner of natural catastrophes" (261). Moreover, circulating
conspiracy theories, that cast the Jews in the demonic role of planning
to dominate the world, had been synthesized in *The Protocols of the
Elders of Zion*. This was "forged in France, in the midst of the Dreyfus
Affair," in which a Jewish officer in the French army was falsely
accused of treachery, "with the assistance of the Russian secret police,
probably between 1894 and 1899" (263). The imagining of a group of

Jewish elders, plotting to dominate the world and other legends "became ... mechanism[s] through which rightist movements sought to change society" (265). In Germany the contribution these and other factors made to the fascist theory and practice that entailed the Holocaust has often been considered. We shall, in this section, therefore, only be concerned with aspects of the use of the concept of community and of German law in these processes.

93 Stolleis also notes that

> The National Socialist state established its public interest in the policy of procreation through changes in the law of adoption, in the procedure of contesting legitimacy, in government loans to young married couples, and in child support. It pursued this further through the Law for the Prevention of Genetically Diseased Offspring of July 14, 1933; the so-called Blood Protection Law of September 15, 1935, forbidding marriage and sexual relations between Jews and non-Jews on the grounds that this constituted "racial pollution," and barring Jews from flying the national colors.
>
> *(The Law under the Swastika*, 17)

94 Cited in Stolleis, *The Law under the Swastika*, 67.
95 Stolleis, *The Law under the Swastika*, 81.
96 Stolleis, *The Law under the Swastika*, 81.
97 Cited in Stolleis, *The Law under the Swastika*, 82.
98 T.S. Eliot, *After Strange Gods: A Primer of Modern Heresy*, London: Faber & Faber, 1934, 19–20.
99 Cited in Anthony Julius, *Trials of the Diaspora: A History of Anti-Semitism in England*, Oxford: Oxford University Press, 2010, 307. Julius argues that this was

> evident in the emergence of fascist parties, in certain aspects of the policy of appeasement, in the reception of Jewish refugees, and in the apparently quite widely held view in late 1939 that "the Jews" were to blame for the anticipated war.
>
> (303–304)

100 Julius, *Trials of the Diaspora*, 303.
101 Julius, *Trials of the Diaspora*, 308.
102 Julius, *Trials of the Diaspora*, 309.
103 Julius, *Trials of the Diaspora*, 313.
104 Enid Bagnold, *The Squire*, with a Preface by Anne Sebba, London: Persephone Books, 2013. All quotations come from this edition.
105 Cited in Sebba, Preface, xiii.
106 See, for example, Thomas Linehan, *British Fascism 1918–39: Parties,*

Ideology and Culture, Manchester: Manchester University Press, 2000, 24–32.

107 Sebba, Preface, viii.
108 Oswald Mosley, *Fascism for the Million*, London: Black House Publishing, 2012, 1.
109 Linehan, *British Fascism 1918–39*, 24–31.
110 Sebba, Preface, xv.
111 Bagnold, *The Squire*, 118–119.
112 Bagnold, *The Squire*, 79.
113 Bagnold, *The Squire*, 175.
114 Bagnold, *The Squire*, 101.
115 Bagnold, *The Squire*, 130–131.
116 Bagnold, *The Squire*, 154.
117 Philippa Levine, "Anthropology, Colonialism and Eugenics," in Alison Bashford and Philippa Levine, eds., *The Oxford Handbook of the History of Eugenics*, Oxford: Oxford University Press, 2010, 55.
118 Levine, "Anthropology, Colonialism and Eugenics," 55–56.
119 Rattansi, *Racism*, 46. See also 46–55.
120 Rattansi, *Racism*, 47.
121 Rattansi, *Racism*, 52.
122 Bagnold, *The Squire*, 1–2.
123 Bagnold, *The Squire*, 106.
124 Bagnold, *The Squire*, 49.
125 Bagnold, *The Squire*, 2–3.
126 Bagnold, *The Squire*, 54.
127 Bagnold, *The Squire*, 54.
128 Bagnold, *The Squire*, 166.
129 Bagnold, *The Squire*, 16.
130 Bagnold, *The Squire*, 104.
131 Bagnold, *The Squire*, 32; see also 47, 48.
132 Bagnold, *The Squire*, 99.
133 Bagnold, *The Squire*, 118.
134 Bagnold, *The Squire*, 132.
135 Bagnold, *The Squire*, 152.
136 Bagnold, *The Squire*, 155.
137 Bagnold, *The Squire*, 47.
138 Bagnold, *The Squire*, 94.
139 Bagnold, *The Squire*, 125.
140 Bagnold, *The Squire*, 131.
141 Bagnold, *The Squire*, 165.
142 Bagnold, *The Squire*, 173.
143 Bagnold, *The Squire*, 178.

4

SLAVERY AND RACE

In certain examinations of slavery it is argued that a distinction needs to be made between slavery and racism. Thus it is sometimes proposed that ancient civilizations may have taken slavery for granted, because, as Benjamin Isaac has observed, "there was no assumption that a person had a natural or moral right to freedom" and, further, that "the subjection of one people by another was not in itself morally condemned." Hence "the urge to build a systematic and consistent theory proving that one set of human beings was inferior to another was less strong than in modern times."[1]

We will not attempt to illustrate or to take issue with contentions such as these. Rather, the focus will be on examples of recent research into how aspects of slavery from the Classical period onwards coincide with, or intersect with, imaginings of race. The emergence of Africa as a source of slaves for international exportation to both West and East is a crucial feature in this narrative. Another case in point is provided by instances in the history of British slaving, together with emerging data related to British slave-ownership and its effects. This work, together with imaginative readings of subsequent slave experiences in North America, insists on the importance of slavery and related labor systems of domination and servitude as significant markers of "race."

"Natural" slavery

There is an important distinction between naturalized beliefs and natural phenomena. Naturalized beliefs are those that have been culturally manufactured to appear natural. Benjamin Isaac proposes a racist dimension to the installation of certain humans as items of property during the Classical period: he notes the "environmental determinism which made it possible for Greek and Roman texts to describe foreign peoples in terms of fixed physical and mental traits, determined by climate and geography."[2] He couples this notion of environmentalism, which "posits an essential contrast between a sturdy but mentally inadequate Europe and a soft Asia ... suffering from deficient masculinity and an insufficient sense of individual and collective independence," with the belief that "the Greeks occupied the ideal environment between Europe and Asia and were therefore supremely capable of ruling others."[3] To this he adds "the claim that the inhabitants of Asia were servile by nature, or natural slaves, and therefore suited to be subjects of the Greeks."[4] Noting that "Roman authors took over these ideas, duly substituting themselves as the ideal rulers," Isaac maintains that "assuming the environment to determine human character and quality, combined with a belief in the heredity of acquired characters, leads to an outlook almost as deterministic as modern racist theory."[5] These two complementary ideas, when applied to human groups

> attribute to them characteristics which, in due course of time, become uniform and constant ... they are a powerful tool justifying imperial rule: those who have been conquered must, because of their defeat, be inferior by nature to their conquerors and then, once they have become subjects and slaves, they rapidly acquire and transmit to their descendants the qualities of being born slaves as formulated by Aristotle.[6]

Paul Lovejoy notes that slavery is "a form of exploitation."[7] It entails, at the very least, the legal ownership of a person or group of people by another person or group of people. In such an arrangement the enslaved are deemed to be property, and their personhood is deemed less valuable than others. They are permanently subordinate to their owners. Aristotle notes that:

> A slave is a living possession, ... He who is by nature not his
> own but another's man is by nature a slave ... Some men are
> by nature free, and others slaves, and ... for these latter,
> slavery is both expedient and right.[8]

This permanently disadvantages the humans whom Aristotle imagines
as "natural slaves." Lovejoy further defines slavery as an extreme
form of subordination:

> Slaves are outsiders who are alien by origin or who could be
> denied their heritage through judicial or other sanctions. With
> slaves, coercion could be used at will, and their labor power
> was at the complex disposal of the master. They did not have
> the right to their own sexuality or, by extension, to their own
> reproductive capacities and gender options. Enslaved women
> separated from their children and eunuchs are examples of
> this complete subordination. Slave status was inherited unless
> provision was made to ameliorate that status. Slavery was
> fundamentally a means of denying outsiders the rights and
> privileges of a particular society so that they could be
> exploited for economic, political and/or social purposes.[9]

Ancient and medieval beliefs about color difference and about the
proximity of some humans to animals also feature in slavery discourse. Even in Antiquity, "inferior foreigners and slaves are to some
extent approximated to animals."[10]

At different moments in history this contention informs presentations of slave labor. Aphra Behn (1640–1689), the English dramatist
and writer who was married to a Dutch man, imagined Montaigne-
like enlightened sentiment when characterizing the natives of the
colony of Surinam in the Americas. In her prose work *Oroonoko*
(1688) Behn registers a form of racism that is evident in the practices of Surinam slavers. She does this through the voice of the hero
in her narrative:

> Caesar [Oroonoko], having singled out these men from the
> women and children, made a harangue to them of the miser-
> ies and ignominies of slavery; counting up all their toils and

sufferings under such loads, burdens and drudgeries as were fitter for beasts than men; senseless brutes, than human souls ... *we are bought* [he said] *and sold like apes or monkeys, to be the sport of women, fools and cowards.*[11]

Isaac records that "Thomas Jefferson, in his discourse about the differences between whites and blacks, repeatedly describes the latter as being closer to animals."[12] He notes that "many authors in the eighteenth and nineteenth centuries such as Buffon, Voltaire, Le Bon, and Rousseau were preoccupied with, or rather, confused as regards the differences between various groups of humans and animals, especially blacks and apes."[13] Isaac also provides an extreme twentieth century example. Heinrich Himmler, Hitler's head of Gestapo Unit from 1929 and German Minister of the Interior, stated in an order to his men:

Whether during the construction of an anti-tank ditch ten thousand Russian women collapse from exhaustion or not, interests me only insofar as the ditch is finished for Germany. We shall never be hard and heartless when that is unnecessary. So much is clear. We Germans are the only people on earth that has a decent attitude towards the animal and we will also assume a decent attitude towards these human animals, but it is a crime against our own blood to worry about them.[14]

Himmler became head of the State secret police in 1943. Regarding this incidence, Isaac notes that the

metaphorical reduction of foreigners and minorities to animals is frequent in the nineteenth century. Friedrich Engels, for instance, observes that the "lowest savages can revert to an animal-like condition." Himmler ... does not say that the Russian women should be exterminated because they were animals or even vermin, although that was a familiar line taken by Nazi propaganda. The women were, for Himmler, slave labor working for Germany, and as such he calls them human animals and orders his men to treat them like work animals, no better and no worse.[15]

Himmler's crude reapplication of this classical notion differs from the more complex instance of someone like Jefferson who combined his equivocal attitude to black people "with a genuine democratic outlook and a firm belief in the equality of men, which, after all, is generally considered to be the Greek heritage."[16] Such a doubleness in the Classical articulation both of notions of equality and of a contradictory imagined condition of "natural" slavery, suggests a more equivocal contribution from Greek culture than is usually claimed for it.[17] In the light of observations we have made in previous chapters, together with Jefferson's contradictory views, this points also to the endemic ambiguity to many post-Classical projects that claim an enlightened approach to slavery while simultaneously and often silently ratifying underlying systems of racist exploitation.

African slaves

As we know, slavery occurs at almost every moment in history, from ancient periods to the medieval Christian and Islamic periods, the Renaissance, the Enlightenment, the periods of colonialism, and into the twentieth century. It endures even today, in instances such as that of human trafficking, and it is practiced, if illegally in a number of locations, in the present-day world.[18] Recent work, such as that by David Wallace, is significant in arguing how the movement of the European slave trade over time, and representations of it, increasingly reflect medieval as well as earlier negative beliefs about race. It argues that this occurs in ways that also anticipate the growing use of Africa as the primary source of slave labor.[19]

Medieval Genoa, for example, traded in slaves from Caffa, on the Black Sea, a place that in its time housed one of Europe's largest slave markets. Wallace notes that "as Chaucer saw at Genoa in 1373, [the Genoese] also shipped slaves ('Tartars' or 'Scythians') across the Mediterranean."[20] They moved "from west to east to west again between ca 1150 and 1500."[21] Thus, "Saracens from Spain make up the majority of slaves ... until the Genoese negotiate their way into the Black Sea and the Crimea in the later thirteenth century" and by "the later fourteenth century there are Greek, Russian, Slav, Bosnian, and Circassian slaves at Genoa and Florence ... the great majority ...

described as 'Tartars.' "[22] Then, "with the fall of Constantinople in 1453 and then of Caffa in 1475, the focus of the trade swings back to the west (which includes the North African coastline)."[23] Wallace argues that "many features of later European colonialism—as the slaving Mediterranean prepares to enter the black Atlantic—are clearly forming throughout this earlier period," although he is not suggesting "seamless continuity with later, full-blown plantation slaving in the Americas":[24]

> certain discursive and material practices of slaving, familiar from more recent times ... are [in the late medieval and early modern periods] becoming well-established, such as, for example, racial profiling. Deeds of sale do not yet figure skin color as an absolute criterion of worth or enslavement, but figure it rather as one aesthetic criterion among many. Toward the end of the period, however, "Ethiopian" begins to stand in for Africans of any provenance and "black" begins to be deployed as a racial term. The marking, scarring, and tattooing of enslaved bodies is commonplace; there are complex arrangements for runaways.[25]

Wallace observes that, despite this, the "study of Genoa continually confronts us with historical practices (enslavement, forced conversion, colonization) upon which cultural history has chosen not to dwell."[26] He charts other instances of avoidance or silence, as in the cases of Petrarch and Scythia, and Spenser and Ireland,[27] what he refers to as the "lethal re-mappings of premodern places from classicizing models,"[28] with its consequent euphemism about the concomitant reality of the practice of racist systems of slavery. Again, in his study of unfolding representations of Somerset,[29] he argues that the

> rustication and ruination of Somerset culture by one set of political, economic and ideologically driven religious forces— the Reformation—came eventually to serve and disguise the ends of another: the transatlantic slave trade, generative of the wealth that built the neoclassical mansions still dotting the Somerset landscape.[30]

Wallace also maintains that "the whole apparatus of Greek and Latin humanist scholarship ... had earlier helped rationalize slavery by reviving the absolute, mutually imbricated, classical notions of liberty and servitude"[31] and, more generally, that in the post-classical world the "process of mapping othering discourses, sharpened and refined through scholasticism, neoclassicism and anti-Jewish polemic, *onto* blackness is long and complex."[32] Citing aspects of the medieval tale of Heloïse and Abelard, Wallace also argues that the

> academic rationalism pioneered by Abelard and institutional-ized by his heirs could be employed to exile certain groups from humanity, declaring them brute-like; the profit-driven economic rationalism of later centuries—spearheaded by Genoese expeditions to the Canaries and beyond—could prove just as uncompromising with equivalent results.[33]

The focus of slaving began to shift in the fifteenth century from the Mediterranean to the Atlantic with an ever-increasing number of slaves transported from Africa. The Portuguese were the most active, particularly in the trans-Atlantic slave trade, during this period while, by the end of the fifteenth century, Spain had the largest number of black slaves in Europe. In the sixteenth century, during the reign of Elizabeth I, Captain John Hawkins made three slaving voyages to Africa, capturing over 1200 Africans and selling them as goods in the Spanish Colonies in the Americas. The Stuarts founded the Royal African Adventurers in 1660, granting it a monopoly of the English African slave trade, and Wallace notes that "between 1672 (when the Adventurers were relaunched as the Royal Africa Company) and 1689, just under 90,000 slaves were exported from Africa (many of them branded with the initials R.A.C.)."[34] The "importation of African slaves to work sugar plantations, massively accelerated between 1688 and 1738."[35] During this process the medieval and subsequent succes-sors of "the Roman *servus* or slave" came into being. And the "moral character" of what Wallace calls "this unfreedom, this bondage to the earth" finds negative "physiological expression,"[36] much of which

> will be mapped onto the blacks who succeed the whites as unfree field labor in New World plantations. Particular canons

of medieval representation will facilitate this transition: first, and especially in France, the depiction of peasants as dark-skinned or black; and second, Biblical Ham's twin medieval roles as a founder of peoples, including black Africans, and as the forefather of European serfs. By the sixteenth century these traditions will conflate to make Ham the progenitor of black slaves.[37]

Recent research emphasizes also that, within the interior of Africa, slavery long preceded the development of the trans-Atlantic slave trade. African Chiefs and other leaders actively worked to perpetuate the commodification and sale of Africans to European traders in the West and Muslim and other traders in the East.[38] After the British emancipation of slaves in 1834, itself initiating complex and often token versions of freedom, the practice of slavery continued within many parts of Africa. This reminds us that the discrimination against, and the exploitation of, particular groups is not always color-determined. We glanced in Chapter 3 at how, in the age of nineteenth century European nationalism, intra-group hatred manifested itself. We also noted above that in the medieval period, Europeans sold other Europeans into slavery. In certain instances of contemporary human trafficking, at least, they still do.

In the case of African merchants and rulers selling Africans into slavery, Trevor Burnard maintains that "Europeans came to Africa upon sufferance and were dependent on local leaders for access to goods, including slaves" and that "the whole Atlantic slave trade was founded on the willingness of Africans to sell other Africans to Europeans, and on the ability of African rulers to conduct such sales without facing local rebellion."[39] Elements of intra-group race discrimination are, disconcertingly, recognizable: the victimized are demarcated as alien. Africans "generally sold peoples they considered foreigners and enemies, although they would make some exception for countrymen guilty of serious offences … [the] African merchants seldom saw the victims of the Atlantic slave trade as their brothers and sisters."[40] Lovejoy argues, further, that "the European demand for African slaves [in such contexts had] a transforming impact on African societies," changing "Africans' understanding of slavery":

According to William Snelgrave, a slave trader on the coast of the Bight of Benin in the 1720s, "It has been the Custom among the Negroes, time out of Mind, and it is so to this day, for them to make Slaves of all Captives they take in War ... [to] employ in their own Plantations." Now, Snelgrave noted, Africans "had an opportunity of selling them to white People." Snelgrave understood that the demand for slaves in the Americas transformed a local method of labor exploitation into an intercontinental system that was now based on racial categories.[41]

We should, however, bear in mind that Africa was the target of slavers for trade to the East as well as to the West in addition to the notorious Atlantic slave trade.[42] More research is needed into the characteristics, the implications of the exportation of Africans as slaves to the East and the nature of their treatment there. By contrast, the nature and effects of the notorious triangular trade route that led from Europe to West Africa and then to the Americas, and its effects, have been explored extensively and it is to examples of this that we will now turn.

History of the British slave trade

Aspects of the narrative of the English struggle to enter the trans-Atlantic slave trade and to establish its own settlements in the Americas, in the sixteenth, seventeenth, and early eighteenth centuries, suggest, as Betty Wood argues, a strong and recurring racist dimension.[43] By the mid-sixteenth century the Spanish and Portuguese had established themselves as the dominant European powers in South America, the Caribbean basin, and the lands surrounding the Gulf of Mexico. There the production of sugar on plantations involved enslaved African labor from the 1530s onwards. Although Englishmen such as John Hawkins had attempted to enter the slave trade, Anglo-Spanish rivalries led to the exclusion of the English from it for another century, leaving it open to the Dutch. Wood argues, however, that

what these early English attempts to penetrate the slave trade reveal is abundantly clear: not only willingness to be complicit in the enslavement of West Africans by other Europeans, but also the possibility, should the need ever arise, they too would not demur from the brutal exploitation of West Africans in any colonies that they might establish at some future date.[44]

Dutch domination of the trade was displaced by the English in the latter part of the seventeenth century.[45] During this period of exclusion from the trans-Atlantic slave trade channels English voyagers returned home with West and West Central Africans thus forming the beginning of a black presence within England. But Wood maintains that there was a lingering ambiguity in defining the status, within England, of these slaves. English common law favored personal liberty and the Christian tradition suggested that personal freedom was the norm. However, for the English, enslavement meant the complete loss of freedom and slaves were thought of as beasts. This ambiguity of the legal status of Africans in sixteenth and early seventeenth century England provided, further, an equivocal model for colonial proprietors and colonists. However, as Wood also argues, because of the "riches that stemmed from slavery and the trans-Atlantic slave trade, successive English monarchs and Parliaments were happy to leave colonial governments to determine the legal status of all members of their populations as they saw fit."[46]

It is almost unnecessary to add that traditional negative stereotypes of Africans, which we noted in previous chapters, prompted this indifference. "Blackness" was taken as a sign of impurity and sinfulness, seen as divine punishment and taken as indicative of a non-human condition. These attitudes, as we shall see in a moment, informed the English management of its holdings in the Caribbean, Virginia, Carolina, and New England.

David Wallace argues that such attitudes are heralded in Aphra Behn's *Oroonoko.* In 1647 Lord Willoughby received from the English government a "twenty-one-year lease of property rights in the Caribee" when he "became governor of Barbados."[47] He wanted to found a new colony in Surinam. The region of Surinam, in the Central Americas, was not effectively controlled by the Spanish or the Portuguese in the sixteenth and seventeenth centuries. It became a target for colonial activity by the French, Dutch, and English.[48] Plantations were begun along the Surinam river and "by the 1660s the colony's purpose was largely to produce sugar for the English market."[49] Wallace captures the increasing English tendency to practice, in such contexts, what was becoming a markedly black- or color-distinct system of slavery when he writes of Aphra Behn's *Oroonoko*, which is located in Surinam and which was "the most widely read pre-modern Anglophone imagining of white/black relations,"[50] that it

> sits on a cusp between losing ... "feudal mutuality" and assuming the harsher logic of the later period ... Skin color ... is migrating from an accidental trait of personhood to an absolute determinant of freedom and lack of freedom; differences of religion, considered in this greater scheme of things, no longer really matter.[51]

With regard to the early establishment of the settlement of Virginia, the English who hoped to break into the seventeenth century Atlantic slave trade to the Americas had never, in contrast to their attitude towards Africans, denied the "humanity" of Native Americans: that is, as they saw it, their potential for conversion to Christianity. At first in the settlement of Virginia they found it convenient to rely on their labor, together with indentured laborers from England. In the aftermath of the Native American Jamestown rebellion (1622), which almost wiped out the English settlement of Virginia, however, they began to depict them as treacherous and also lazy. The Virginian settlers did not, despite this, immediately demand more African slaves as an alternative to Native Americans. Economic factors, such as the initially steady availability of English-settler indentured labor, together with the Dutch lack of interest in the dubious profitability of supplying African slaves to the struggling Virginia settlement largely given to the production of tobacco, deterred them. But in the 1620s the English also acquired their first two possessions in the Caribbean: St Kitts and Barbados. At first these acquisitions were run on the model of the tobacco plantations in Virginia, which relied largely on the flow of indentured laborers from England. In the 1630s, however, a shift from tobacco to sugar production occurred in Barbados, modeled on the example of Brazil, which used the African slave trade to acquire the cheapest and economically most productive workforce. Wood points out that, unlike Virginia, "Barbados was on the direct route between West Africa, Brazil and the Caribbean basin, and its demand for labor gave Dutch traders every incentive to shorten their voyages and exploit this new market for their human cargoes."[52]

It is important to note that Barbadian planters readily drew on this new source of labor. Furthermore, in 1636 Governor Henry Hawley decreed that any "Negroes that come here to be sold [would] serve for life,"[53] unlike indentured laborers who were always released, in some cases to buy land of their own, after a specified time:

> His decree went unchallenged not only in Barbados, but also in England. Neither politicians nor Anglican Churchmen saw fit to intervene and seek to overturn this momentous declaration. On the contrary, in the decades that followed, influential Englishmen, motivated by self-interest would both defend and promote a Barbadian policy soon to be emulated by English colonists everywhere on the North American mainland.[54]

Thus, in 1689, the Earl of Shaftesbury and the political thinker John Locke, produced the "Fundamental Constitutions" for Carolina, which had been established by the English in the mid-1660s. The right to hold property in the form of slaves was legitimated in this document, which may be set against examples of British self-admiration after the moment of emancipation and beside claims as to an alleged history of British liberalism, both to be noted in the following section. The racist consequences of this legislation are also evident from Wood's observation that the ensuing rapid growth of Carolina's enslaved black population "stemmed from the trans-Atlantic slave trade," which had "fundamentally altered during the 1660s and 1670s with England's defeat of its major commercial rival, the Dutch."[55] As a result of this defeat English participation in the slave trade increased significantly.

In the last two decades of the seventeenth century, the settlement of Virginia also underwent changes. Partly as a result of the Civil War in England, the flow of indentured labor from England had diminished dramatically. Wood notes that "England's entry into the trans-Atlantic slave trade" had by then made "African peoples an economically more attractive type of labor" for Virginia's tobacco planters because "now it was possible for slave traders to sell an entire human cargo at one location":

> For their part, Virginia planters knew that in Barbados and South Carolina, as well as in the sugar economies of Brazil, Africans were being forced to work not for a legally limited term of years, but for their entire lives. Moreover, any children born to enslaved mothers were forced to inherit their status. Africans offered the prospect of a perpetual agricultural workforce in a way that indentured Europeans did not. Not only this but, if necessary through harsh physical coercion, Africans not only could be made to work longer hours than Europeans, but also could be maintained much more cheaply.[56]

In view of its ever-increasing population of African slaves, Virginia simultaneously embarked on a program of legislation decreeing that Africans formed part of their "master's" property, proposing laws that prohibited interracial sex and marriage, and restricting black people's freedom of movement; in effect stripping blacks of all their rights. Moreover, on the argument that one Christian could not hold another Christian in perpetual bondage,

> like the Anglican planters and churchmen of the other plantation colonies, those of Virginia took the self-serving position that, provided they attended to the spiritual needs of those in their service, it was perfectly legitimate for Christian masters to hold other Christians as slaves.[57]

This was a notion endorsed by the Anglican authorities in England and remained its official position during the era of the American Revolution. The victory over the Dutch also secured for England "New Netherland," divided during the late seventeenth century into the English colonies of New York, Pennsylvania, and the Jerseys. The English unquestioningly administered the Dutch slave system they had inherited, with all its cruelties left intact. The agricultural and urban economies of what was now "New England" had, however, different needs from the plantation colonies but, even so, in 1641, the Puritans embarked on familiar legislation relating to black enslavement. Unlike Carolina and Virginia, Wood points out that they did, however, accept that

> bond servants should not be totally denied their humanity,
> but should continue to enjoy a cluster of rights ... [thus] those
> who came to be enslaved in Massachusetts would enjoy, or
> endure, the ambiguous status of being considered both as
> property and as person in the eyes of the law.[58]

New Englanders also derived economic benefits from slavery. This was at first indirectly, by way of "transportation of commodities produced by enslaved labor elsewhere in English America ... and, eventually, by their wholehearted participation in the trans-Atlantic slave trade."[59]

The slave trade was then, for England, importantly a matter of economics, but it was always complex, involving also the systematic reiteration and recirculation of racist beliefs, and the often self-interested introduction of racist laws of bondage. All this, despite the fact that, as Wood emphasizes, "everywhere in English America, including New England, the racially based slave systems that emerged during the seventeenth century were rooted in pragmatism":

> The English did not begin their colonization of the Americas
> with a view to enslaving West and West Central African
> peoples, but turned to these peoples—to those whom they
> could depict as the Sons of Ham—as irredeemable sub-
> humans, as and when they deemed it both possible and in
> their economic self-interest to do so.[60]

The British slave economy with its racist underpinnings may have indeed been partly a matter of pragmatism. This may also partly account for the extent to which the mention of slavery, and its markings of race, appears to be both there, and not there, in British political, social, and literary discourse. Thus John Richardson argues that even in the eighteenth century, when the British presence in the slave trade became ever more extensive,[61] contemporary political discourse "included little open and explicit discussion of slavery."[62] He notes that while

> the spoor of slavery shows everywhere in shipping[63] and
> company details, in figurative language, in casual references,

> and in newspaper reports of trading difficulties or losses at
> sea or rebellions ... there are few extended commentaries
> devoted either to the trade for slaves in Africa or to the use of
> them in America ... the facts of slavery were known but rarely
> written of at length.[64]

Yet, as Richardson points out, early eighteenth century Englishmen "of even modest information knew that English merchants bought slaves in Africa for transportation to the Americas, and that English plantations in North America and the Caribbean depended on slave labor."[65] However, references to this involvement were brief and often laced with commonly held European shibboleths about race. Thus William Bosman (1672 to after 1703), chief agent of the Dutch East India Company on the African coast, in his *New and Accurate Description of the Coast of Guinea: Divided into the Gold, the Slave and the Ivory Coasts*, published in English in London, 1705, writes:

> The *Negroes* are all without exception, Crafty, Villainous and
> Fraudulent, and very seldom to be trusted; being sure to slip
> no opportunity of cheating an *European*, nor indeed one
> another. A Man of Integrity is as rare among them as a white
> Falcon ... they indeed seem to be born and bred Villains.[66]

Richardson provides several other examples of brief references to the racist dimension inherent in slavery. In an attack on the abuses of the military press gang, the *Examiner* of October 12, 1712, confirms, in its use of the slave metaphor, the lower human status routinely assumed for slaves: "Our Fellow-Subjects were tethered like Slaves, cudgell'd by merciless Serjeants, beaten worse than Dogs, and thrown aboard our Ships, to reinforce the Army."[67]

The reaction of two Franciscans who board a ship carrying 680 slaves, reported in John and Awnsham Churchill's anthology *Collection of Voyages and Travels* (1704), reads

> It was a pitiful sight to behold, how all these people were
> bestow'd. The Men were standing in the Hold, fastned one to
> another with Stakes, for fear they should rise and kill the
> *Whites*. The Women were between the Decks ... the Children

> in the Steeridge press'd together like Herrings in a Barrel, which caus'd an intolerable heat and stench.[68]

Such descriptions went largely unremarked.

It is true that a few declarations by the poet Alexander Pope (1688–1744), suggest a posture of open disapproval for the institution of slavery. For example, in his "Windsor Forest" (written 1704–1713; published 1713), towards the end of the poem, the River Thames delivers a visionary panegyric on the glorious future predicted for British trade.[69] Pope's lines are also, however, a reiteration of that, significantly "fair," British superiority, before whose "Thunder, and her Cross" all other trading nations[70] will "bend." British trading power will also effect a neat, that is, poetically skillful inversion, when "Earth's distant Ends our Glory shall behold,/And the new World launch forth to seek the Old." But Pope's gracefully implemented antithetical statement belies the more equivocal trading situation his poetic device encapsulates. The doubleness evident in his presentation of slavery emerges in his allusion to a tributary visit by Native Americans to Queen Anne in 1710, in lines that also lead to his "open" denunciation of the practice of slavery:

> Then Ships of uncouth Form shall stem the Tyde,
> And Feather'd People crowd my wealthy Side,
> And naked Youths and painted Chiefs admire
> Our Speech, our Colour, and our strange Attire!
> Oh stretch thy Reign, fair *Peace*! From Shore to Shore,
> Till Conquest cease, and Slav'ry be no more:
> Till the freed *Indians* in their native Groves
> Reap their own Fruits, and woo their Sable Loves,
> *Peru* once more a race of Kings behold,
> And other *Mexico's* be roof'd with Gold.
> Exil'd by Thee from Earth to deepest Hell,
> In Brazen Bonds shall barb'rous *Discord* dwell.[71]

British trading power in the Americas is strikingly figured in the first four lines above, by means of exotically presented Native Americans who, in the wit of another of Pope's inversions, have come to England to "admire our Colour." The following lines then express the hope that, in this imagined glorious future of British trade, "fair *Peace*" will ensure that "Slav'ry be no more." "*Indians*" will be freed, from Peru to Mexico, and thus the "barb'rous" practices or "*Discord*" of, especially, the Spanish Americas will be stopped. We need to recall in this context that Pope's confidence in the second decade of the eighteenth century, in the future of British trade, was, as Richardson argues, partly politically based.[72] Indeed the writers Swift and John Gay (1685–1732) as well as Pope

> were ... connected with the Tory ministry of 1710–1714, and with its leader Robert Harley. His ministry made the slave trade a principal ... element in its financial planning ... to solve the problem of the national debt which had built up during the first years of the War of Spanish Succession (1702–1713). It founded the South Sea Company in 1711 in order to exploit the *Asiento*, the lucrative slave-trading contract with Spanish South America which was ... the major concession of the peace agreed in the Treaty of Utrecht in 1713 ... This is not to suggest that the ministry invented the slave trade or reveled in its cruelty, but simply that Tory financial policy set out to increase its importance to the British economy.[73]

Pope's generalized and apparently open disapproval of slavery in the lines from "Windsor Forest" reflect then that declarations of enlightened postures towards slavery are often far from "simple," as the English procedure in the settlements in the Caribbean and on the North American mainland, which we have just been tracing above, arguably also suggests. It is equally significant that Pope chooses in these lines to acknowledge slavery by an exclusive focus on the experience of Native Americans in the Spanish Americas. Leaving aside current Tory projects, English slave traders were by the time of Pope's poem, already firmly engaged in the African trans-Atlantic slave trade. In such contexts it is also interesting that Pope excised from the published edition the line, "His hissing axle in th'*Atlantic* deeps."[74] Richardson remarks of this omission:

> In the published version,[75] the passage conforms to the vague, euphemistic geography of most other peace poems and of the

title of the South Sea Company. Just as the company's name obscures the fact that the bulk of its business is in the Atlantic, so the new lines send Windsor's oaks east, north and to the southern Pacific—anywhere but Africa, the Caribbean and the Atlantic between them ... The only British ships for which the peace [Treaty of Utrecht 1713] opened the waters of the "South Seas," and the way to the Peruvians and the Mexicans, were those of the South Sea Company. The first legs of their South Sea voyages were to be Africa to collect slaves, and to the Caribbean or Spanish South America to drop them off ... The removal of the Atlantic and the Caribbean from the poem removes all trace of this.[76]

In the years that followed "the South Sea Company became a major slave trading enterprise ... according to the records that survive, 81,570 Africans were embarked as slaves on voyages that began in Britain; the South Sea Company embarked 12,598"[77] between 1716 and 1720. And Pope's dedication[78] of his later "An Essay on Man" (written 1730–1732; published 1733–1734) to St. John, saluted a man who, throughout his career, "retained a lively interest in slavery, the slave trade and their benefits for Britain."[79] Thus St. John maintains in a *Craftsman* of 1728 that "Her Prosperity and Safety in great Measure depend upon Trade, and *Trade* on the *Plantations*."[80] St. John also argues, in another *Craftsman*, against the monopoly granted to the Royal African Company, which in his view, stifles the growth of companies within England and weakens England's competitiveness abroad,

The *Sugar Colonies*, being then in their Infancy, were stinted in their Growth, by being scantily supplied with Negroes, which were absolutely necessary in them, and labored [that is, the Sugar Colonies] under many other *Hardships* and *Oppressions* from that *Company*.[81]

In the later "An Essay on Man,"[82] Pope expresses sympathy for the predicament of slaves, but again focuses on the instance, in the Spanish Americas, of Native American slavery.

Moreover, when set against what we now know of the treatment of Native Americans, even Pope's presentation of them, as enslaved by the Spanish, also emerges as misleadingly reticent, generalized, and at times delusionally pastoral. Spanish examples notwithstanding, Woods notes, for instance, that English involvement in Native American slavery in fact predated any systematic English trade in African slaves. Native American slavery, compared to African slavery may, furthermore, have been minor but it had important consequences:

> English enslavement of Indians raised ... questions about the status of Indians in civil society. In the eighteenth century, Britons and Americans were concerned to try and reject the very idea of Indian bondage but that rejection did not entail a rejection of the idea of Indian subordination. As Indians were released from bondage, they tended, especially in the new United States, to be denied the status of citizen. Those Indians who remained within areas of white settlement were redefined using categories of "blackness" which suggests a considerable overlap between how Indians and African Americans were viewed by Europeans, and indicates how the manner in which Native Americans were freed established a way in which African Americans could be freed but not given civil equality.[83]

Pope's condemnations of racist slavery in these instances are thus characterized by understatement of, or misleading data about, English involvement in slavery and the slave trade. Furthermore, Richardson's contention that "Pope's later poetry is beset by fears for the integrity and survival of the self, fears which are often conceived and expressed in terms of [a debased representation of] femininity or slavery"[84] relates to the doubleness, which we noted in Chapter 2, to be found in writers such as Voltaire and Defoe. Implicit in the work of John Gay (1685–1732) there is also to be discerned, "both opposition against and support for slavery."[85] The need for a possibly self-admiring, condemnation of a palpable moral injustice often appears to coexist with unquestioned racist assumptions, acts of evasion, or silence that contribute, albeit sometimes incidentally, to the perpetuation of the very injustices against which such writers inveigh.

We also hinted in Chapter 2 that one aspect of Swift's tone in "A Modest Proposal" appears, similarly, to challenge by implication the institution of slavery. Swift's tone in the essay often points to the ruthlessness of the slave traders' treatment of victims presented as animals or dehumanized as saleable commodities.[86] But Richardson argues that in *Gulliver's Travels* by contrast, although there is "a strong emphasis on the desirability of freedom in some of the general political passages and in many of Gulliver's predicaments," there is also "the powerful image of slavish Yahoo/humans" which "implies that [most] people do not deserve freedom and are unfitted for it."[87] Some of Swift's passages "have resonances both of the 'savage' in general and of Africans in particular,"[88] for instance, in Gulliver's description of a Yahoo's physiognomy:

> The Face of it was indeed flat and broad, the Nose depressed, the Lips large and the Mouth wide: But these Differences are common to all savage Nations, where the Lineaments of the Countenance are distorted by the Natives suffering their Infants to lie groveling on the Earth, or by carrying them on their Backs, nuzzling with their Face against the Mother's shoulders.[89]

Similar to slaves, the Yahoos "are ordered about, tied up by their necks, brought to tameness, set to work, and ... once hunted down ... destroyed like Caribbean rebels."[90] Swift, furthermore, "makes this seem natural and right."[91] Thus Gulliver's version of their nature is that

> The *Yahoos* appear to be the most unteachable of all Animals, their Capacities never reaching higher than to draw or carry Burthens. Yet I am of Opinion, this Defect ariseth chiefly from a perverse, restive Disposition. For they are cunning, malicious, treacherous and revengeful. They are strong and hardy, but of a cowardly Spirit, and by Consequent insolent, abject and cruel.[92]

"The almost-human Yahoos," then, are, as Richardson emphasizes, associated "with 'primitives' and Africans," so that they "deserve to be treated like cattle."[93] Such a representation, "at a time when real Africans were treated like cattle, works against the libertarian, anti-colonial and anti-slavery sentiments elsewhere in the book."[94]

British slave-ownership

As we remarked earlier, our focus in this study is on examples of those structurations of "race," which have negative effects, and which often, disturbingly, endure over time. Positive presentations of difference have regrettably not produced, in different periods, positive alternatives to negative fabrications. On slavery, for example, Simon Gikandi notes that, looking at Theodore de Bry's illustrations in the eighteenth century of the attire of Congo noblemen, "one can assume that the famous engravers did not make any distinction between Africans and Europeans, that blackness was not a negative or remarked feature in their imagination of the other."[95] However, despite such instances, he adds that:

> the discourse of similitude was always marginal and ephemeral ... the political and moral economy of slavery mandated the separation of black and white, even in similar conditions of servitude, as was the case in colonial Virginia, and the isolation of the African from what was considered human under law and convention ... It is difficult to think of modern slavery without its manifest racism."[96]

The current exploration of data regarding the extent to which slave-ownership and its eventual abolition worked to the general benefit of the slave-owners themselves, rather than to that of the slaves who prior to abolition had been exploited, provides another example of how recent research illuminates the racist dimensions of slavery.[97] Thus the payment of compensation upon emancipation to slave-owners rather than to the slaves who were again being demeaned by this additional indifference to their prior enslavement, reflects systemic racism. Moreover, the substantial existence of British slave-ownership has been noticeably understated even though the profits produced by this system, and the wealth that compensation often engendered and perpetuated, actually contributed to the growth of the Victorian economy.

Despite practices of concealment, we now know, for example, that a wide range of British people were slave-owners or absentee slave-owners. Small-scale ownership of enslaved men and women included widows and single women with land- and slave-holdings particularly in the Caribbean. In certain instances existing letters found in the slave compensation records from small-scale slave-owners appealing for "adequate" remuneration in the face of what it was claimed would otherwise precipitate personal and familial ruin, blatantly indicate that sympathy for the predicaments of the slaves themselves was both non-existent and inconceivable. In addition, 5–10 percent of the British elite is recorded in compensation records as owners, mortgagees, legatees, trustees, and executors, for 40 or 50 years following the end of slavery. Records also show that the English and, notably, the Scots predominate as slave-owners, while, in England, and in addition to Bristol and Liverpool, there were large concentrations of slave-ownership in the south-east and south-west of England. Catherine Hall and her group of researchers show also how some compensated slave-owners used the money they received to increase their wealth. For two-thirds of the nineteenth century they remain an identifiable wealthy group, which diversified notably into manufacturing. Hall notes that even though many slave-owners were swept away by the changes which industrialization brought,

> many more not only adapted to the new world order but also were among the most active agents of change, transferring financial and human capital generated in slavery to the new industrial and commercial economy ... Slave-ownership was one component of many in the consolidation of Britain, and specifically the City, as the centre of global capital in the mid- and late nineteenth century.[98]

In this way former slave-owners and their families moved from the Caribbean to the east to participate in Britain's industrial penetration of Asia during the nineteenth century.[99] Emancipation was also implemented, with more than the dimension of freedom in view, indeed, in 1833 slave-owners secured concessions in return for their acceptance of abolition. The system of "apprenticeship" ensured that those previously enslaved were compelled to work on the estates of their masters for a further period of four to six years. Slavery was, moreover, only abolished in the British Caribbean, Mauritius, and the Cape. Elsewhere it continued.[100]

John Edwin Mason maintains that, as the abolitionist movement's support grew in the Cape Colony, figurations of "paternalism" motivated slave-owners to challenge the reforms of 1826 and 1830 and the approaching likelihood of emancipation.[101] Mason notes the example of an eastern Cape slave-owner who spoke of paternalism in a manner that

> had little to do with mutual affection and everything to do with violent domination. "I could not rule [my slaves]," he told an assistant protector, "unless ... I had the power of exacting prompt obedience and repressing insolence with an occasional correction with my hand or whatever I chanced to have in it, *they are children and must be treated as such or [be] spoiled.*" The language of everyday life reflected the slave owners' commitment to paternalism. Dutch-speaking slave owners referred to their slaves as their *volk* ["people"], and at least one English-speaking master called his twenty slaves "my family." Slaves were not simply part of the family, they were children. Slave-owning society referred to a slave man as a *jong* [boy] and a woman as a *meid* [girl]. Adult slaves were not literally children, and, being adults, they were [also imagined to be] dangerous ... slave owners in Stellenbosch wrote to local officials of their need to defend their wives and children "from the dagger of incited slaves. Not alone our Wives and Daughters, but also yours, will in a libidinous manner be prosecuted by our Slaves with rape and defloration.[102]

The historian R.L. Watson also records that many white South Africans were hit by the challenge of abolition to their sense of social propriety. When they left the Cape Colony they took their notions of race and the procedures of enslavement and the notions that went with them to the places beyond the Cape Colony to which they trekked. According to the stipulations of the emancipation such places could still practice slavery. Thus when, in the late 1830s, thousands of Dutch farmers emigrated from the Cape Colony in what became known as the "Great Trek," the trekker Anna Steenkamp declared that it was not just the slaves' freedom that caused the Trek, but also the idea that they were being placed "on an equal footing with Christians, contrary to the laws of God and the natural distinctions of race and religion.'"[103] Such qualifications of the extent of actual freedom emancipation help us see a more complex picture of Britain's limited interventions in slavery. For example, the British Empire implemented forms of labor restraint that arguably approached the harshness of slavery itself, as we have noted in earlier chapters in the case of South Africa. Other contradictions seriously undermined claims to an enlightened British liberalism. Thus, in the case of the demands of imperial economic policies, coercion, intervention, and the subjugation of indigenous identities became, whenever necessary, the order of the day.

Despite the data about various euphemisms, qualifications, and contradictions evident in the processes of slave-ownership, compensation, and emancipation that recent research has uncovered, after the abolition of slavery slave-owners displayed no guilt for their part in maintaining the institution for so long. Instead, they laid claim to an imagined British moral superiority, erased any acknowledgement of the benefits that slave-owning and compensation had accorded them, and castigated "other, less progressive, slave-owning nations."[104] But this apparent amnesia did not betoken the demise of racism, and even in the 1820s, pro-slavery writers were still presenting slave-ownership as benign. From 1829 onwards Michael Scott (1789–1835) wrote a series of sea adventures set in the West Indies, which were then published as a book entitled *Tom Cringle's Log* (1833) in which Jamaica emerged as a "benevolent patriarchy"[105] within which slavery was regarded as a "civilizing institution."[106] In his "Scenes in Jamaica," for example, he describes one of the villages on an established estate that he visited in terms that manage to transform the harsh reality of slavery into a benign carnival:

> While I was pursuing my ramble, a large conch-shell was blown at the over-seer's house, and the different gangs turned in to dinner; they came along dancing and shouting, and playing tricks on each other in the little paths, in all the happy anticipation of a good dinner and an hour and a half to eat it in, the men well clad in Osnaburg frocks and trousers, and the women in baize petticoats and Osnaburg shifts, with a neat printed calico sort-gown over all. "And these are slaves," thought I, "*and this is West Indian bondage*! Oh that

some of my well-meaning anti-slavery friends were here, to judge from the evidence of their own senses![107]

Hall notes that Samuel Taylor Coleridge (1772–1834) "regarded the book as 'excellent' and as close to Smollett as anything he could remember."[108] Moreover, she also registers the doubleness in the behavior of anti-abolitionists after emancipation. Even as they disavowed their own past and now praised Britain as an enlightened state, essayists, travel writers, novelists, poets, and others[109] worked to reinforce the traditional hierarchical social order that this narrative of enslavement reiterated. Thus,

after abolition they subscribed to the orthodoxy that slavery was an anathema ... alternatively that slavery had been a benign institution, totally misrepresented by its enemies, an essential tool *in the difficult work of civilizing Africans. The cruelties and atrocities associated with slavery—the everyday practices of violence, of punishment and of humiliation*—were sectioned off as if having nothing to do with them. At the same time they constructed themselves as the unfortunate victims of Emancipation and *denigrated the African.* The horrors of slavery were erased, all excoriation reserved for foreigners who continued to trade in slaves.[110]

It is ironic, then, that the very movement to abolish slavery also prompted narratives that were designed to reconfigure negative contours of race.

Solomon Northup's *Twelve Years a Slave* and Toni Morrison's *Beloved*

The profound impact slavery has had on the circulation of negative imaginings of "black" or "colored" people, particularly Africans, and the terrible exploitation which such negative markings of particular human groups legitimate or encourage, also emerges from North American representations of slavery and its effects. *Twelve Years a Slave* (1853), written by Solomon Northup (1807–unknown), for example, is referred to by Henry Louis Gates Jr. as, "one of our canonical slave narratives."[111] He notes that 101 such narratives were published between 1760 and the end of the Civil War.

Northup's text is about his own kidnap in Washington by agents of slave-owners in the American South, and, until his escape, his subsequent experience of being a slave for the following 12 years of his life. He begins his story by stressing that although he was born in the American North and that he was, as a young man, "resolved to enter upon a life of industry," he was aware that, even in the North he was disadvantaged by his skin color, although,

> notwithstanding the obstacle of color, and the consciousness of [his] lowly state, [he] indulged in pleasant dreams of a good time coming, when the possession of some humble habitation, with a few surrounding acres, should reward [his] labors, and bring [him] the means of happiness and comfort.[112]

His experience with his descent into slavery proves that despite these hopes, to be the opposite, as Gates remarks, of the so-called American Dream.

Northup's narrative draws our attention to the discursive struggle that imaginings of race entail. For example, he remarks,

> having all my life breathed the free air of the North, and conscious that I possessed the same feelings and affections that find a place in the white man's breast; conscious, moreover, of an intelligence equal to that of some men, at least, with a fairer skin, I was too ignorant, perhaps too independent, to conceive how any one could be content to live in the abject condition of a slave.[113]

These remarks counter-identify the prevailing negative stereotype of "black" men as willfully inferior, one of many disparaging representations of blacks in the nineteenth century. Indeed, the Rev. Theodore Wright (1797–1847), with such representations of African-Americans in view, observed that

> the prejudice peculiar to our country, which subjects our colored brethren to a degrading distinction in our

worshipping assemblies, and schools, which withholds from them that kind and courteous treatment to which as well as other citizens they have a right, at public houses, on board steamboats, in stages, and in places of public concourse, is the spirit of slavery.[114]

In the face of such imaginings of inferior and slavish black "natures," Northup declares, "I could not comprehend the justice of that law or religion which upholds or recognizes the principle of Slavery."[115]

Northup is, moreover, on occasion openly explicit about ironies in the Union's claims to promote human freedom. Emphasizing that slavery and its circulation of imagined characteristics of race work sadistically and systemically to dominate and subdue the human identity of its victims, he observes of Williams's slave pen in Washington, where he is first imprisoned and tortured after his kidnap, that "it was like a farmer's barnyard in most respects, save it was so constructed that the outside world could never see the human cattle that were herded there." He continues, "a stranger looking at it would never have dreamed of its execrable uses" and he notes the trenchant irony of the juxtaposition of an opulent civilization and its barbaric underpinning:

Strange as it may seem, within plain sight of this same house, looking down from its commanding height, upon it, was the Capitol. The voices of patriotic representatives boasting of freedom and equality, and the rattling of the poor slave's chains almost commingled. A slave pen within the very shadow of the Capitol![116]

When these prisoners are taken under cover of night to commence their journey to a life of slavery in the American South, the narrative again ponders the systemic governmental and legislative promotion, but simultaneous concealment of this brutality:

we passed, hand-cuffed and in silence, through the streets of Washington—through the Capital of a nation whose theory of government, we are told, rests on the foundation of man's inalienable right to life, LIBERTY, and the pursuit of happiness! Hail! Columbia, happy land, indeed![117]

Set against imaginings of African-American childish ineptitude, Northup's narrative demonstrates acute powers of geographical observation, knowledgeable and detailed descriptions of work such as carpentry or the methodology of cotton picking, and, ironically, canny depiction of the physiognomy of various white slave-masters whom he encounters. The abolitionist Rev. John Pierpoint (1785–1846) writes, during the same period, in one of his anti-slavery poems:

> Our tobacco they plant, our cotton they pick,
> And our rice they can harvest and thrash
> They feed us in health, and they nurse us when sick
> And they earn—while we pocket—our cash
> They lead us when young, and they help us when old
> And their toil loads our tables and shelves
> But they're "niggers" and therefore (the truth must be told)
> They cannot take care of themselves![118]

The stereotypical racism of the cutting sarcasm of Pierpont's last two lines is counter-identified by the preceding lines, which point to just how much slaves do take care of. Indeed, much of the knowledgeable detail in Northup's wide-ranging narrative functions to undercut existing racist premises. Moreover, his detailed and informative passages describing the labors of workers, "inasmuch as some may read this book who may never have seen a cotton field,"[119] underlines the system's economic ruthlessness:

> The fastest hoer takes the lead row. He is usually about a rod in advance of his companions. If one of them passes him he is whipped. If one falls behind, or is a moment idle, he is whipped. In fact the lash is from morning until night, the whole day long ... When a new hand, one unaccustomed to the business, is sent for the first time into the field, he is whipped up smartly, and made for that day to pick as fast as he can possibly [sic]. At night it is weighed, so that his capability in cotton picking is known. He must bring in the same weight each night following. If it falls short, it is considered evidence that he has been laggard, and a greater or lesser number of lashes is the penalty.[120]

Such detail in the narrative challenges racial stereotypes of the "naturally" enslaved, errant, and lazy black body which is always in need of guidance and control. Indication of the capacity, moreover, on the part of the enslaved for what emerges as heroic labor within desperate conditions, itself stands in opposition to these disparaging allegations. Such negative articulation of race may thus be understood as indicative of discursive struggle over the institution and exploitation of cheap labor.

In addition to his methods of counter-identification, Northup sometimes shows the discursive imagination literally coming apart in the face of material realities. Thus when the slaves are permitted to unshackle themselves in order to eat, during their transportation from one place to another on their way to a life of slavery in the American South, discursively imposed allegations of their "animality" disintegrate. The violence, again, of sexual exploitation and abuse, alluded to at points in the narrative, is irrefutably heinous. We may argue that in less overtly violent situations, although never in a way that presumes to legitimate or apologize for such enforced sexual behavior, levels of personal intimacy that emerge during these incidents counterbalance negative imaginings about race. Such intimacy is, arguably, glimpsed in the example of the long-term relationship of President Thomas Jefferson (1743–1826) with a slave after the death of his wife, manifest in the offspring that this relationship apparently produced.

Northup's narrative strives for omniscience but given the hostility of the discourse within which he writes, it is little wonder that his writing is occasionally punctuated by anticipations of possible denial on the part of his readers. He stresses that

> it is necessary in this narrative, in order to present a full and truthful statement of all the principal events in the history of my life, and to portray the institution of Slavery as I have seen and know it, to speak of well-known places, and of many persons who are yet living … what I am about to say, if false, can be easily contradicted.[121]

Furthermore, Northup's text makes it repeatedly clear that such processes of willful denial of the veracity of his text, and more especially the dismissal of the torments it identifies, are *knowingly* sadistic and cruel. Thus, when he finds himself incarcerated in the Washington slave pen and insists on his identity as a free man, he is ferociously beaten:

> When his unrelenting arm grew tired, he stopped and asked if I still insisted I was a free man. I did insist upon it, and then the blows were renewed, faster and more energetically, if possible, than before. When again tired, he would repeat the same question, and receiving the same answer, continue his cruel labor ... All his brutal blows could not force from my lips the foul lie that I was a slave ... A man with a particle of mercy in his soul would not have beaten even a dog so cruelly.[122]

This determined attempt to beat the identity out of the victim implicitly assumes, at the same time, the existence of an inalienable personhood which is hated and under premeditated attack. Conversely, it also points to the animality of the individual who sadistically initiates brutal tortures or programs of dehumanization. When Northup notes how "we were each provided with blankets, such as are used upon horses—the only bedding I was allowed to have for twelve years afterwards."[123] He remarks that "I who had been so lonely, and who had longed so ardently to see some one, I cared not who, now shuddered at the thought of man's approach. A human face was fearful to me, especially a white one."[124] In this instance, he effectively names in his text the animal brutality of his "white" slave masters. As he puts it on another occasion, "it was difficult to determine which I had most reason to fear—dogs, alligators or men!"[125] This, together with the narrative's accounts of moments such as those of resistance or attempts to escape, all register responses that contest the stereotypes of the "natural" slave or the "slavish natures" of demarcated groups of people and the allegedly civilized nature of the whites who "own" them and "control" them.[126]

The recent film version of *Twelve Years a Slave* is directed by Steve McQueen. Its screenplay is by John Ridley and the film has a noted group of predominantly male producers. The camera's antislavery gaze, together with its evocations of period realism both endeavor to contain and order its audience's exposure to its subject within the conventions of slave narratives. Its mode of linear narrative presentation works, as in Northup's literary presentation, to distance the reader's reception from what offers itself as a cruel but now concluded past. This reflects an arguably masculinist inclination for at least a narrative ordering of the "history" it delineates.

By contrast Toni Morrison, in her much admired novel, *Beloved* (1987),[127] written over 100 years after Northup's text, focuses on how the narration of the impact of slavery upon African-American experience may be discursively and chronologically complicated. Stories are always related from a particular point of view. "Past" experience is also perceived as continuously impinging upon the present, whether or not they are presented in a linear fashion as ostensibly distance stories of the past. Narratives of slavery and the history of its racism, are here shown to deal with episodes and material events that repeatedly and disturbingly still intrude upon and intersect with current African-American life. The possibility of a form of containment by means of linear presentation of various experiences is repeatedly undone by the persistent intrusion into the present of this inexplicable past.

We may look, by way of example, at Morrison's treatment in her novel of the newspaper article which she discovered when helping to edit *The Black Book.* The clipping, a photograph of which may be found on page 10 of the volume, reports that a slave woman who escaped enslavement by fleeing from her Kentucky plantation to a relatively safe house in Cincinnati, killed one of her own children in her attempt to save them from a life of slavery.

In drawing upon an actual newspaper report, from which her own "story" emerges, Morrison meditates on the way history itself may be said always to be mediated by the language which represents it. Her employment of multiple narrative techniques also attests to this complication: several different characters attempt to comprehend what happened. For instance, Paul D, a companion slave of the mother, Sethe, has also escaped the euphemistically labeled "Sweet Home," on which they were enslaved and has now, 18 years after the incident involving the death of her child, formed a relationship with her. He understands aspects of her pain, how the choke cherry tree she wears like a burden on her back is also a "revolting clump of scars,"[128] a sign of whipping and enslavement. But he does not know about the infanticide. He is shown the original newspaper article describing the incident by Stamp Paid, another escaped companion. Stamp, it subsequently emerges, in his own guilty recollections later in the novel about his equivocal revelation, believes he should not remain silent about the past of a woman with whom his friend, ignorant of this "past," may now be entering into a permanent relationship.

In the course of presenting the moment of attempted revelation of this past event, Morrison focuses on Stamp Paid's as well as Paul D's histories, at times interweaving responses to the newspaper clipping. Thus Paul D thinks:

> That ain't her mouth ... From the solemn air with which Stamp had unfolded the paper, the tenderness in the old man's fingers as he stroked its creases and flattened it out, first on his knees, then on the split top of the piling, Paul D knew that it ought to mess him up. That whatever was written on it should shake him.[129]

The two men are also pointedly located in the present realities of their laboring lives:

> Pigs were crying in the chute. All day Paul D, Stamp Paid and twenty more had pushed and prodded them from canal to shore to chute to slaughterhouse ... Cincinnati was still pig port in the minds of Ohioans ... For a month or so in the winter any stray man had work, if he could breathe the stench of offal and stand up for twelve hours, skills in which Paul D was admirably trained.[130]

But the past continually hovers insistently around the edges of Morrison's detailed and vivid descriptions:

> A hundred yards from the crying pigs, the two men stood behind a shed on Western Row and it was clear why Stamp had been eying Paul D this last week of work; why he paused when the evening shift came on, to let Paul D's movements catch up to his own. He made up his mind to show him this piece of paper—newspaper—with a picture drawing of a woman who favored Sethe except that was not her mouth.

> Nothing like it ... Paul D slid the clipping out from under Stamp's palm. The print meant nothing to him so he didn't even glance at it.[131]

Against Paul D's avoidance of what is being presented to him, Stamp's own *largely unspoken* recollections also unfold in the following pages, of how "not anybody ran down ... to say some new white-folks with the Look just rode in," the "righteous Look [that] every Negro learned to recognize along with his ma'am's tit"[132] and of how, now in Stamp's narrative, although also *not spoken* to Paul D, Sethe

> flew, snatching up her children like a hawk on the wing; how her face beaked, how her hands worked like claws, how she collected them every which way: one on her shoulder, one under her arm, one by the hand, the other shouted forward into the wood-shed filled with just sunlight and shavings now because there wasn't any wood.[133]

The attention in the text to what was *not spoken* hints at the unspeakable nature of certain events, as well as at the complexity of private perceptions of them. What also emerges from such mingling of narrative interaction and private response is the sense of shared predicament and challenge in addressing what is a common past and the inescapability of multiple perceptions of past as well as present events that forms part of the narration of this harrowing history. Paul D cannot read, but he reflects upon the kind of sensationalist, openly prejudiced representation that a popular newspaper might offer to its readers:

> And no at whatever it was those black scratches said, and no to whatever it was Stamp Paid wanted him to know. Because there was no way in hell a black face could appear in a news-paper if the story was about something anybody wanted to hear. A whip of fear broke through the heart chambers as soon as you saw a Negro's face in a paper, since the face was not there because the person had a healthy baby, or outran a street mob. Nor was it there because the person had been killed, or maimed or caught or burned or jailed or whipped or

evicted or stomped or raped or cheated, since that would hardly qualify as news in a newspaper. It would have to be something out of the ordinary—something whitepeople would find interesting, truly different, worth a few minutes teeth sucking if not gasps. And it must have been hard to find news about Negroes worth the breath catch of a white citizen of Cincinnati.[134]

Eventually Stamp reads the clipping to Paul D, who in turn shows it to Sethe. Paul D is trying to avoid what the article might contain, but now he has been fully exposed to its contents. The

love she saw in his eyes ... made her go ahead and tell him what she had not told Baby Suggs [her mother-in-law, who has offered Seth and her children the relative safety of her Cincinnati house on 124 Bluestone Road], the only person she felt obliged to explain anything to.[135]

Again different narrative voices present the ensuing intersections and interactions. This time we shift to Sethe's and then to Paul D's points of view as they grapple to articulate or comprehend a painful, almost unspeakable, past:

"I couldn't let all that go back to where it was, and I couldn't let her nor any of em live under schoolteacher [the slave-owner who has come to track his escaped slaves down]. That was out" ... Sethe knew that the circle she was making around the room, him, the subject would remain one. That she could never close in, pin it down for anybody who had to ask. If they didn't get it right off—she could never explain ... she was squatting in the garden and when she saw them coming and recognized schoolmaster's hat ... And if she thought anything, it was No. No. Nono. Nonono. Simple. She just flew. Collected every bit of life she had made, all the parts of her that were precious and fine and beautiful, and carried, pushed, dragged them through the veil, out, away over there where no one could hurt them. Over there. Outside this place, where they would be safe ... "I stopped him," she said ... "I took and put

> my babies where they'd be safe" ... The roaring in Paul D's head did not prevent him from hearing the pat she gave to the last word, and it occurred to him that what she wanted for her children was exactly what was missing in 124: safety. Which was the very first message he got the day he walked through the door. He thought he had made it safe, had gotten rid of the danger; beat the shit out of it.[136]

During the development of his relationship with Sethe, Paul D resents Beloved's ghostly presence in the house but he confesses that "it was one thing to beat up a ghost, quite another to throw a helpless colored girl out in territory infected by the Klan" which was "desperately thirsty for black blood, without which it could not live."[137] The ambiguities attached to Beloved's presence in the novel as ghost, as young woman pretending to be Beloved, as Sethe's imagined daughter, sometimes all of these at once, encapsulates the novel's concern with the presentness for all African-Americans of the past. But even though Paul D recognizes the dangers that he and Sethe or Beloved still face as black ex-slaves, his response to Sethe is torn:

> This here Sethe was new ... This here Sethe talked about love like any other woman; talked about baby clothes like any other woman; but what she meant could cleave the bone. This here Sethe talked about safety with a handsaw ... Suddenly he saw what Stamp Paid wanted him to see: more important than what Sethe had done was what she claimed. It scared him ... "What you did was wrong, Sethe" ... and right then a forest sprang up between them; trackless and quiet ... Later he would wonder what made him say it ... How fast he had moved from his shame to hers ... Meanwhile the forest was locking the distance between them, giving it shape and heft ... He didn't rush to the door. He moved slowly and when he got there he opened it before asking Sethe to put supper aside for him because he might be a little late getting back. Only then did he put on his hat ... Sweet, she thought. He must think I can't bear to hear him say it. That after all I have told him ... "goodbye" would break me to pieces. Ain't that sweet. "So long," she murmured from the far side of the trees.[138]

In the novel the presentation of these various points of view, and the juxtapositions of different kinds of pain which they indicate or cause also include the perspective of Schoolmaster, who had, 18 years ago, come with a slave-catcher and his two nephews in order to take the "pickaninies they hoped were alive ... back to Kentucky, take back and raise properly to do the work Sweet Home desperately needed."[139] Before the escapes, Schoolmaster had taken over management of the plantation, and had instituted a rigid regime of beatings. He also witnesses the rape of Sethe by his sons/nephews, taking notes all the while. He views slaves as animals to be trained, and at another point reprimands one boy for his excessive punishment of a slave, asking what would the boy's own horse do "if you beat it beyond the point of education."[140] But, confronted by the scene in the woodshed, he and his companions retreat with language that is indifferent to their suffering; the damaged family will for them no longer hold value as potential slaves:

> Enough nigger eyes for now. Little nigger-boy eyes open in sawdust; little nigger-girl eyes staring between the wet fingers that held her face so her head wouldn't fall off; little nigger-baby eyes crinkling up to cry ... the worst ones were those of the nigger woman ... All testimony to the results of a little so-called freedom imposed on people who needed every care and guidance in the world to keep them from the cannibal life they preferred.[141]

Beloved grapples discursively in this and other ways with the effect of North American racist slavery upon the African-American present. The absence in the novel of an omniscient voice or a Master/Mistress narrator, the shifts of points of view, the use on occasion of techniques such as stream of consciousness, all attest to the difficulty of any authoritative speaking of the unspeakable, and to the pain and destruction still there as a ghostly presence still capable of burning into the substance of domestic life. Thus number 124 is tellingly, still 18 years later, "full of a baby's venom,"[142] an image that goes straight to the heart of Morrison's "story" and to the complex troubled environment where members of the African-American community must still today live out their lives. "We could move," Sethe once suggests to her mother-in-law, Baby Suggs, who replies, "What'd be the point? ... Not a house in the country ain't packed to its rafters with some dead Negro's grief."[143] Sensing the sadness in Sethe's house when he first comes to it, Paul D tells himself, "if a Negro got legs he ought to use them. Sit down too long, somebody will figure out a way to tie them up."[144]

Morrison notes also the complexities wrought on discursive utterance of place and identity by factors such as ambiguity, repression, and the concept of "rememory." "Sweet Home," belies a place that different narrative voices in the novel register as unsettled and ambiguous, a "home" as much of violence as it may have also been one of beauty. Sethe recalls the plantation "rolling, rolling, rolling out before her eyes and although there was not a leaf on that farm that did not make her want to scream, it rolled itself out before her in shameless beauty."[145] Sweet Home "never looked as terrible as it was" so that "it made her wonder if hell was a pretty place too ... fire and brimstone all right, but hidden in lacy groves."[146] She finds the "lively spite" that the house on 124 Bluestone Road "felt" for its inhabitants just as troublingly ambiguous. To it comes a strange ghost-like young woman called Beloved whom Sethe in the course of the novel, construes to be her daughter Beloved. She is haunted by intimations of her, here only indirectly acknowledged infanticide, for

> counting on the stillness of her own soul, she had forgotten the other one: the soul of her baby girl. Who could have thought that a little old baby could harbor so much rage? ... Not only did she have to live out her years in a house palsied by the baby's fury at having its throat cut but those ten minutes she spent pressed up against dawn-coloured stone studded with star chips, her knees wide open as the grave, were longer than life, more pulsating than the baby blood that soaked her fingers like oil.[147]

The house in Sethe's present time is still "palsied" by intimations of the novel's "ten minutes" from its terrible past that has only been alluded to but not dealt with explicitly. This is a complex past; Morrison's language points implicitly to Sethe's hope of giving birth, to her child's escape from a future life of unmitigated pain. It is mixed also with her act of infanticide. Thus she is, in partial recollection, "pressed up against" the house's "stone" floor, which is simultaneously "dawn-coloured" with reflections, "studded with star chips." Her attempt to give to her child a star-like birth of freedom is also, "her knees wide open as the grave," a birth-gift of blood. Those ten minutes in this house's past remain for her, in her present, "longer than life, more pulsating" than the terrible "baby blood" whose imagined liberation soaks her fingers "like oil."

Sethe attempts to handle such intimations from the past by means of repression. To her, "the future was a matter of keeping the past at bay," the "better life" she believes she and Denver, the daughter she now lives with in 124 Bluestone Road, have together, "was simply not that other one"[148] in Sweet Home. Such avoidance is for her like "kneading bread in the half light of the restaurant kitchen"[149] where she is now employed, "working dough. Working, working dough. Nothing better than that to start the day's serious work of beating back the past."[150] Talking to Denver, Sethe acknowledges the pain that represses a history that needs at the same time to be confronted and articulated. Recollection of an unspeakable past involves a picture of what it insists on, intruding into a present that, because of it, remains nonetheless still unspeakable, impenetrably resistant to any particular narrative attempt:

> I was talking about time. *It's so hard to believe in it.* [emphasis added] Some things go. Pass on. Some things just stay. I used to think it was my rememory ... Some things you forget. Other things you never do. But it's not. Places, places are still there. If a house burns down, it's gone, but the place—the picture of it—stays, and not just in my rememory, but out there, in the world. What I remember is a picture floating around out there outside my head ... Someday you be walking down the road and you hear something or see something going on ... And you think its you thinking it up. But no. It's when you bump into a rememory that belongs to someone else. Where I was before I came here, that place is real. It's never going away. Even if the whole farm—every tree and grass blade of it dies. The picture is still there and what's more, if you go there—you who never was there—if you go there and stand in the place where it was, it will happen again; it will be there for you, waiting for you. So

> Denver, you can't never go there. Never. Because even though it's all over—over and done with—it's going to always be there waiting for you. That's how come I had to get all my children out. No matter what.[151]

Retellings and sometimes revised memories of the past, as in the case of the multiple narratives of infanticide, are communal endeavors to handle a common past. Thus Denver tells Beloved of her mother's and her grandmother's story of her birth, when Sethe has run away to join her children:

> Denver began to see what she was saying and not just to hear it: there is this nineteen-year-old slave girl—a year older than herself—walking through the dark woods to get to her children who are far away. She is tired, scared maybe, and maybe even lost. Most of all she is by herself and inside her is another baby she has to think about too. Behind her dogs, perhaps; guns probably; and certainly mossy teeth [a reference to Schoolmaster's two sons/nephews who rape her, by stealing her milk while he observes and takes notes]. She is not so afraid at night because she is the color of it, but in the day every sound is a shot or a tracker's quiet step. Denver now was seeing it and feeling it—through Beloved. Feeling how it must have felt to her mother.[152]

The shift in tense brings the terror and feelings of Denver's memory of her mother's past into her own sentient present. That past becomes also in this way part of both Denver's and Beloved's present. In her preaching Baby Suggs calls for her community to unlearn School-master's "proprietary models of identity that slavery has literally trained into their bodies."[153] In the novel:

> the bodily effects of enslavement on men and women are linked through images of "animality" and "iron" suggesting [also] that Sethe and Paul D must alike unlearn the mechani-zation of slavery's signifying disciplines of dressage ... Like the iron bit schoolteacher forces Paul D to wear ... [Sethe is] linked to his ... inscription of her enslaved body as half-consisting of

animal characteristics. Paul D must unlearn the sensation of
the coffle irons ... just as Sethe must unlearn the choke-hold
... around her throat that is both the collectively rememoried
sensation of the Middle Passage and ... Beloved's rage.[154]

The powerfully moving section III of *Beloved* is mostly narrated in
the third person in a manner reminiscent of a traditional slave narrative. But there are two shifts from the past-tense record of Paul D's
return to Sethe, the communal recognition of Sethe's pain, Denver's
self-assertions, to a predominantly present-tense account of a past that
remains insistently there as well. Both shifts encapsulate again some
of the novel's central concerns about time.

The first shift occurs when the narrative records how the white
man who has offered a job to Denver and whose family helped Baby
Suggs when she first came to Cincinnati, drove a cart to 124 Bluestone Road, the house he lived in as a child. He had "promised ... a
detour to pick up [the] new girl."[155] Suddenly the narrative shifts to
the present tense:

Sethe feels her eyes burning and it may have been to keep
them clear that she looks up. The sky is blue and clear. Not one
touch of death in the definite green of the leaves. It is when
she lowers her eyes again ... that she sees him. Guiding the
mare, slowing down, his black hat wide-brimmed enough to
hide his face but not his purpose. He is coming into her yard
and he is coming for her best thing ... And if she thinks anything, it is no. No no. Nonono. She flies. The ice pick is not in
her hand; it is her hand ... rising from his place with a whip in
his hand, the man without skin, looking. He is looking at her.[156]

The second shift in the narrative from past tense into present tense
also ponders the painful impact upon the present moment when the
past is invoked. This narrative is a picture of loneliness, wrought by
the past upon the present, both within Sethe, and between her and her
lost daughter, Beloved:

There is a loneliness that can be rocked. Arms crossed, knees
drawn up; holding, holding on, this motion, unlike a ship's,

> smooths and contains the rocker. It's an inside kind—wrapped
> tight like skin. Then there is a loneliness that roams. No
> rocking can hold it down. It is alive, on its own. A dry and
> spreading thing that makes the sound of one's own feet going
> seem from a far-off place.[157]

At its conclusion the novel turns to a mixture of past and present
tenses. It repeats the formulation, "It was not a story to pass on,"[158]
three times, in a way that also recognizes the unspeakability in the
very presentness of pictures of a communally experienced and variously related past:

> Down by the stream in back of 124 her footprints come and
> go, come and go. They are so familiar. Should a child, an adult
> place his feet in them, they will fit. Take them out and they
> disappear again as though nobody ever walked there. By and
> by all trace is gone, and what is forgotten is not only the foot-
> prints but the water too and what is down there. The rest is
> weather. Not the breath of the disremembered and unac-
> counted for, but wind in the eaves, or spring ice thawing too
> quickly. Just weather. Certainly no clamor for a kiss.[159]

Recurrent and noticeable in this chapter is the tendency in negative
imaginings of race to adopt strategies of silence or evasion. We have
noted how various modes of denial informed eighteenth century
avoidance of complicity in slave trading and nineteenth century presentations of slave-ownership. This is a concern in the North American
fiction of Alice Walker and Toni Morrison at which we have just
discussed.

In this regard, we may add that the sociologist, Stanley Cohen, notes
that "one common thread runs through the many different stories of
denial: people, organizations, governments or whole societies are presented with information that is too disturbing, threatening or anomalous
to be fully absorbed or openly acknowledged."[160] He observes that such
information, in sometimes complicated ways, "is therefore somehow
repressed, disavowed, pushed aside, or reinterpreted."[161] But it may be
worth remembering, in the context of our ongoing analysis of complexity of race, that he also argues that, "despite the complex obstacles

between information and action … no humanitarian, educational or political organization should even consider limiting its flow of knowledge."[162] On the subject of denial he especially insists that in the task of examining such complexities, this at least means "making *more* troubling information available to more people."[163]

Notes

1 Benjamin Isaac, "Racism: A Rationalization of Prejudice in Greece and Rome," in Miriam Eliav-Feldon, Benjamin Isaac, and Joseph Ziegler, eds., *The Origins of Racism in the West*, Cambridge: Cambridge University Press, 2009, 56. Or it is argued that while

> slavery was common in Arab societies where Islam took hold, and while stereotypes of slaves as stupid can be found, these did not appear to have led to any specific identification of particular cultural and territorial populations as naturally inferior and therefore suitable for permanent servitude.
> (Ali Rattansi, *Racism: A Very Short Introduction*, Oxford: Oxford University Press, 2007, 18)

2 Benjamin Isaac, *The Invention of Racism in Classical Antiquity*, Princeton: Princeton University Press, 2004, 503.
3 Isaac, *The Invention of Racism*, 503.
4 Isaac, *The Invention of Racism*, 503.
5 Isaac, *The Invention of Racism*, 503.
6 Isaac, *The Invention of Racism*, 503.
7 Paul E. Lovejoy, "Slavery in Africa," in Gad Heuman and Trevor Burnard, eds., *The Routledge History of Slavery*, London: Routledge, 2012, 36.
8 Cited in Brian Niro, *Race*, Basingstoke: Palgrave Macmillan, 2003, 28.
9 Lovejoy, "Slavery in Africa," 36.
10 Isaac, *The Invention of Racism*, 194.
11 Aphra Behn, *Oroonoko*, ed. Janet Todd, London: Penguin Books, 2003, 61–62. All quotations come from this edition.
12 Isaac, *The Invention of Racism*, 195.
13 Isaac, *The Invention of Racism*, 195.
14 Cited in Isaac, *The Invention of Racism*, 194–195.
15 Isaac, *The Invention of Racism*, 194–195.
16 Isaac, *The Invention of Racism*, 195.
17 Indeed these and many of the other instances he provides, prompt

Isaac to argue that in the

> attempt to give the Greeks and Romans their due: if they have given us, through their literature, many of the ideas of freedom, democracy, philosophy, novel artistic concepts and so much else that we regard as essential in our culture, it should be recognized that the same literature also transmitted some of the elementary concepts of discrimination and inequality that are still with us.
>
> (*The Invention of Racism*, 516)

18 See Joel Quirk, "Modern Slavery" in Gad Heuman and Trevor Burnard, eds., *The Routledge History of Slavery*, London: Routledge, 2012, 331–346. Quirk notes the persistence of present-day "classical" slavery in places such as Niger and Mauritania, Burkino Faso, Cameroon, Chad, Ghana, Guinea, Mali, Nigeria, and Western Sahara, the persistence of bonded labor in places such as India, Pakistan, and Nepal, forced prostitution in "most corners of the globe," the incidence of "enslaved" migrant domestic workers in Singapore, Saudi Arabia, and Haiti, forced labor for the state in North Korea and northern China and the persistence of incidents of wartime enslavement in places such as Sudan, Uganda, and the Democratic Republic of Congo. Quirk estimates the number of people caught up in present day forms of slavery to be 27 million. Arguably also, Chinese labor forces in present-day Chinese manufacturing and production policy earn the kind of minimum wages and are subject to the kind of restrictions of their human rights that suggest a de facto condition of slavery.

19 David Wallace, *Premodern Places: Calais to Surinam, Chaucer to Aphra Behn*, Oxford: Blackwell Publishing, 2006.

20 Wallace, *Premodern Places*, 5.

21 Wallace, *Premodern Places*, 188.

22 Wallace, *Premodern Places*, 189, notes:

> The overwhelming majority of these slaves were young teenage (and often not quite teenage) girls. In a list of slaves sold in Florence between July 4, 1366, and March 2, 1397, for example, 329 of the slaves are women or little girls; only four of the 28 males are over 16. Some 98 percent of Florentine domestic slaves in this period, it has been argued, were female.

23 Wallace, *Premodern Places*, 188.

24 Wallace, *Premodern Places*, 189.

25 Wallace, *Premodern Places*, 189.

26 Wallace, *Premodern Places*, 187.

27 Wallace, *Premodern Places*, 190–194.

28 Wallace, *Premodern Places*, 194.

29 Wallace, *Premodern Places*, 139–166.

30 Wallace, *Premodern Places*, 5.

31 Wallace, *Premodern Places*, 166.

32 Wallace, *Premodern Places*, 249.

33 Wallace, *Premodern Places*, 249.

34 Wallace, *Premodern Places*, 249.

35 Wallace, *Premodern Places*, 240.

36 Wallace, *Premodern Places*, 250.

37 Wallace, *Premodern Places*, 250.

38 Lovejoy, "Slavery in Africa," 44, notes that:

> the relative impact of external trade in slaves on internal developments within Africa varied with proximity to the Sahara, the Indian Ocean and, after the late fifteenth century, along the Atlantic coast. There were wide-ranging networks that were dominated by Muslim merchants, along the East African coast and from the Red Sea to the Atlantic shores of the upper Guinea coast, and from these areas far into the interior. While some of these merchants came from North Africa, the Middle East and India, there were also many merchants who were resident in Sub-Saharan Africa and East Africa, and who dominated the trade in slaves well before the opening of trans-Atlantic commerce … Most estimates of the numbers of enslaved Africans who were shipped to the Americas after the early sixteenth century through the nineteenth century range in the order of 12.5 million people. The numbers of people sent as slaves across the Sahara Desert, the Red Sea and the Indian Ocean have been more difficult to establish, but the scale of this trade was historically very large as well.

39 Trevor Burnard, "The Atlantic Slave Trade," in Gad Heuman and Trevor Burnard, eds., *The Routledge History of Slavery*, London: Routledge, 2012, 83. Burnard notes also that "Islamic societies were particularly keen on enslavement … prepared to enslave anyone, regardless of colour, as long as they were people who were not Muslim" (83).

40 Burnard, "The Atlantic Slave Trade," 83. At the same time such loaded discriminatory practices intersect with demands for cheap labor, other economic needs, as the next section indicates, or warfare. The willingness, argues Burnard, for example, to engage in the slave trade is

accounted for by "long experience with slavery within northern and western Africa," and "the nature of political authority in much of West Africa encouraged slavery ... like ... the Caucasus, the Balkans and pre-Norman England West Africa was politically fragmented" ("The Atlantic Slave Trade," 83).

41 Lovejoy, "Slavery in Africa," 39. After the Portuguese, the British were the biggest carriers, "taking 3,259,440 Africans to the British West Indies and British North America" (Burnard, "The Atlantic Slave Trade," 91). Others participating in the trade included, over time, Dutch, French, Spanish, and Danish carriers. Racism also underlay aspects of the management of the Middle Passage, the name given to the slave crossing of the Atlantic from Africa to the Americas, "a forced migration, but one that was fundamentally different ... [because] what slavers tried to do to captives was to deny their personhood ... [before] their full commodification as slaves" (Burnard, "The Atlantic Slave Trade," 90). On arrival in the Americas, "the process of sale increased the degree of social alienation that Africans faced" with victims being sold "as individuals or as a set of a few people in a several-stage process that encompassed being treated like livestock" ("The Atlantic Slave Trade," 93).

42 Lovejoy, "Slavery in Africa," 44, remarks, again on the numerical impact of the African slave trade, that

> about 17.5 million people were forcibly moved from Africa between 1500 and 1900, of which more than 70 per cent went to the Americas and the rest to the Muslim regions of North Africa, the Middle East and the Indian Ocean world

although he points out that "these estimates do not include the number of slaves sent into the Muslim world before 1500, which was considerable, or indeed after 1900."

43 Betty Wood, "The Origins of Slavery in the Americas 1500–1700," in Gad Heuman and Trevor Burnard, eds., *The Routledge History of Slavery*, London: Routledge, 2012. I am indebted to Wood for much of what follows. Wood notes (67) that "Las Casas' fiery denunciation of the Spanish treatment of Indians" notwithstanding, "the English, too, fostered slavery, despite their protestations that they were different from the cruel Spaniards in what became the ... legend of Spanish depravity."

44 Wood, "The Origins of Slavery in the Americas," 65, 68–69.

45

> The planters who bought captive Africans literally could afford to work their slaves to death. They were able to replace dead workers

with newly imported men and women. In fact, the average life expectancy of an enslaved worker on the sugar estates of Brazil and the Caribbean was only around seven years after arrival from Africa. As long as the trans-Atlantic trade continued, sugar planters showed little interest in exploiting the reproductive, as well as the productive, potential of African women by encouraging them to have children. Enslaved women and men struggled against horrendous odds to carve out for themselves something resembling familiar and secure relationships.

> (Wood, "The Origins of Slavery in the Americas," 65)

46 Wood, "The Origins of Slavery in the Americas," 69.
47 Janet Todd, "Introduction," in Aphra Behn, *Oroonoko*, ed. Janet Todd, London: Penguin Books, 2003, xxi.
48 Todd, "Introduction," xxi.
49 Todd, "Introduction," xxii.
50 Wallace, *Premodern Places*, 240.
51 Wallace, *Premodern Places*, 240–241, 239–284. Wallace reminds us that Surinam, "the most prized and lucrative [slaving] colony possessed by the United Provinces ... became a byword for European cruelty and excess" (240). Surinam is the place to which Voltaire brings Candide. Moreover the sea over which slaves travel, increasingly comes to serve over time as a literary image of racialized complexity:

> The sea itself, or the crossing of it, both foments a hope of newness (the perennial great white hope) ... and interpellates those who lose through negritude. Behn complies with this paradigm: her Oroonoko comes from no place (beyond the sea) to a new place that can never be his; and he is black ... For Behn ... the first and foundational difference is no longer a matter of religion but of color, specifically of white/black.
>
> (Wallace, *Premodern Places*, 243)

52 Wood, "The Origins of Slavery in the Americas," 72.
53 Wood, "The Origins of Slavery in the Americas," 72.
54 Wood, "The Origins of Slavery in the Americas," 72–73.
55 Wood, "The Origins of Slavery in the Americas," 73.
56 Wood, "The Origins of Slavery in the Americas," 75.
57 Wood, "The Origins of Slavery in the Americas," 76.
58 Wood, "The Origins of Slavery in the Americas," 77.
59 Wood, "The Origins of Slavery in the Americas," 77.
60 Wood, "The Origins of Slavery in the Americas," 78.

61 See John Richardson, *Slavery and Augustan Literature: Swift, Pope, Gay*, London: Routledge, 2004, 7–9.

62 Richardson, *Slavery and Augustan Literature*, 29.

63

> Shipping news in the London newspapers usually advert to the third leg of the triangular voyage by listing returns from the Americas. However, there are also sometimes references to the first leg in news ... and to the middle passage ... Perhaps more tellingly, contributions to the public debate about free or monopoly trading assume familiarity with the triangular trade. In 1714 the Royal African Company, the would-be monopolists, argued that the existence of their forts had kept the price of African slaves down and had been [an economic] benefit to Britain.
>
> (Richardson, *Slavery and Augustan Literature*, 15)

64 Richardson, *Slavery and Augustan Literature*, 29.

65 Richardson, *Slavery and Augustan Literature*, 15.

66 Cited in Richardson, *Slavery and Augustan Literature*, 23. Bosman's discussion of the calculation of the value of slaves recalls Swift's ironies in his presentation of calculation in *A Modest Proposal*, which we noted in Chapter 3. It reflects at the same time the racist representation of slaves as animals:

> But yet before we can deal with any person, we are obliged to buy the king's whole stock of slaves at a set price, which is commonly one third or one fourth higher than ordinary; after which, we obtain free leave to deal with all his subjects, of what rank soever. But if there happen to be no stock of slaves, the factor must then resolve to run the risk of trusting the inhabitants with goods to the value of one or two hundred slaves; which commodities they send into the inland country, in order to buy with them slaves at all markets, and that sometimes two hundred miles deep in the country. For you ought to be informed, that markets of men are here kept in the same manner as those of beasts with us.
>
> (William Bosman, *A New and Accurate Description of the Coast of Guinea, Divided into the Gold, the Slave, and the Ivory Coasts*, 2nd ed., trans. from Dutch, London: 1721, Barnes & Noble, 1967, 353a–365a)

67 Richardson, *Slavery and Augustan Literature*, 17–18.

68 Richardson, *Slavery and Augustan Literature*, 18.

69 The lines on which the following discussion is based are:

I see ... a new *White-Hall* ascend!
There mighty Nations shall inquire their Doom,
The World's great Oracle in Times to come;
There Kings shall sue, and suppliant States be seen
Once more to bend before a *British* QUEEN.
Thy Trees, fair *Windsor*! Now shall leave their Woods,
And half thy Forests rush into my Floods,
Bear *Britain*'s Thunder, and her Cross display,
To the bright Regions of the rising Day;
Tempt Icy Seas, where scarce the Waters roll,
Where clearer Flames glow round the frozen Pole;
Or under Southern Skies exalt their Sails,
Led by new Stars, and born by spicy Gales!

....

The Time shall come, when free as Seas or Wind
Unbounded Thames shall flow for all Mankind,
Whole Nations enter with each swelling Tyde,
And Seas but join the Regions they divide;
Earth's distant Ends our Glory shall behold,
And the new World launch forth to seek the Old.

(ll. 379–402)

They come from Alexander Pope, "Windsor Forest," in The Poems of Alexander Pope, ed. John Butt, London: Methuen, 1963, 208–210. All quotations from Pope's poetry come from this edition.

70 Pope's reference to "suppliant States" recalls that, in 1575 and 1585, "the sovereignty of the United Provinces was offered to Queen Elizabeth and her aid was solicited in the struggles of the Dutch against Philip of Spain" (Butt, *The Poems of Alexander Pope*, 209).

71 Pope, "Windsor Forest," 403–414; Butt, *The Poems of Alexander Pope*, 210.

72 See Richardson, *Slavery and Augustan Literature*, 1–2.

73 Richardson, *Slavery and Augustan Literature*, 1.

74 From line 389, the original version read:

Now shall our Fleets the bloody Cross display
To the rich regions of the rising day
Or those green isles, where headlong *Titan* steeps
His hissing axle in th'*Atlantic* deeps.
Tempt icy seas &c.

(Butt, 209)

75 See n. 70 above.

76 See Richardson, *Slavery and Augustan Literature*, 67–68.

77 Richardson, *Slavery and Augustan Literature*, 59.

78 Epistle I. 1–6.

79 Cited in Richardson, *Slavery and Augustan Literature*, 103.

80 Richardson, *Slavery and Augustan Literature*, 103.

81 Richardson, *Slavery and Augustan Literature*, 104.

82 I. 99–112.

> Lo! The poor Indian, whose untutor'd mind
> Sees God in clouds, or hears him in the wind;
> His soul proud Science never taught to stray
> Far as the solar walk, or milky way;
> Yet simple Nature to his hope has giv'n,
> Behind the cloud-topt hill, an humbler heav'n;
> Some safer world in depth of woods embrac'd,
> Some happier island in the watry waste,
> Where slaves once more their native land behold'
> No fiends torment, no Christians thirst for Gold!
> To Be, contents his natural desire,
> He asks no Angel's wing, no Serap's fire;
> But thinks, admitted to that equal sky,
> His faithful dog shall bear him company.

(I. 99–112)

83 Wood, "The Origins of Slavery in the Americas," 68.

84 Richardson, *Slavery and Augustan Literature*, 94.

85 See Richardson, *Slavery and Augustan Literature*, 109–120.

86 See Richardson, *Slavery and Augustan Literature*, 120–136.

87 Richardson, *Slavery and Augustan Literature*, 138; see also 136–145.

88 Richardson, *Slavery and Augustan Literature*, 141.

89 Cited in Richardson, *Slavery and Augustan Literature*, 141.

90 Richardson, *Slavery and Augustan Literature*, 142.

91 Richardson, *Slavery and Augustan Literature*, 143.

92 Cited in Richardson, *Slavery and Augustan Literature*, 143.

93 Richardson, *Slavery and Augustan Literature*, 143.

94 Richardson, *Slavery and Augustan Literature*, 143.

95 Simon Gikandi, *Slavery and the Culture of Taste*, Princeton: Princeton University Press, 2011, 45.

96 Gikandi, *Slavery and the Culture of Taste*, 45. Gikandi also argues that at the end of the eighteenth century, "racialization seems to have increased rather than diminished," even as the impetus of the emancipation movement was increasing

whether we are dealing with the belated attempt by agents of the slave trade—the Liverpool interest, for example—to deploy the specter of race to justify their profits; or the abolitionist's imposition of a pathos of suffering on the black body, as was evident in Josiah Wedgewood's famous medallion for the committee on the abolition of the slave trade; or Blake's attempts to imagine the African woman in the comity of nations.

(*Slavery and the Culture of Taste*, 49)

97 See Catherine Hall, Nicholas Draper, and Keith McClelland, "Introduction," in Catherine Hall, Nicholas Draper, Keith McClelland, Katie Donington and Rachel Lang, eds., *Legacies of British Slave-ownership: Colonial Slavery and the Formation of Victorian Britain*, Cambridge: Cambridge University Press, 2014, 1, 21–22. I am indebted to Hall *et al.* everywhere in this section.

98 Hall *et al.*, "Introduction," 22–23.

99 Evident in

the explosion of British overseas trade; the reorientation of British long-distance commerce towards Asia, Latin America and the settler colonies; the consolidation of the City of London as the centre of global capital flows, with its concomitant growth in financial services, in the professions supporting the City and in merchant banking; the emergence of the joint-stock company; the increased integration of Britain through the railway and of the world through the steamship and the telegraph; and the birth of the free-trade nation.

(Hall *et al.*, "Introduction," 23)

100

Slavery was still being legislated against in India in 1976. Illegal slave trading, [as we noted earlier] continued in the nineteenth century alongside variegated forms of free and bonded labor that persisted well into the twentieth century, and beyond ... the freedom of labor was restricted in many ways both at home and in the empire, not least in the regulation of masters and servants.

(Hall *et al.*, "Introduction," 6–7)

101 John Edwin Mason, *Social Death and Resurrection: Slavery and Emancipation in South Africa*, Charlottesville: University of Virginia Press, 2003, 70.

102 Mason, *Social Death and Resurrection*, 71–72.

103 R.L. Watson, *Slave Emancipation and Racial Attitudes in Nineteenth-Century South Africa*, Cambridge: Cambridge University Press, 2012, 130.

104 See Hall *et al.*, "Introduction," 7, 17, 19–20.

105 Catherine Hall, "Reconfiguring Race: The Stories the Slave-Owners Told," in Catherine Hall, Nicholas Draper, Keith McClelland, Katie Donington and Rachel Lang, eds., *Legacies of British Slave-ownership: Colonial Slavery and the Formation of Victorian Britain*, Cambridge: Cambridge University Press, 2014, 163.

106 Hall, "Reconfiguring Race," 163–164.

107 Michael Scott, *Tom Cringle's Log*, Ithaca: McBooks Press, 1999, 141–142.

108 Hall, "Reconfiguring Race," 163.

109 See Hall, "Reconfiguring Race," 170–196.

110 See Hall, "Reconfiguring Race," 169–170, emphasis added.

111 Henry Louis Jr. Gates, "Afterword," in Solomon Northup, *Twelve Years a Slave*, Introduction by Ira Berlin, New York: Penguin Books, 2013, 236. All quotations are from this edition.

112 Northup, *Twelve Years a Slave*, 10.

113 Northup, *Twelve Years a Slave*, 10–11.

114 *The Black Book*, eds. Middleton A. Harris, Morris Levitt, Roger Furman and Ernest Smith, New York: Random House, 2009, 11.

115 Northup, *Twelve Years a Slave*, 10–11.

116 Northup, *Twelve Years a Slave*, 21–22.

117 Northup, *Twelve Years a Slave*, 31.

118 Cited in *The Black Book*, 78.

119 Northup, *Twelve Years a Slave*, 107.

120 Northup, *Twelve Years a Slave*, 108.

121 Northup, *Twelve Years a Slave*, 27.

122 Northup, *Twelve Years a Slave*, 23.

123 Northup, *Twelve Years a Slave*, 27.

124 Northup, *Twelve Years a Slave*, 25.

125 Northup, *Twelve Years a Slave*, 91.

126 This is not to suggest that the narrative ignores problems of interpellation or of strategic submission to overwhelming domination, as in its acknowledgement of certain individuals, "brought up in fear and ignorance as they are, it can scarcely be conceived how servilely they will cringe before a white man's look" (Northup, *Twelve Years a Slave*, 41).

127 Toni Morrison, *Beloved*, London: Vintage Books, 2007. All quotations are from this edition.

128 Morrison, *Beloved*, 25.
129 Morrison, *Beloved*, 181.
130 Morrison, *Beloved*, 181–182.
131 Morrison, *Beloved*, 182–183.
132 Morrison, *Beloved*, 184–185.
133 Morrison, *Beloved*, 185.
134 Morrison, *Beloved*, 183.
135 Morrison, *Beloved*, 190.
136 Morrison, *Beloved*, 192–193.
137 Morrison, *Beloved*, 79.
138 Morrison, *Beloved*, 193–195.
139 Morrison, *Beloved*, 175–176.
140 Morrison, *Beloved*, 176–177.
141 Morrison, *Beloved*, 177.
142 Morrison, *Beloved*, 3.
143 Morrison, *Beloved*, 6.
144 Morrison, *Beloved*, 11.
145 Morrison, *Beloved*, 7.
146 Morrison, *Beloved*, 7.
147 Morrison, *Beloved*, 3–4.
148 Morrison, *Beloved*, 51.
149 Morrison, *Beloved*, 86.
150 Morrison, *Beloved*, 86.
151 Morrison, *Beloved*, 43–44.
152 Morrison, *Beloved*, 91.
153 April Lidinsky, "Prophesying Bodies: Calling for a Politics of Collectivity in Toni Morrison's *Beloved*," in Carl Plasa and Betty J Ring, eds., *The Discourse of Slavery: Aphra Behn to Toni Morrison*, London, Routledge, 1994, 194.
154 Lidinsky, "Prophesying Bodies," 205.
155 Morrison, *Beloved*, 305.
156 Morrison, *Beloved*, 308–309.
157 Morrison, *Beloved*, 323.
158 Morrison, *Beloved*, 323–324.
159 Morrison, *Beloved*, 324.
160 Stanley Cohen, *States of Denial: Knowing about Atrocities and Suffering*, Cambridge: Polity Press, 2015, 1.
161 Cohen, *States of Denial*, 1.
162 Cohen, *States of Denial*, 295.
163 Cohen, *States of Denial*, 296.

PART III

LOOSENING THE FETTERS OF RACE

5

RACE AND EPISTEMOLOGIES
OF OTHERNESS

When confronted with the unknown, many societies tend to transfer observations of unfamiliar phenomena onto their mental map of what is already known. Just as twenty-first century's effort to search for extra-terrestrial life forms on other planets is based on the idea of "life as we know it," ideas of people of other races have historically been based on what is familiar, what is considered to be "known." Race as a category is entangled with empirical knowledge, misinformation, and ideology, all of which seek to justify and sustain particular beliefs. This chapter will explore how knowledge about otherness is socially constructed and justified in the areas of drama and literature. Knowledge of race results from taxonomical observations made for colonial, medical, bureaucratic, or other purposes such as political movements. This knowledge is often articulated in the form of inaccurate stereotypes deriving from perceived behavioral patterns, political shorthand that condenses biological features such as skin color and other bodily characteristics, racialized cultural artifacts such as hip-hop or chopsticks that are associated with particular groups or cultures, and check boxes on government forms that require information that encode racial characteristics.

Race is an inescapable part of social life but it takes on particular and disturbing meaning when it becomes absorbed into the hierarchical structures of institutional life as reflected by politics and bureaucratic procedures. In contemporary United States, it is common for governments and educational institutions to compile statistics of the number of members of specific races and ethnicities with the aim of formulating policies designed to increase cultural diversity. In addition to the U.S. Census, a decennial census mandated by the U.S. Constitution, on bureaucratic forms it is common to find a box labeled race or ethnicity that the citizen is expected to fill in. In contrast, while contemporary France has its unique racial problems and vocabulary, French bureaucratic forms are generally averse to categorizing citizens based on race. For historical reasons after World War II, the French government goes to great lengths to avoid identifying racial differences in order to deter racial profiling. Whether race as a category is customarily articulated, as is the case of the United States, or remains unarticulated, as is the case of contemporary France, latent and explicit forms of racism continue to exist,[1] and information gathered for an ostensibly laudable political purpose is sometimes used to exacerbate racial difference. Indeed, at times, racism can be obscured by superficial measures of "diversity" that are used to show that the institutions are free from racial discord, as Sara Ahmed suggests. She writes: "A stranger experience can be an experience of becoming noticeable, of not passing through or passing by, of being stopped or being held up."[2] One does not become a stranger until the moment of epistemological impasse. This is why understanding the production and circulation of what we might call epistemologies of race can be socially productive in laying bare opaque institutional processes and analyzing unexamined assumptions about otherness.

In this chapter we will consider narratives that reflect the impact of epistemologies of otherness upon our understanding of race. We shall begin by examining how race intersects with other social factors such as class, cultural citizenship, and gender. We draw on case studies of artists in exile or diaspora who interrogate their own identities, because exile brings racial tensions into stark relief. Exile highlights race in personal identities. We will then explore how narratives engaged with epistemologies of otherness inform works about exile and works produced in exile. We will consider how the recent emergence of whiteness changes notions of race. Lastly, it is important to take a step back and examine the process of knowledge production. We will explore select cases of intellectuals in diaspora and in exile, particularly those who are located within the Western metropolis, and whose work is at the same time marked by the experience of their multicultural backgrounds.

Signifying relationally: race and nation

As is often the case, without contact with or the threat from other groups, there is generally no perceived need for self-definition. Is one born black, or does one become black? European observers associated red with American Indians' skin color because of their war paint and because of the sun-screening substance they used to anoint themselves.[3] American Indians became red when the need for distinction between the European settlers and the natives arose. Meanwhile when the West encountered African culture in the sixteenth century, "the most arresting characteristic of the newly discovered African was his color. Travelers rarely failed to comment upon it."[4] In pre-modern China, peoples of many ethnicities and cultural origins became black in the Chinese consciousness. Increased cross-cultural contacts seemed to have only broadened the idea of blackness. Numerous peoples were given the label "black." Initially the Nam-Viet peoples and Malayans, China's Southeast Asian neighbors, were designated black in the Tang dynasty, but with China's increased encounters with slaves from Africa (modern-day Somalia, Kenya, Tanzania) from the seventh to the seventeenth centuries, the "blacks" in Chinese consciousness expanded to include peoples from various parts of the world, including Bengali peoples of the Indian subcontinent, who were deemed different from the local population.[5]

Likewise East Asians became "yellow" after the eighteenth century physician Johann Friedrich Blumenbach categorized them as such. The pseudo-scientific classification of human features during the enlightenment and epistemologies of race derived from them formed a mutually validating and energizing synergy. The system of knowledge that emerges from this combination is then put to political use. As Michael Keevak observes, "there was something dangerous, exotic, and threatening about East Asia that yellow ... helped to reinforce, [as the term is] symbiotically linked to the cultural memory of a series of invasions from that part of the world."[6] In many contemporary societies across the globe, skin color "as a biological concept," as K. Anthony Appiah notes, is shorthand for racial identification along with "a few visible features of the face and the head."[7] However, as we will show in this chapter, linguistically constructed epistemologies of race play an important role among strategies of racialization both for the purpose of solidarity, of binding groups together, and alienation or the exclusion of individuals or groups from the mechanisms of power.

Epistemologies of race signify relationally, which means a group that suffers from discrimination can themselves discriminate against other groups based on any combination of the factors of race, class, gender, religion, and politics. Take East Asia for example. While Taiwanese women are fighting for economic and social equality, at the same time they are known to mistreat their darker-skinned live-in Indonesian and Filipino maids. Pei-Chia Lan's ethnographic study, *Global Cinderellas: Migrant Domestics and Newly Rich Employers in Taiwan*, argues that "the integration of the global economy has simplified the gendered household burden for more privileged women by complicating the racial and class divisions of domestic labor on a global scale."[8]

Along similar lines, there is the phenomenon of what is sometimes called internal racism, or intra-group hatred as we examined in Chapter 4, where a community has internalized its former colonizer's outlook. In politically post-colonial but culturally colonial societies such as Singapore, where the state apparatus openly uses race as a category in its promotion of institutionalized multiculturalism, whites are typically placed above the local race in the social hierarchy while darker-skinned migrant workers are placed below.[9]

As fundamentally personal forms of self-expression, arts and literature are a fertile area to explore the expressions of racialized experience. During the early twentieth century, images of cultural others arising from exile or displacement were central to the brutalities of World War I and the decline of imperial power. The experience of exile and diaspora informed writers' and artists' responses to socially constructed cultural otherness. Who is an insider, and who is an outsider? To whom do these categories apply? For example, the modernist movement registered a predominantly conservative sense of the breakdown of traditional conceptualizations of order. The Irish poet W.B. Yeats who famously observed in his poem "The Second Coming" (1919) that "[t]hings fall apart; the centre cannot hold" lived most of his life in exile from his native Ireland.[10] The experience of living and writing outside his culture shaped Yeats' writing and worldview. The phrase "things fall apart," echoed in Nigerian novelist Chinua Achebe's novel *Things Fall Apart*, depicts the clash between Nigeria's white colonial government and the Igbo people, although Achebe's verbatim use of Yeats' line raises complex questions about the extent to which the novelist's experience has been absorbed into a colonizing culture.

Exile can take many different forms, ranging from forced movement across geopolitical borders in order to escape an oppressive government, to distancing oneself intellectually from undesirable ideologies or even self-exile. Beyond Yeats and Achebe, some other twentieth and twenty-first century writers and theatre directors who are exiles or descendants of diasporic parents include Bertold Brecht, Salman Rushdie, Eugenio Barba, Ariane Mnouchkine, Suzuki Tadashi, Ong Keng Sen, and French-Chinese Nobel laureate Gao Xingjian. While the project of Anglo-European modernity and modernism is often defined by the emergence and struggles of the individual against the society, Gao's works examine the moral agency of the collective by activating what he calls apolitical, personal voices that are placed in opposition to institutionalized national and racial identity. In this context he wishes to be seen as an individual rather than as a Chinese artist in more limiting ethnographic imaginations.[11]

The modernist belief in decaying values was paradoxically combined with an unexpected readiness to experiment with the aesthetic forms that might give expression to the apprehension of a disintegrating value system. T.S. Eliot, who was born in North America but who lived most of his life in London, registered the decline in traditional values after World War I in "The Waste Land" (1922), by way of experimental, fragmented language. The poem projects a persistent but obscure apprehension of loss when, for example, it asks:

What is that sound high in the air
Murmur of maternal lamentation

> Who are those hooded hordes swarming
> Over endless plains, stumbling in cracked earth
> Ringed by the flat horizon only
> What is the city over the mountains
> Cracks and reforms and bursts in the violet air
> Falling towers
> Jerusalem Athens Alexandria
> Vienna London
> Unreal[12]

Eliot's citation in his notes to these lines indicate that the earth over which sinister undecipherable "hooded hordes" swarm alludes to the Swiss writer Hermann Hesse's (1877–1962) sense of the decay of Eastern Europe.[13] The allusion is however mingled with images of spiritual loss suggested in phrases such as "maternal lamentation," or the dryness of the "cracked earth," or the featurelessness of the "flat horizon." Such phrases resonate with the loss of the Son in the narrative of the Crucifixion of Christ even as they point to a spiritual dryness that can only long for, but is unable to realize in the poem's present, its original religious signification. Thus the "violet air" that should be indicative of spiritual wholeness, "cracks" even as it "reforms" and then "bursts." Such intimations of a wholeness that is glimpsed but simultaneously lost emerges again in Eliot's lines, which present a disjunctive collocation of cities important to European notions of civilization. The past "real"-ness of the social, historical, and spiritual city glimpsed within the word "unreal" is threatened by the coexistent and barbarous condition of unrealizabilty, in which the negative and the positive are suggested within the same word.

During the modernist period, many other so-called English writers had non-English origins or followed in their life experiences non-English trajectories. Like Yeats, the Irish-born writer James Joyce (1882–1941) lived most of his life in self-imposed exile, in Joyce's case, in Europe. The Polish-born writer Joseph Conrad (1857–1924) took British citizenship out of necessity. As we noted above, T.S. Eliot can be considered a displaced North American electing to live most of his life in London. Ford Maddox Ford (1873–1939), who experimented with the use of unreliable narratives in *The Good Soldier* (1915) and who collaborated with Joseph

Conrad in the writing of three other novels, was born in England. His father was German and his mother English. But he spent much of his life abroad, in the company of émigré writers during the modernist period in Paris, later teaching in Michigan and finally living in France where he died. The writer D.H. Lawrence (1885–1930) whose father and mother both came from the mining town of Eastwood in Nottinghamshire, traveled widely, but was very critical in his writings of the English world he grew up in, a world which T.S. Eliot, who also engaged in travel writing, reviled in *After Strange Gods*. After 1922, and largely as a result of the hostility his work met with in Britain, Lawrence spent most of his life in self-imposed exile including Australia and New Mexico. Travel narrative involves the fragmentation of shared values and foregrounds the subjective encounter with difference. A more sympathetic view of unconscious bias against racial others or "unintended racism" might be Eliot's own theory that all knowledge is simply "a matter of degree," because "you cannot put your finger upon even the simplest datum and say 'this we know'."[14]

The imagined superiority of the national category of English, which was used during the modernist period to describe such writers, who were actually in one way or another displaced from their countries of birth, implicitly devalued in their lived experience of ethnic and racial malleability and diversity. As Brian Niro observes, "in modernism, the exoticism of difference ... internalized with a desire for a 'new' method of expression ... brings the exiled, the colonial, the displaced, and the other into the discursive fold."[15] Despite their incorporation into English culture, otherness remained apparent from the evidence of their life experiences, and in their writings.

Narratives of otherness also characterized the movement known as Négritude during the twentieth century. During the 1930s the North American writers Langston Hughes (1902–1967) and Richard Wright (1908–1960) described to several Francophone African writers gathered in Paris the significance in the 1920s of the cultural, social, and artistic explosion in which they had been involved known as the Harlem Renaissance. This movement advocated a revised cultural assessment of blackness. In so doing African-Americans proposed racial difference as the starting point for a new cultural, rather than biological, understanding of black consciousness.

Taking its inspiration from the Harlem Renaissance, Négritude also considered blackness as a given. The African writers Aimé Césaire (1913–2008) from Martinique, Léopold Senghor (1906–2001) from Senegal, and Léon Damas (1912–1978) from French Guiana together proposed renditions of their identities that were based on their own racial humanity that existed independently of colonialism's demonizations of them.

In this way these writers, poets, social activists, and intellectuals hoped to counter the Western world's negative cultural constructions of their blackness, by means of their own equally cultural, but positive conceptions of, African consciousness and philosophy. Césaire noted

> we thought that Africa was not some sort of black page [but that] our Negro heritage was worthy of respect and that this heritage was not relegated to the past [so that] its values ... could still make important contributions to the world.[16]

Later the French philosopher, activist, and novelist Jean Paul Sartre (1905–1980) argued provocatively that the movement exemplified an "anti-racist racism."[17]

This "anti-racist racism" can lead to nationalist sentiments. Perhaps not surprisingly, in early twentieth century China, sociopolitical reformers took a similar approach to the self-definition of the Chinese race. According to Frank Dikötter, nationalism articulated as racial cohesion and the discourse of race as nation was seen as a key to the country's survival.[18] Radical magazines between 1903 and 1915 often hailed the Yellow Emperor (Huangdi, reign 2697–2597 BC), a mythical figure, as the point of origin of the Han race, the dominant ethnic group in mainland China. Sun Yat-sen (1866–1925), leader of the Republican revolution in 1911, resorted to biological purity to define the Han group in opposition to other ethnic groups within China and the result is an argument for racial nationalism:

> The Chinese race totals four hundred million people; of mingled races there are only a few million Mongolians a million or so Manchus, a few million Tibetans ... These alien races do not number altogether more than ten million, so

> that, for the most part, the Chinese people are of the Han ...
> race with common blood, common language, common reli-
> gion, and common customs—a single, pure race.[19]

In contrast, though also similar in some aspects, to the Négritude
movement, Sun and his fellow reformers focused on the Han in their
construction of a territorially and biologically predetermined Chinese
race. Sun's theory echoes the Romanticist idea of *Volksgeist* (national
spirit) proposed by Johann Gottfried Herder (1744–1803), who has
commonly been regarded as the originator of modern nationalism and
the first person to articulate elements of *Volksgeist* in a coherent
manner, which we examined in Chapter 3.

Other instances of lived, embodied experiences of one's own and
others' races use metaphors of illness to describe an entire people,
because "the body [is seen as] a model for political community" in
the metonymic frame of understanding race.[20] In 1895, after China's
defeat in the first Sino-Japanese War (1894–1895), both Kaiser
Wilhelm II of Germany and the Chinese scholar Yan Fu used the
phrase yellow peril and the metaphor of a "sick man" (*die gelbe
Gefahr* and *bingfu*) to describe East Asian and particularly Chinese
people. In 1898, the concept became the title of British novelist M.P.
Shiel's short story *Yellow Danger*.[21] Resistance of this metaphor of an
ill race took center stage in an anonymous poem in Chinese that was
very widely circulated over the Internet in the months leading up to
the 2008 Beijing Olympics. Entitled "To the West," the poem self-
consciously comments on the contradiction behind the image of a
threatening sick man: "When we were called the Sick Man of Asia,
we were also called the yellow peril. Now when we are billed as the
next superpower, we are called a threat."[22] The biopolitics and the
colonial history of the metaphor continue to inform modern day
encounters between Asian and Western epistemologies of race.

Signifying relationally: race and gender

Race and gender are interconnected categories. Similar to other categories of identity, racial difference is often imagined as an inversion
of what are perceived to be gender norms. Ania Loomba points out
that "patriarchal domination ... provided a model for establishing

racial hierarchies and colonial domination," as evidenced in a number of once prevalent beliefs, such as the ideas that Jewish men menstruate, Egyptian women urinate standing up, and Muslim men engage in sodomy.[23] In terms of the "yellow peril," which we discussed earlier, the concept has intersected in twentieth century United States with gender stereotypes: yellow fever. For example, punning on the disease of the same name, David Henry Hwang uses yellow fever in his play *M. Butterfly* (1988) to describe white men with a sexual fetish for East Asian women who are imagined to be subservient, dainty, and more feminine than their Western counterparts. In contemporary American media and popular discourse on dating, the term is used to identify and sometimes to critique the social phenomenon of white men exclusively preferring East Asian women. This Orientalist tendency is captured in Debbie Lum's 2012 documentary film, *Seeking Asian Female*, in which the director interviews white men who exhibit "yellow fever" in San Francisco.[24] The fetish makes Asian women interchangeable. East Asian women are seen as erotic because they are perceived to be exotic in physique and manners. The interviewees pointed to East Asian women's facial features: "it's the long black hair that is really eye catching." They also mentioned their love interests' perceived submissive personalities: "they are kind of subtle and kind of quiet," as reasons for their dating preference. In Lily Wong's study of the role that Asian women are compelled to perform in this context, she argues that racial and sexual discourses repurpose and recode Asian-ness "from legacies of colonial discourse" to govern and consume the Asian female body.[25]

Not all critics believe that sexualized depictions of Asian-American women in popular culture can only be understood in a negative light. In *The Hypersexuality of Race*, Celine Parreñas Shimizu makes a case for a more nuanced approach to understanding the self-performance and public perception of sexuality. In an attempt to move beyond denunciations of sexualized representations as necessarily demeaning, Shimizu believes that the female "productive perversity" allows women of color to lay claim to their own sexuality and desires as performers and spectators.[26] The political and emotional landscapes of race and gender have changed dramatically since Shimizu's 2007 book. In the wake of the vote for Brexit in the UK, a referendum for Britain to withdraw from the European Union, and the U.S.

presidential election in 2016 there have emerged prominent groups known as white nationalists.

The racialized myth about Asian women provides a partial explanation of the baffling phenomenon of white supremacists in the U.S. exclusively dating Asian women. This phenomenon has only recently begun to attract journalistic attention. While proclaiming publicly that the United States is a "white country designed for [the whites] and [their] posterity," Richard B. Spencer has dated a series of Asian-American women.[27] Spencer told the award-winning progressive magazine *Mother Jones* (founded in 1976) during a 2016 interview that "there is something about the Asian girls. They are cute. They are smart. They have a kind of thing going on."[28] Likewise, Mike Cernovich, John Derbyshire, and Kyle Chapman are all married to Asian women or have a partner who is an Asian woman. A January 6, 2018, op-ed in the *New York Times* by Audrea Lim is one of the latest attempts to explain the "confusing mix" of "the white supremacists on the far right's yellow fever." They seem to fetishize Asian women. The exceptionalism that white nationalists have granted to Asian-Americans falls neatly along a gendered fault line. While Asian-Americans are often seen as the hard-working model minority who assimilate well into North American society, it is specifically, and only, Asian women who the white nationalists embrace. On the one hand, the mainstream society has the prerogative to determine who is sufficiently well behaved to deserve acceptance, hence the label of "model minority." On the other hand, a form of racially inflected misogyny informs the alt-right's imagination of Asian women as subservient and hypersexual individuals who are "naturally inclined to serve men."[29] This perceived quality sets Asian women apart from white women.

There is a long legal and institutional history behind the phenomenon of yellow fever and the idea of yellow peril. The United States's often self-contradictory, love–hate relationship with female Asian immigrants can be traced back to the era of the Chinese Exclusion Act, which was in force from 1882 to 1943, a time when whiteness became the dominant racial norm in the United States. It was also a time when, as Frank Dikköter observes, the country's "Anglo-Saxon foundation coalesced with other 'assimilable' European immigrant ethnicities."[30] Lily Wong has argued that the legalization of discrimination effectively marked Chinese workers "unfree and feminized laborers who undermine white workingmen's ownership of their 'free' labor." Chinese immigrants were both the desirable other in service of the United States and a codified threat.[31] Female Chinese immigrants were assumed to be sex workers unless proven otherwise under the Page Act (1875) which was enacted under the guise of anti-trafficking laws. Similar restrictions were imposed on Indian women in British colonial Caribbean.[32] At work here are both the "yellow peril" discourse and an imperial civilizing rescue mission. Before 1922, if a female U.S. citizen married a foreign man, she would assume the citizenship of her husband and lose her U.S. citizenship. The Cable Act of 1922 partially amended the situation by allowing married women to retain their U.S. citizenship if their husbands were "aliens eligible to naturalization." Asians were not eligible for U.S. citizenship, and American women who married Asian men would not be protected by the Cable Act.

The intersectionality of race, gender, and nation is articulated in the context of colonial India by E.M. Forster in his novel *A Passage to India*. Drawing on the author's own trips to colonial India in 1912 and 1921, the novel offers both a critique and inadvertent affirmation of racial stereotypes of both Indians and the British colonizers.[33] Even as Forster attempts to unravel the stereotypes of the "Orientals," his novel is marked by broad generalizations about British and Indian sexuality and by its implicit acceptance of an Anglo-European epistemology of race. For example, in some instances the narrator seems to agree with the stereotypes of the "Orientals" circulating among the colonizers. The narrator suggests, for example, that the local doctor, Dr. Aziz, is in touch with his own sexuality despite the pressures imposed upon him by the colonial "European" social order:

> His mind here was hard and direct, though not brutal. He had learnt all he needed concerning his own constitution many years ago, thanks to the social order into which he had been born, and when he came to study medicine, he was repelled by the pedantry and fuss with which Europe tabulates the facts of sex.[34]

From early on, the novel makes numerous connections between race and gender, showing how they signify relationally. The intertwining signifiers of race and gender create a complex landscape of self-identification and social hierarchy. For example, Mrs. Turton tells the more open-minded Adela that she should regard herself as superior to the Indians: "You're superior to them, anyway. Don't forget that. You're superior to everyone in India except one or two of the Ranis, and they're on an equality [*sic*]."[35]

Meanwhile, from the Indian perspective, the colonizers display a new attitude of entitlement upon arriving in India. In Hamidullah's brutally honest words: "They all become exactly the same, not worse, not better. I give any Englishman two years, be he Turton or Burton. It is only the difference of a letter. And I give any Englishwoman six months."[36] Hamidullah receives more dignified treatment when he visits England as a guest. In India, however, the English administrators and their wives tend to be more hostile towards the local populace, and the Englishwomen, whose interactions with locals are mostly in the domestic setting in the novel, are even more class conscious, treating Indians as servants.

Here imperialism and sexuality intersect to form a space where identities are reexamined and could be reformulated.[37] The friendship between Dr. Aziz, the Muslim Indian surgeon, and Cyril Fielding, a British Principal at the Government College, is subjected to stress on several occasions. Fielding believes in Aziz's innocence during the trial of his alleged rape of Adela. Later, after Adela changes her testimony, Fielding is the only one to take her in as she faces a backlash against her actions. Consequently, Fielding's friendship with Aziz suffers as a result. Clearly in Forster's novel, the concepts of race and nation operate on a delicate and nuanced scale.

One of the most challenging and controversial events in the narrative is Adela Quested's false accusation, and subsequent retraction of the allegation, of Aziz's attempted rape of her in the Marabar Caves. In a conversation with Fielding, Aziz expresses in direct terms his frustration with English stereotypes of Indian men, and their consequences:

"We will rob every man and rape every woman from Peshawar to Calcutta," I suppose, which you get some nobody to repeat and then quote every week in the *Pioneer* in order to frighten us into retaining you! We know![38]

In this way, the trial of Aziz is not about admissible evidence but rather about solidified, ideologically over-determined epistemologies of race. The popular racial discourse of the time demands that Aziz be classified as a rapist, and positions Adela as an emblem of white feminine victims under Indian threat. The trial sets in opposition rapacious Indian masculinity at odds with fragile white womanhood. Yonatan Touval speculates that the

> imperial misogyny fuels this fantastical chain from the start with sincere wishes that Adela had been raped—or how else to read the aftermath of a trial in which everyone's greatest irritation seems to lie less in the fact that Aziz is vindicated than that Adela wasn't raped after all?[39]

As such, the trial espouses journalistic racism and racially inflected sexism directed at both Aziz and Adela. Aziz is framed as the ultimate other who preys upon innocent white women, while the case affirms that Adela is nothing more than a weak female prone to hysterical illusion. The novel makes clear that Adela is vexed because "she was both in India and engaged to be married, which double event should have made every instant sublime" in her pursuit of the understanding of the exotic and of an ideal life with her future husband.[40] She and Mrs. Moore, of course, never come to understand India, and they never achieve their dream of building an ideal family, either. Adela's allegation of rape may be her hallucination that emerges as she pursues the sublime. She is on the lookout for some sort of sublime experience to make up for her bland engagement. The immateriality of Adela's account of what happens in the cave fuels and authenticates the court's verdict:

> I went into the detestable cave. ... There was this shadow, or sort of shadow, down the entrance tunnel, bottling me up. It seemed like an age, but I suppose the whole thing can't have lasted thirty seconds really. I hit at him with the glasses, he pulled me round the cave by the strap, I escaped, that's all.[41]

Before Adela walks in to explore the caves she laments that "Not to love the man one's going to marry! Not to find it out till this moment!

Not even to have asked oneself the question until now!"[42] Critics have linked Adela's indeterminacy and frustration in her romantic relationship to her fantasizing of an attack while in the caves because we first learn of the accusation only when Aziz is arrested. All that is revealed is that Mrs. Moore becomes ill in the first cave, and Adela and Aziz carry on exploring deeper caves with their guide. At one point Adela asks Aziz if he has more than one wife, a suggestion that the doctor thought was appalling and hideous. There are reasons to believe that Adela, as an Englishwoman, has a particular set of preconceptions about Indian men.

Historically, scholars have debated whether the rape actually does take place in the novel, and why Adela later retracts her accusation. June Perry Levine argues that the assault is entirely imagined, because Adela's breakdown is a result of her confusing mental turmoil with physical assault.[43] Brenda Silver, on the other hand, suggests that while in the cave Adela realizes in terror what it means to be "rapable": "Before the caves, Adela had defined herself, as Fielding does, through her intelligence. After the caves, having been absorbed by the male discourse that surrounds rape, she herself disappears."[44] In connection with readings of the veracity and impact of Adela's claim, Forster criticism has devoted substantial energy to interpreting the metaphorical significance of the caves as the location of the alleged rape. Frances L. Restuccia notes that the Marabar Caves are "female morphologically." She also notes that the caves are also configured to be female linguistically.[45] Yonatan Touval believes that the caves are a queer space that thrives on indeterminacy, which parallels the ambiguity in Adela's account. The indeterminacy itself constitutes the possibility of the attempted rape.[46] Building upon her reading of the caves, Restuccia suggests that the "Eastern indeterminacy ... keeps alive the theoretical possibility of an attempted rape whose vagueness precludes the act from being prosecutable."[47]

It is useful to consider Forster's drafts of this particular episode in the novel. His manuscript describes Adela's assault in the Marabar Caves in greater detail than the final published account, and from the narrator's point of view:

> She struck out and he got hold of her other hand and forced her against the wall, he got both her hands in one of his, and

> then felt at her breasts. ... The strap of her field glasses
> tugged suddenly, was drawn across her neck, she was to be
> throttled as far as necessary and then ... silent, though the
> echo still raged up and down, she waited and when the
> breath was on her wrenched her hand free, got hold of her
> glasses and pushed them into her assailant's mouth.[48]

It is notable that the published version of Forster's novel erases these
details of physical violation and offers only Adela's ambiguous words
that could be read as her hallucination in the caves. Thus, Aziz's
alleged attempted rape of Adela is symbolic in the published version.
The racially inflected hostility between Indian men and white women
reaches a climax when Adela goes public with her accusation. In the
published version, Adela's accusation is a self-fulfilling prophecy
about Indian masculinity. The English characters support Adela
during the trial not because the violation is or can be substantiated,
but because they are invested in the veracity of the idea that an Indian
man would rape a white woman.

Reading the contrast between Forster's draft and the published
version of this event in the light of the post-Kavanaugh, post-#MeToo
movement era gives us pause for thought. The new cultural context
compels us to examine more closely the weight given to the presumably masculine narrator's voice in the draft and readers' and characters'
suspicion of Adela's own statement in the final version of the novel.
The phrase "me too" was first proposed by Tarana Burke. Following
the revelation of sexual misconduct allegations against American film
producer Harvey Weinstein, actress Alyssa Milano popularized the
phrase in October 2017 to encourage women to tweet their own experiences of sexual assault in order to "give people a sense of the magni-
tude of the problem."[49] The core message is to turn the tables and have
the court of public opinion, and by extension the legal system, trust
women when they come forward with accusations of sexual assault.
The clarity in the description of Adela's assault in Forster's draft is
informed by a colonial rescue narrative that echoes the long literary tradition of pitching men of color against white womanhood. In contrast,
Forster's published version amplifies the indeterminacy of Adela's
experience and invites questions about the validity of her account. Aziz
emerges as the victim when Adela retracts her accusation and it appears

that in the novel Forster is attempting to avoid a sexual critique of imperial racial discourses while struggling to engage with an intertwined racial and gender identity politics. More importantly, it is likely that Forster and his narrator do not wish to look at their own society's colonial practice, instead preferring to locate the origin of patriarchal domination in India, in a world elsewhere, beyond England. Time and again *A Passage to India* points to Indian colonization of women, or claims that the feeble mind of the Indian is the problem to be remedied by a Western civilizing mission. The same pattern of evasion can be observed in Western anthropology as a field of academic study, where scholars neglect the inequality at home "out of a more or less conscious fear of having to take into consideration ... the society of the colonial power to which they themselves belong."[50]

In the novel, male friendship between the colonizer and the colonized seems to be complicated, if not threatened, by English women, such as Adela and her chaperone Mrs. Moore. The English bureaucrats in India are torn between alliance with their wives and befriending Indian men. Through his friendship with Aziz, Fielding becomes a traitor to the British empire, while Mr. McBryde, the District Superintendent of Police, believes that Aziz did sexually assault Adela, even though she merely implies that such an attack took place. McBryde's attitude is evidenced by his clearly orientalist remark that: "The darker races are physically attracted by the fairer, but not vice versa—not a matter for bitterness, not a matter for abuse, but just a fact which any scientific observer would confirm."[51]

There is a long history of cultural anxiety concerning the threat from hypersexualized racial others to white women who are in need of protection throughout Anglo-American drama and literature from *Othello* to contemporary romance. The language of predetermined criminality permeates *A Passage to India* and other texts in the literary tradition of depicting non-white masculinity as threatening and the defense of white womanhood as the West's collective responsibility. In her study of inter-racial sexual relationships in Anglo-American literature, Celia R. Daileader argues that from the Renaissance onward,

> the masculinist racist hegemony used myths about black male sexual rapacity and the danger of racial "pollution" ... to

> exorcise its own collective psychological demons: the slave-master's sexual guilt, and his fear of the products—filial and social—of the inter-racial trysts.[52]

All of these cases show again and again that the Western epistemology of race is predicated upon a gendered presence of otherness, and the cultural anxiety that this produces.

Double consciousness

This duality of racialized existence between two communities has been articulated by various critics, most notably by W.E.B. Du Bois. In 1897, Du Bois used the term "double consciousness," or a double life, to describe the black experience in the United States a "peculiar sensation ... of always looking at one's self through the eyes of others, of measuring one's soul by the tape of a world that looks on in amused contempt and pity." He speaks of the black community's two irreconcilable strivings and compares the "history of the American Negro" to a history of the struggle between "two souls, two thoughts, two warring ideals in one dark body ... [as one attempts to be] both a Negro and an American without being cursed and spit upon by his fellows."[53] The repression of black identity in the United States has made it difficult for African-Americans to unify their black and American identities.[54]

How do white Americans react to the black community's double consciousness? Whiteness as a racial category emerged in public consciousness and journalistic discourse after white supremacist Dylann Roof murdered several African-Americans in one of the United States's oldest black churches in Charleston, South Carolina, in a mass shooting in June, 2015. A series of violent clashes occurred at a white-nationalist rally in Charlottesville, Virginia, in August, 2017, which initiated more public discourse about whiteness and race. As one of the usually unmarked identities, whiteness has not been regarded as being in need of analysis or definition simply because it is the default mode of existence. In his study of the agency of black workers during the Civil War and Reconstruction Era in late nineteenth century United States, Du Bois argued that the black emancipation movement clashed particularly with whites who were poor. Du

Bois suggested that the white working class was progressively manipulated into racism.[55] David Roediger pinpoints the Reconstruction as the time when the white working class "comes to think of itself and its interests as white."[56] While blackness is a burden for African-American laborers, whiteness provides, in Du Bois's words, "a public and psychological wage" to compensate for the low wage for white workers. This package and its benefits come in many forms. For example, the workers "were admitted, with all classes of white people, to public functions and public parks." Historically, their votes "selected public officials." This is an example of how race is often privileged above other factors of self-identification such as class. The white working class distinguishes itself from the non-whites in the same class, but while its votes do not necessarily improve the personal economic situation, "it had great effect upon their personal treatment."[57] In the twenty-first century, even as the white working class is repeatedly betrayed by politicians, they are manipulated into deriving a sense of superiority and psychological satisfaction by placing their whiteness above their own socioeconomic inequality. This cultural "schizophrenia" is captured by U.S. President and Southern politician Lyndon Baines Johnson. He told journalist Bill Moyers in 1960 upon seeing some racial epithets in Tennessee that "if you can convince the lowest white man he's better than the best colored man, he won't notice you're picking his pocket. Hell, give him somebody to look down on, and he'll empty his pockets for you."[58] So powerful is race as a category of self-identification that it supersedes socioeconomic forces of socialization.

The double-consciousness of the black community is sometimes captured in code switching and choices between the colonizer's language and the native tongue. This can be seen in the dilemma that has been vividly articulated by Chinua Achebe. While Achebe concedes that he must write in English due to the history of colonialism, he laments "the fatalistic logic of the unassailable position of English in our literature."[59] If early modern geo-humoral theory defines a person's race by their "native habitat" and its climate, the modern era defines a person's identity by their languages and accents. For people in the diaspora, in exile, and in minority communities, language is both a unifying force and an unbearable burden as they oscillate between the imperialist tradition and a resistance tradition.[60] Asian accents are depicted as interchangeable and can be consolidated into one unifying identity, as in the film *Falling Down* (dir. Joel Schumacher, 1993). The white-collar worker William "D-Fens" Foster lashes out at a Korean shopkeeper:

D-Fens: You give me seventy "fie" cents back for the phone. What is a fie? There is a "V" in the word. Fie-vuh. Don't they have "v"s in China?

Shopkeeper: Not Chinese. I am Korean.

D-Fens: Whatever. What differences does that make? You come over here and take my money and you don't even have the grace to learn to speak my language.

Accents, particularly those that distort the predominant language in a community, are intimately connected to racial thinking, and identities become collapsible. As this scene shows, the burden of communication is typically placed on the non-native speaking diasporic subject who exists between two accents and two cultural realms. The protagonist has been unemployed, and his family has disintegrated. His life story is a snapshot of the breakdown of society. The final shoot-out on the pier enacts a perverse fantasy of the American dream, the kind of death-wish that is there at the end of Willy Loman's life in *Death of a Salesman*. As Kenyan writer Ngũgĩ wa Thiong'o opines, "language has always been at the heart of the two contending social forces in the Africa of the twentieth century," namely using the colonizer's language as a vehicle to reach a global audience and privileging the local language as a tool of resistance, such as Gikuyu and Kiswahili, in the case of Ngũgĩ after 1977.[61] It is with this in mind that Ngũgĩ gave up writing in English.

These writers' anxieties about the uses of language can be traced back to the Classical era. Skin color may be privileged as the primary signifier in the modern understanding of the racialized body, but language and accent have always been important denominators in the formation of political solidarity and fictions of racial differences. Ian Smith's research shows that the Greek and Roman empires defined aliens "not because of their color but as a result of their language difference or errors."[62] Indeed as Anthony Pagden summarizes, in the eyes of Hellenistic Greeks, a barbarian, or *barbaros* in Greek was, "before he was anything else," someone "who was a babbler, one who spoke not Greek but only barbar."[63] In early modern England, language supersedes color as the primary factor used to distinguish race. For example, Rosalind remarks in *As You Like It* that the affective power of language outweighed physical appearance "such Ethiop words, blacker in their effect/Than in their countenance" (4.3.).[64] The characters mock the Ethiop's language, believing that the effect of linguistic transgression is "blacker" than their complexion. Language here is taken to be an important marker of racial difference. Portia in *The Merchant of Venice* tells her waiting woman Nerissa that one of her suitors, Falconbridge, the baron of England, is "a dumb show" with whom she cannot converse. Falconbridge "hath neither Latin, French, nor Italian." Portia unabashedly admits that she has "a poor pennyworth in the English" (1.2.65–1.2.69), but places the blame of non-communication on her suitor. Patricia Akhimie points out there is a "system of social differentiation that … intermingles [the] two categories [of] class [and] race." As Portia's bias attests, "systems of social differentiation are cultural specific rather than universal."[65]

Race and hospitality

The examples above demonstrate a long history of institutionalized racialization of strangers, strangers considered necessary as political and cultural supports, or those who seek shelter or hospitality. The relationship between race and hospitality has been taken up by French philosopher Jacques Derrida in the following question: "Isn't the question of the foreigner [*l'étranger*] a foreigner's question?" he asks. It is a question that is a challenge from "the foreigner, from abroad [*l'étranger*]." In their book *Of Hospitality*, Derrida's co-writer, Anne Douformantelle argues that "the question of the foreigner is a question asked [about] the foreigner, the one who brings [my] identity into question."[66] For Derrida, the mere presence of the other puts into question our own identity, and since genuine hospitality operates as a gift whose very nature is that it is only possible on condition of the impossibility of reciprocity. The idea of hospitality and accommodation in the context of race theory refers to a sense of belonging, a mode of belonging that enables "cultural, linguistic, or historical participation" in a community, as Derrida writes in *Monolingualism of the Other*.[67] While one's native language, like one's skin color, has often been assumed to be one's inborn features and even birth right, Derrida demonstrates that linguistic purity, and by extension racial purity, is a fiction, for "every culture institutes itself through the unilateral imposition of some politics of language." We master our native language, or any language and culture, "through the power of naming, of imposing and legitimating appellations."[68] Here Derrida registers the challenge of the intersection of the discourses of race, prescriptive markings, and the concept of hospitality. Drawing on his own experience as a Maghreb-Algerian and a naturalized citizen of France, Derrida reminisces that "never was I able to call French 'my mother tongue.'" While French is supposed to be his "maternal" language, its "source, norms, rules and law were situated elsewhere."[69]

In the context of asking for hospitality and for accommodation from their newly found local communities, diasporic and intercultural subjects face a dilemma, because they are caught between pursuing authenticity and "selling out." A recent example of the Royal Shakespeare Company's (RSC) English-language productions of two plays, one Chinese and the other Shakespearean, have reignited debates about cultural authenticity. The first is Gregory Doran's adaptation of *Orphan of Zhao* with an almost exclusively white cast of 17. British actors of East Asian heritage have spoken out against the practice of what Doran calls "non-culturally specific casting," or colorblind casting.[70] The politics of recognition can be a double-edged sword. One the one hand, intercultural theatre is an important testing ground for ethnic equality and raises equal employment opportunity questions in the UK. On the other hand, we might pose the following question: can an all-white cast not do justice to the *Orphan of Zhao* just as a performance of *Richard III* by an all-Chinese cast performed at the London Globe and in Beijing cannot? We may go on to ask: why would an English adaptation of a Chinese play have to be performed by authentic-looking East Asian actors?[71]

Another production that poses relevant questions is Iqbal Khan's *Much Ado About Nothing* that was set in contemporary Delhi and staged at the Courtyard Theatre in Stratford-upon-Avon in August, 2012. In her essay in the RSC program, Jyotsna Singh reminds the audience that "the romantic, sexual and emotional configurations underpinning the centrality of marriage in Shakespeare's romantic comedies" are elements that "richly resonate within the Indian social and cultural milieu."[72] Clare Brennan, writing for the *Guardian*, believed that the transposition of Messina to contemporary Delhi worked well, because it "plays to possible audience preconceptions about the communality and hierarchical structuring of life in India that map effectively onto similar structuring in Elizabethan England."[73] Performed by a cast of second generation British Indian actors to Bollywood-inspired music as part of the World Shakespeare Festival (WSF), the "postcolonial" production (in Gitanjali Shabani's words)[74] was quickly compared by the press and reviewers to the two more "ethnically authentic" productions at the Globe from the Indian Subcontinent (Arpana Company's *All's Well That Ends Well* directed by Sunil Shanbag in Gujarati, and Company Theatre's *Twelfth Night* directed by Atul Kumar in Hindi). Cultural, linguistic, and ethnic pedigrees are part of the picture,[75] but some critics questioned the RSC's type of internationalism. Birmingham-born director Khan's treatment of Indian culture was regarded as too simplistic in that it occluded historical differences, and modern cultural complexities of hybrid Anglo-Indian identity.

It should be pointed out that Khan resisted the perception that his production offered "any kind of *Best Exotic Marigold* Indian Shakespeare experience." RSC artistic director Michael Boyd suggested to Khan that one possible concept for the production might be an adaptation in "an Indian setting" since it was to be part of the WSF. It was clear, however, that the possible direction of adaptation was never to be a "condition of employment" of Khan who wrote that "all my experiences of Shakespeare as a practitioner before *Much Ado* had little to do with being Asian."[76] There was, nonetheless, clearly a gap between the production's intention and its reception by the general public and media.

Kate Rumbold wished that the production had "ironized the company's inevitable second-generation detachment from India."[77] Moreover, taking issue with the production's "pastiche of 'internationalism', with apparently second generation British actors pretending to return to their cultural roots in a decidedly colonial way," Kevin Quarmby thought that the production offered "the veneer of Indian culture, served on a bed of Bradford or Birmingham Anglicized rice." He concluded that "as the World Shakespeare Festival and Globe to Globe seasons have shown, 'international' is best understood in the context of the nations who embrace Shakespeare as their own."[78] The more difficult part of these debates concerns commercialized cultural and ethnic identities. Obviously art and commerce are not antithetical activities, but they have become inescapable predicates in the debates about the sociological and expressive values of touring and intercultural Shakespeare performances.

Identities in exile

Some artists in the diaspora or in exile deliberately maintain an ideological and psychological distance from their homeland. Born in Jiangxi province in China in 1940, Gao Xingjian is a prolific playwright, director, poet, novelist, and painter based in France, and who writes in French and Chinese. He fled from China to Paris through Germany in 1987. He had enjoyed a successful career in mainland Chinese theatre before his exile. In France, he was honored with the title Chevalier d'Ordre des Arts et des Lettres in 1992. He was awarded the Nobel Prize for Literature in 2000. Despite Gao's statements in interviews and in his theoretical writings that he does not seek to embody an authentic voice of the Chinese diaspora or China per se, the award of the Nobel Prize has initiated heated debates about his identity politics.[79]

His post-1987 theatre works challenge national and nationalist paradigms. He coined the term "cold literature" (*leng de wenxue*) to describe his philosophy, which he defines as "a literature that regains its original nature," that is, a literature that differs from "the literature of moral teaching, of political criticism, of social engagement." He defines literature as "a personal affair."[80] Gao's stance can be traced back to his time in China when he believes that he was prevented from using theatre as a medium to search for alternative voices that have been alienated in the process of Chinese modernization.

Although Gao feared political attacks and prosecution in China, once he was in France, he found it difficult to deal with the excessive amount of freedom that he now had. A different type of pressure emerged; seeing how fellow Asian diasporic artists catered to the European appetite for traditional Chinese cultural relics (especially the Chinese opera, *feng shui*, *qi gong*, and *kung fu*) that had become the hallmark of "Chinese-ness," Gao asked: "Can a Chinese intellectual living abroad preserve his spiritual independence without embracing a nationalist doctrine, or seeking solace in traditional Chinese culture?" He observed that the Chinese diasporic artists often sell Chinese "antiques" that fuel and reinforce essentialized views of cultural difference. He criticized the opportunist tendency, writing that "an artist ... does not need to sponge a living off [his] ancestors ... He should not sell himself as a local product or handicraft."[81] In short, Gao has refused to become a native informant.[82] He believes that "the most important thing for a writer is to keep aloof above himself, that is, not selling the inheritance passed down from his ancestors."[83] He champions the dearly bought opportunity to "record one's personal voice through arts and literature." He believes pursuing this new path could counter what he recognizes in the history of modern and contemporary Chinese literature as nationalistic obsession. Gao posits that literature provides the "fragile individual or writer" with the opportunity to find his own voice.[84] This leads to a much larger question that is beyond the scope of this book: to what extent is the "individualism" that Gao has encountered in Europe part of an alternative ideology that now leads him to recognize a "double" identity, that leaves him open to the pressures of hybridity, or the simultaneous inhabitation of the values of two cultures?

Nevertheless, what Gao relinquishes is a nostalgia for an "imaginary" China that is common not only among the early twentieth century reformers, but also among his fellow Chinese diasporic artists. His theory of "cold literature" is defined by its resistance to being "strangled by society in its quest for spiritual salvation." Or, to put the matter a little differently, because of its independent non-utilitarian nature, cold literature has to flee "in order to survive."[85] His emphasis on artistic individuality and personal voice rather than collective cultural identity is most evident in his 1993 essay on nationalist myth:

> Chinese intellectuals have never been able to separate the idea of the State from the idea of their own. They have been extremely timid in freethinking. ... While there have been quite a number of heroes in the past century who willingly sacrificed themselves for the Party or the State, there have

been extremely few who dared to challenge the entire society in defense of individual freedom of thinking and writing.[86]

As an émigré, Gao turned his gaze away from a racially defined, ideological China to an aestheticized personal voice. He further elaborated this position in his Nobel lecture in December 2000, emphasizing that he wanted to use the opportunity to "speak as one writer in the voice of an individual." He went on to argue that

literature can only be the voice of the individual. ... Once literature is contrived as the hymn of the nation, the flag of the race, the mouthpiece of a political party or the voice of a class or a group, it can be employed as a mighty and all-engulfing tool of propaganda. Such literature loses what is inherent in literature, ceases to be literature, and becomes a substitute for power and profit.[87]

Gao's, Ngũgĩ wa Thiong'o's, and Chinua Achebe's resistance of the imposition of a racially determined national culture is understandable when we see even scholars trained to analyze social discursive practices make assumptions about national heritage. Stephen Owen, for example, criticizes Chinese poet-in-exile Bei Dao and many "third world" poets for pandering to Western tastes and by abandoning their "national identity." Owen believes that is why some works lend themselves to easy commodification and translation for cross-cultural consumption.[88] The idea of a national cultural heritage, when framed in this way, is problematic in that it assumes an alignment between cultural affiliation and race.

Coda: locating the epistemology of otherness

Who produces knowledge about race? In what context? The material we covered in this chapter might be summarized by the concept of hybridity, which is one of the terms that have been widely employed in postcolonial studies. As a practice in horticulture, hybridity is a cross-breeding process in which two species are grafted or cross-pollinated to form a new species. Frequently associated with the work of Homi K. Bhabha, the idea of hybridity refers to the interdependence of the colonizer and the colonized. In Bhabha's framework, all cultural identities exist in the ambivalent "third space of enunciation" and cultural purity is untenable.[89] Examples of hybridity, as we mentioned in this chapter, include pidgin and creole languages.

Each of the co-authors of this book has his and her origins outside Anglo-European metropolitan centers. Martin Orkin writes, self-consciously and critically, about race from Haifa, Israel, though he grew up in South Africa and was educated in Johannesburg and London. Born in Taiwan, educated in the United States, Germany, and the United Kingdom, and married to a Frenchman, Alexa Alice Joubin is based in Washington, DC, where she is conscious of her positionality as a diasporic subject—on both sides of the Atlantic and the Pacific—in her writings on globalization in a number of different languages. John Drakakis, the general editor of the Routledge New Critical Idiom series, of which this book is a part, is half Italian and half Greek in heritage and culturally Welsh and British.

Consideration of the interplay between their current positions within the Western academic metropolis and the implications for markings of race of their particular non-Western origins characterizes the crucially significant intervention of a group of scholars working on theoretical narratives concerned with identity and difference during the mid- and late twentieth century. We will examine only selected aspects of their substantial contributions to this debate, in order to suggest the kind of impact they had in the specific registering of epistemologies of otherness.

The French philosopher Jacques Derrida (1930–2004), who was Director of Studies at the École des Hautes Études en Sciences Sociales, Paris and a Professor of Humanities at the University of California, Irvine, considered in his writings the impact on him of his experiences as a Jewish native Algerian. Similarly the U.S. literary theorist Edward Said (1935–2003) who was a Professor at Columbia University, New York, repeatedly figured his birth in Palestine/Israel as a crucial marker of otherness. The French writer and essayist Albert Memmi (1920–) who is a Professor of Sociology at the University of Paris, Nanterre, also considers the impact of his conception of race on the fact of being born in Tunisia. Aimé Césaire was similarly concerned with the consequences of having been born in Martinique, another place of "otherness." The French Afro-Caribbean psychiatrist and social activist Frantz Fanon

(1925–1961) who worked in Lyon, France, and Algiers, also regarded his birth in Martinique as formative. Gayatri Chakravorty Spivak (1948–) the U.S. literary theorist who is a Professor at Columbia University, writes of the continuing importance of aspects of her birth and early experiences in Kolkata, India. And the U.S. critical theorist Homi K. Bhabha (1949–) who is a Professor of literary studies and of Postcolonial Studies at Harvard University has developed crucial literary and post-colonial notions in his conceptualization of the markings that are the result of his experience of being born in Mumbai, India.

Locations matter and locations of knowledge matter. Racial identities evolve and move with various types of immigration. Critical theorists of the Frankfurt School, led by Max Horkheimer, relocated to Los Angeles in 1941 during the war. Walter Benjamin, on the other hand, refused to leave Europe, while the new cultural location and vantage point of Herbert Marcuse and Theodor Adorno affected their writings on mass culture. For instance, Adorno and Horkheimer's concept of the "culture industry" as mass deception (*Kulturindustrie*), as outlined in their book, *Dialectic of Enlightenment* (1944), reflects their diasporic positionality. Their view that popular culture operates in the form of a factory churning out standardized products is influenced by their experience of Hollywood which was dominated by studio monopolization. As Jewish German émigrés, Adorno and Horkheimer were both outsiders in U.S. culture and insiders with regard to the operating principles of global entertainment industries. Likewise, after June 4, 1989, Chinese intellectuals working in the West have been unwilling or unable to return to China and instead remain in the diaspora.

Rey Chow self-consciously reflected on the evolving relationship between diasporic scholars and their objects of study "at home." She wrote that "internationalized Chinese women intellectuals" may become "a privileged class vis-à-vis the women in China." The study of race takes on an ethical urgency as Chinese women's writings are used as the "raw material" for research in the West. Scholars in the metropolitan West who study race are both insiders as native informants and outsiders as supposedly impartial observers. The imbalance within the relationship between diasporic scholars and their subject positions echo the relationship between a master narrative and native informant.[90] On the one hand, readers sometimes defer to, or even privilege, a racially charged perception of diasporic scholars' ethnic authenticity. On the other hand, the re-inscription of their alterity by others and by some diasporic scholars themselves encourages the production of unexamined assumptions of the production of specific epistemologies of otherness.

We have spoken of border crossings of all kinds, and nowhere is racial discourse more palpable and visible than at airport checkpoints. We will conclude this part of the discussion with an anecdote offered by Madhavi Menon in her book *Indifference to Difference: On Queer Universalism*. An immigration officer who quizzed Menon on her profession revealed his preconceptions of the naturalized alignment of race and subject of study. Upon hearing that Menon taught English literature, the officer asked if she specializes in V.S. Naipaul and Salman Rushdie. Because she was Indian and held an Indian passport, he was surprised to learn that she was a Shakespeare scholar. The assumption here is English literature scholars from India should teach Indian authors. Menon stated in the autobiographical opening of her book that she has frequently encountered this kind of surprise when traveling. At times she has been asked if she "worked on Indian authors who'd traveled out of India," because the immigration officer "wanted to know about traveling Indians from a traveling Indian." Once again, the location of knowledge is the key. As Menon concludes, "despite being motivated by a desire for difference, this thirst for knowledge detailed in advance the parameters within which that difference could be known and disseminated."[91] Epistemologies of otherness are invigorated and challenged at once by the cultural locations from which they emerge and to which they are transported.

Notes

1 Dorian Bell, *Globalizing Race: Antisemitism and Empire in French and European Culture*, Evanston: Northwestern University Press, 2018), 217–282; Rita Chin, Heide Fehrenbach, Geoff Eley, and Atina Grossmann, *After the Nazi Racial State: Difference and Democracy in Germany and Europe*, Ann Arbor: University of Michigan Press, 2009; John R. Bowen, *Why the French Don't Like Headscarves: Islam, the State, and Public Space*, Princeton: Princeton University Press, 2007;

Herrick Chapman and Laura L. Frader, eds., *Race in France: Interdisciplinary Perspectives on the Politics of Difference*, New York: Berghahn Books, 2004.

2 Sara Ahmed, *On Being Included: Racism and Diversity in Institutional Life*, Durham: Duke University Press, 2012, 2.

3 Michael Keevak, *Becoming Yellow: A Short History of Racial Thinking*, Princeton: Princeton University Press, 2011, 1.

4 Winthrop D. Jordan, *White over Black: American Attitudes toward the Negro, 1550–1812*, Chapel Hill: University of North Carolina Press, 1968, 4.

5 Don J. Wyatt, *The Blacks of Pre-modern China*, Philadelphia: University of Pennsylvania Press, 2009, 17–18.

6 Keevak, *Becoming Yellow*, 4.

7 K. Anthony Appiah, *Color Conscious: The Political Morality of Race*, Princeton: Princeton University Press, 1996, 69.

8 Pei-Chia Lan, *Global Cinderellas: Migrant Domestics and Newly Rich Employers in Taiwan*, Durham: Duke University Press, 2006, 4.

9 Daniel P.S. Goh, Matilda Gabrielpillai, Philip Holden, and Gaik Cheng Khoo, eds., *Race and Multiculturalism in Malaysia and Singapore*, London: Routledge, 2008, 2.

10 W.B. Yeats, *The Collected Poems of W. B. Yeats*, London: Macmillan, 1958, 211.

11 Alexa Alice Joubin, "The Theatricality of Religious Rhetoric: Gao Xingjian and the Meaning of Exile," *Theater Journal*, 63.3, 2011, 365–379.

12 T.S. Eliot, "The Waste Land, V: What the Thunder said," 366–376, in *Collected Poems 1909–1962*, London: Faber, 1974.

13 Eliot, *Collected Poems*, 85.

14 T.S. Eliot, *Knowledge and Experience in the Philosophy of F. H. Bradley*, London: Faber & Faber, 1964, 151.

15 Brian Niro, New York: Palgrave, 2003, 130. See also Terry Eagleton, *Exiles and Émigrés: Studies in Modern Literature*, London: Chatto & Windus, 1970.

16 Cited in Niro, *Race*, 141.

17 Niro, *Race*, 141–142.

18 Frank Dikötter, *The Discourse of Race in Modern China*, Hong Kong: Hong Kong University Press, 1992, 107–108.

19 Sun Wen (Sun Yatsen), *San minzhuyi* [*The Three Principles*], Shanghai: Shangwu yinshuguan, 1927, 4–5; translation from F.W. Price, *San min chu i: The Three Principles of the People*, Shanghai: China Committee, Institute of Pacific Relations, 1927, 11–12; and Dikötter, *The Discourse of Race in Modern China*, 124.

20 Carlos Rojas, *Homesickness: Culture, Contagion, and National Transformation in Modern China*, Cambridge: Harvard University Press, 2013, 11.

21 Rojas, *Homesickness*, 2–3.

22 http://blog.renren.com/share/247670697/4666114019, accessed February 1, 2018, Alexa Alice Joubin's translation.

23 Ania Loomba, *Shakespeare, Race, and Colonialism*, Oxford: Oxford University Press, 2002, 7.

24 Debbie Lum, dir., *Seeking Asian Female: A Documentary*, Chicken and Egg Pictures, 2012, DVD.

25 Lily Wong, *Transpacific Attachment: Sex Work, Media Networks, and Affective Histories of Chineseness*, New York: Columbia University Press, 2018, 147.

26 Celine Parreñas Shimizu, *The Hypersexuality of Race: Performing Asian/American Women on Screen and Scene*, Durham: Duke University Press, 2007, 1–29.

27 Daniel Lombroso and Yoni Appelbaum, " 'Hail Trump!': White Nationalists Salute the President-Elect," *Atlantic*, November 21, 2016, www.theatlantic.com/politics/archive/2016/11/richard-spencer-speech-npi/508379/, accessed February 10, 2018.

28 Josh Harkinson, "Meet the White Nationalist Trying to Ride the Trump Train to Lasting Power," *Mother Jones*, October 27, 2016, www.motherjones.com/politics/2016/10/richard-spencer-trump-alt-right-white-nationalist/, accessed February 22, 2018.

29 Audrea Lim, "The Alt-Right's Asian Fetish," *New York Times*, January 6, 2018, www.nytimes.com/2018/01/06/opinion/sunday/alt-right-asian-fetish.html?mtrref=www.google.com&assetType=opinion, accessed February 21, 2018.

30 Yu-fang Cho, *Uncoupling American Empire: Cultural Politics of Deviance and Unequal Difference, 1890–1910*, Albany: State University of New York Press, 2013, 5–6, 77–102.

31 Lily Wong, *Transpacific Attachment*, 26–27.

32 Kamala Kempadoo, Jyoti Sanghera, and Bandana Pattanaik, eds., *Trafficking and Prostitution Reconsidered: New Perspectives on Migration, Sex Work and Human Rights*, Boulder: Paradigm, 2005, xii.

33 Jeffrey Meyers, "The Politics of *A Passage to India*," *Journal of Modern Literature*, 1:3, 1971, 329–338, 329.

34 E.M. Forster, *A Passage to India*, New York: Harcourt Brace, 1924, Part 1, ch. 9, para. 17.

35 Forster, *A Passage to India*, Part 1, ch. 5, para. 21.

36 Forster, *A Passage to India*, Part 1, ch. 2, para. 16.

37 Yonatan Touval, "Colonial Queer Something," *Bloom's Modern Critical Interpretations: E.M. Forster's A Passage to India*, Philadelphia: Chelsea House, 2004, 111–128, 111.

38 E.M. Forster, *A Passage to India*, New York: Harcourt Brace, 1924, 312.

39 Touval, "Colonial Queer Something," 115.

40 Forster, *A Passage to India*, Part 2, ch. 14, para. 2.

41 Forster, *A Passage to India*, 184–185.

42 Forster, *A Passage to India*, Part 2, ch. 15, para. 4.

43 June Perry Levine, "An Analysis of the Manuscripts of *A Passage to India*," *PMLA*, 85:2, 1970, 284–294, 288.

44 Brenda R. Silver, "Periphrasis, Power, and Rape in *A Passage to India*," *NOVEL: A Forum on Fiction*, 22:1, 1988, 86–105, 100–101.

45 Frances L. Restuccia, "'A Cave of My Own': The Sexual Politics of Indeterminacy," *Raritan*, 9:2, Fall 1989, 110–128, 122.

46 Touval, "Colonial Queer Something," 114–115.

47 Restuccia, "A Cave of My Own," 111.

48 Quoted in Levine, "An Analysis of the Manuscripts of *A Passage to India*," 228.

49 Nadia Khomami, "#MeToo: How a Hashtag became a Rallying Cry Against Sexual Harassment," *Guardian*, October 20, 2017, www.theguardian.com/world/2017/oct/20/women-worldwide-use-hashtag-metoo-against-sexual-harassment, accessed February 1, 2018.

50 G. Balandier, "The Colonial Situation: A Theoretical Approach (1951)," trans. Robert A. Wagoner, in Immanuel Wallerstein, *Social Change: The Colonial Situation*, New York: John Wiley, 1966, 34–61; quoted in Rey Chow, *Writing Diaspora: Tactics of Intervention in Contemporary Cultural Studies*, Bloomington: Indiana University Press, 1993, 6.

51 Forster, *A Passage to India*, Part 2, ch. 24, para. 47.

52 Celia R. Daileader, *Racism, Misogyny, and the Othello Myth: Inter-racial Couples from Shakespeare to Spike Lee*, Cambridge: Cambridge University Press, 2005, 9–10.

53 W.E.B. Du Bois, *The Souls of Black Folk*, New York: Dover, 1903, 2–3. The term was first used in an *Atlantic Monthly* article titled "Strivings of the Negro People" in 1897.

54 Laura Edles and Scott Appelrouth, *Sociological Theory in the Classical Era*, Second Edition, Thousand Oaks: Pine Forge Press, 2010, 351–352.

55 W.E.B. Du Bois, *Black Reconstruction in the United States, 1860–1880*, New York: Harcourt Brace, 1977 (1935), 727.

56 David R. Roediger, *The Wages of Whiteness: Race and the Making of the American Working Class*, Revised Edition, London: Verso, 2007, 12.

57 Du Bois, *Black Reconstruction in the United States*, 700–701.

58 Bill D. Moyers, "What a Real President Was Like," *Washington Post*, November 1988, www.washingtonpost.com/archive/opinions/1988/11/13/ what-a-real-president-was-like/d483c1be-d0da-43b7-bde6-04e10106ff6c/?utm_term=.713830f4aaf0, accessed February 20, 2018.

59 Chinua Achebe, *Morning Yet on Creation Day*, New York: Anchor Press, 1975, xii.

60 Rosina Lippi-Green, "Chapter 15: The Unassimilable Races: What It Means to be Asian," *English with an Accent: Language, Ideology, and Discrimination in the United States*, Second Edition, London: Routledge, 2012, 281–302.

61 Ngũgĩ wa Thiong'o, *Decolonising the Mind: The Politics of Language in African Literature*, London: James Currey, 1986, xiv, 2, 4.

62 Ian Smith, *Race and Rhetoric in the Renaissance: Barbarian Errors*, New York: Palgrave Macmillan, 2009, 15.

63 Anthony Pagden, *European Encounters with the New World: From Renaissance to Romanticism*, New Haven: Yale University Press, 1993, 120.

64 All quotations from Shakespeare are taken from William Shakespeare, *The Riverside Shakespeare*, Second Edition, ed., G. Blakemore Evans, New York: Houghton Mifflin, 1996.

65 Patricia Akhimie, *Shakespeare and the Cultivation of Difference: Race and Conduct in the Early Modern World*, New York: Routledge, 2018, 2.

66 Jacques Derrida, *Of Hospitality: Anne Dufourmantelle Invites Jacques Derrida to Respond*, trans. Rachel Bowlby, Stanford: Stanford University Press, 2000, 3; see also Jacques Derrida, "Racism's Last Word," *Critical Inquiry*, 12:1, 1985, 290–299.

67 Jacques Derrida, *Monolingualism of the Other or, The Prosthesis of Origin*, trans. Patrick Mensah, Stanford: Stanford University Press, 1998, 14–15.

68 Derrida, *Monolingualism of the Other*, 39.

69 Derrida, *Monolingualism of the Other*, 41.

70 Matt Trueman, "Royal Shakespeare Company under Fire for not Casting enough Asian Actors," *Guardian*, October 19, 2012, www.guardian. co.uk/stage/2012/oct/19/royal-shakespeare-company-asian-actors? fb=optOut, accessed October 21, 2012.

71 On the conflicted Asian identities in diaspora, see Alexa Huang, "Asian American Theatre Re-imagined: *Shogun Macbeth* in New York," in Scott Newstok and Ayanna Thompson, eds., *Weyward Macbeth: Intersections of Race and Performance*, New York: Palgrave, 2009, 121–125; on colorblind casting in Shakespearean theatre, see Ayanna Thompson, ed., *Colorblind Shakespeare: New Perspectives on Race and Performance*, New York: Routledge, 2006.

72 Jyotsna Singh, "Wooing and Wedding," RSC program, *Much Ado About Nothing*, n.p.

73 Clare Brennan, Review of *Much Ado About Nothing*, *Guardian*, 4 August 2012, www.guardian.co.uk/stage/2012/aug/05/much-ado-about-nothing-review, accessed October 21, 2012.

74 Gitanjali Shahani, "Fighting the Merry War," RSC program, *Much Ado About Nothing*, n.p.

75 Kate Rumbold (Review of *Much Ado About Nothing*, *Year of Shakespeare* blog, August 10, 2012, http://bloggingshakespeare.com/year-of-shakespeare-much-ado-about-nothing-at-the-rsc, accessed October 21, 2012), for example, writes that

> the combination of the distinctive space of the Globe, the otherness of its foreign visitors, the absence of English language, and even the Globe's seeming proximity to Shakespeare, has evidently ascribed to participants in the "Globe to Globe" festival in particular a new degree of "authenticity".

76 Iqbal Khan, "1960s Birmingham to 2012 Stratford-upon-Avon," in Dalia Jarrett-Macauley, ed., *Shakespeare, Race and Performance: The Diverse Bard*, London: Routledge, 2017, 137–145, 140–141.

77 Rumbold, Review of *Much Ado About Nothing*.

78 Kevin Quarmby, Review of *Much Ado About Nothing*, *British Theatre Guide*, www.britishtheatreguide.info/reviews/much-ado-about-rsc-courtyard-t-7732, accessed October 21, 2012.

79 Kwok-kan Tam, "Gao Xingjian, the Nobel Prize and the Politics of Recognition," in Kwok-kan Tam, ed., *Soul of Chaos: Critical Perspectives on Gao Xingjian*, Hong Kong: Chinese University Press, 2001, 1–20.

80 Gao Xingjian, "Wo zhuzhang yi zhong leng de wenxue" [I advocate a cold literature, July 30, 1990], in *Meiyou zhuyi*, 18–20; Sy Ren Quah, *Gao Xingjian and Transcultural Chinese Theater*, Honolulu: University of Hawaii Press, 2004, 186.

81 Gao Xingjian, "Jinghua ye tan" [Evening talks in Beijing], *Zhongshan*, 5, 1987, 198.

82 Gao's discontent with the role frequently assigned to writers in the exilic realm is shared by many diasporic intellectuals. One recent example is Sylvia Molloy's illuminating article on the topic, in which she recalls her experience as an Argentine and Latin-American studying in France during the 1960s. Her dissertation advisor assigned her a dissertation topic: the reception of Latin-American literature in France. Despite having trained in French and knowing very little about Latin-American literature, she "was ... assigned the role of the native informant, a role

[she has] been asked to play more than once since then." See Molloy, "Postcolonial Latin America and the Magic Realist Imperative: A Report to the Academy," in Sandra Bermann and Michael Wood, eds., *Nation, Language, and the Ethics of Translation*, Princeton: Princeton University Press, 2005, 370–379.

83 Gao Xingjian, "Meiyou zhuyi" [Without isms], *Wenyi bao*, 1, 1995, 46.

84 Gao Xingjian, "Meiyou zhuyi."

85 Gao Xingjian, "Wenxue de liyou" [The case for literature], trans. Mable Lee, *PMLA*, 116:3, 2001, 605.

86 "Guojia shenhua yu geren diankuang" [Nationalist myth and individualistic madness], *Mingbao yuekan*, 8, 1993, 16 (English translation revised from Henry Y.H. Zhao's *Towards a Modern Zen Theatre: Gao Xingjian and Chinese Theatre Experimentalism*, London: School of Oriental and African Studies, 2000, 128).

87 Gao, "Wenxue de liyou," 594.

88 Stephen Owen, "The Anxiety of Global Influence: What is World Poetry?" *New Republic*, November 19, 1990, 28–32, 29, 31–32.

89 Homi K. Bhabha, *The Location of Culture*, London: Routledge, 2004 (1994), 55–56.

90 Rey Chow, *Writing Diaspora: Tactics of Intervention in Contemporary Cultural Studies*, Bloomington: Indiana University Press, 1993, 109–110.

91 Madhavi Menon, *Indifference to Difference: On Queer Universalism*, Minneapolis: University of Minnesota Press, 2015, 1.

CONCLUSION

RACE IN THE WORLD

Humans come to know and experience the world through various categories that organize it into knowable fragments. All rational beings understand the world in terms of space and time, and deploy categories such as cause and effect, substance, unity, plurality, necessity, possibility, and reality. That is, whenever we think about anything, we do so in certain ways; for example, as having causes, as existing or not existing, as being one thing or many things, as being real or imaginary, as being something that has to exist or doesn't have to exist. We think this not simply because we passively reflect the way the world is, but rather because that is the way that our minds order experience. There can be no knowledge without sensation, but sense data alone cannot provide knowledge. Throughout history, people tend to think in terms of categories that help them to demarcate difference. In the process, we also shape the world with the language we use to describe it.

Inevitably some narratives privilege the storyteller's own cultural location as a superior center and the rest of the world as inferior and peripheral. This is a tendency that is especially evident in myths about the origin of human races in various cultures. For example, according to a Chinese myth, different skin tones are related to accidents in the creation process. When the gods created humans out of clay figures, they initially left the clay in the kiln for too long. The figure came out burned and black. The gods threw it as far as they could, and it landed in Africa. They took the second figure out of the kiln too soon, which is pale and white. They threw it away, and it landed in Europe. Once the gods determined the correct timing, they created the perfect figure in gorgeous yellow, who became the ancestor of the superior East Asian yellow races. Along a similar vein of constructing racial hierarchies, early modern Europe devoted significant social energy to the idea of "blue blood," an idea about racial purity, or *sangre azul* in Spanish. The nobility's "blue" veins are visible through their fair skin, because, according to this ideology, their lineage has never been "contaminated" by Moorish or Jewish blood. There can be no knowledge without sensation, but sense data alone, as we have already suggested, cannot provide knowledge either. Throughout history, people tend to think in terms of categories that help them to demarcate difference, and people tend to privilege their own cultural locations. Racialized thinking is often a projection of one's desires, ambitions, anxieties, or ignorance.

Word made flesh

The *Oxford English Dictionary* shows that the word race comes from the twelfth century French word *haraz*, which refers to horse breeding: "an enclosure in which horses and mares are kept for breeding." The word race therefore refers to breeds of horses. In English, race is initially used to indicate a whole range of human differences that include gender and class. It simply refers to differentiated communities rather than specifically to people of different skin colors or heritage, such as "the bounteous race/Of woman kind" in Edmund Spencer's *Faeirie Queene*. As such, men and women might be said to be the first races. As the word evolved, it came to denote not only broad categories of human difference but also ethnicity and national origin, as in such expressions as the race of "the Britons" and "the Spanish race" in Raphael Holinshed's *Chronicles* in 1587.[1] By the seventeenth century, race began to describe complexion and even physiology, though the alignment of positivity, negativity, and particular skin tone is not always obvious. It is notable that the relative hierarchical positions of various races were fluid and mobile depending on contexts. While Shakespeare's *Othello* ascribed positive and negative traits to the Moorish general's cultural and religious origin, Ben Jonson attached positive value to blackness in his 1605 *Masque of Blackness* when he describes the "Fair Niger" and "all his beauteous race."[2] Moreover, the word race was used to refer to various species beyond human beings. The Clown in Shakespeare's *Winter's Tale* uses the word race when he means root, as in "a race or two of ginger" at a sheep-shearing festival.[3] It is not surprising that race is associated with root, because root is a term often used to refer to lineage, heritability, and familial origin. Ayanna Thompson and Jason Demeter refer to this feature in early modern writing as a form of "lexical convergence."[4] Shakespeare, specifically, used "race" to evoke breeds of horses, species of plants, and categories of humans. The overlapping meanings and connotations provide occasions for rich poetic expression and food for thought.

In contemporary American culture, race, too, has multiple and contradictory meanings. On the one hand, race commonly refers to heritable traits of skin color and hair type. On the other hand, race is associated with culturally inflected mannerisms, such as what one eats, how one speaks, and how one carries herself or himself. In current American cultural discourses, race often brings to mind people who are not white, while whiteness remains unmarked and serves as a benchmark category—as if white is not a race. The second feature in American racial discourses is the alignment of a race-based social group with innate or inner qualities rather than class. Third, the focus on black and white sometimes obscures other groups within the United States, such that Hispanics, Latinos, Chicanos, and Native Americans often fall under the rubric of ethnicities rather than "race."

Throughout this book, we have discussed biological markings of difference (Chapter 2), religiously inflected boundaries (Chapter 1), geographical determinism, socially inflected understanding of race (Chapter 3, for example), and intersections of race and gender (Chapter 5). What is important to bear in mind is that, ultimately, race as a concept is profoundly constituted by language, by narratives, and by attempts to codify what exactly the term includes and excludes.

While individuals manifest various qualities and markers of identity, these differences will only emerge once they are noted. In medical science, race is a factor in the study of genetics, statistics, public health, and the calculation of the probability of vulnerability, as in the case of the susceptibility of a certain group to suffer from a particular disease. However, as Kim Hall argues, "The easy association of race with modern science ignores the fact that language itself creates social differences ... and that race was then ... a social construct that is fundamentally more about power and culture than about biological difference."[5] In this regard, one may say that race is a red herring, a signifier that accumulates meaning by a chain of deferral to other categories of difference such as gender, class, education. These categories of difference are dependent upon access to financial resources and the freedom, or lack thereof, to inhabit various forms of subjectivity. In short, the possibilities of social mobility and immigration complicate a society's racial landscape. Race seems to be predicated upon upbringing, which is probably what was meant by the comment that President Obama was "not black enough" by Ben Carson, a candidate for President of the United States in the Republican primaries in 2016. Carson suggested that his upbringing differs dramatically from that of Obama, and therefore Carson will be better able to represent the black experience. Obama was "raised white" and is therefore an "African" American rather than an African-American.[6]

The issue becomes complicated when skin color enters into dialogue with those categories that are dependent upon material circumstances (economics, education). Physiological difference has no cultural meaning until it enters into the discourse of race and the cultural differentiations that it carries with it; that discourse inheres in language and the act of noting. It facilitates racial difference. To this extent, it is not possible to describe race and histories of race without leaving the trace of the observer. In invoking various markings and boundaries, descriptions of racial histories bring these differences to the fore, and can prepare the ground for the possibility of political intervention.

Ocular proof

However, race may exemplify an age old question of which comes first, the chicken or the egg. Race, and the cultural differentiations that it implies, comes into being through language, as language and the act of noting enable racial differences. One cannot describe race and histories of race without the observer leaving her or his mark.

Literary works show us that racial differences emerge once they are noted and narrated. In Shakespeare's *Antony and Cleopatra*, Mark Antony tells Cleopatra that they are about to "wander through the streets and note/The qualities of people" (1.1.55–1.1.56). The race of a homogeneous group may be unremarkable, but the race of a minority group would be a matter of note. Othello's blackness makes the character stand out in his adopted Venetian society, because "blackness" signals a wide range of positive and negative attributes once it becomes notable. Furthermore, Othello is notable for being a white man in blackface make-up. The fact that Othello was a role created for and played by the white early modern English actor Richard Burbage sets the character apart from others in the play.[7] Sethe, a mother who escapes slavery in American novelist Toni Morrison's *Beloved* (1987), carries the burden of past suffering on her back. She has been whipped as a slave, and the scars on her back become a marker of her race and identity. The novel follows her recovery from the emotional and physical scars. In Sethe's own words to Paul D, her scars resemble a tree which turns her body into soil for new life: "I got a tree on my back and a haint [ghost] in my house, and nothing in between but the daughter I am holding in my arms."[8] Amy, the white girl who saves Sethe's life during her escape, identifies the scars as a chokecherry tree.[9] The tree mainly grows in Virginia and Caroline. Othello's blackness becomes notable in contrast to his new communities, and Sethe's tree both marks her suffering and root part of her identity in geographic centers of slavery. Sethe's tree is most likely not notable when she is a slave before her escape, for scars are taken for granted as part of a slave's life. Not only can skin color and scars become notable when contexts change, but eye colors, too, are often the object of the gaze. In Morrison's *The Bluest Eye* (1970),[10] Pecola, a poor black child, believes that possessing blue eyes would give her white privilege and enhance her life. She would literally see the world differently through blue eyes. Ironically, for Claudia blue eyes do not symbolize the cachet of whiteness. She resents the blue eyes on her white dolls. In contrast to what is commonly termed "people of color," as we noted in Chapter 5, whiteness often goes unmarked and unremarked, because it is considered the norm in, for example, modern day United States. As the norm, it is not notable and, when an idea goes unnoticed, it is taken for granted and becomes invisible.

Locations of race

Locations of race matter. In contrast to the continuing Anglo-European West remarking on non-white people, whiteness as a value in contemporary East Asia has become a yardstick of intelligence, beauty, and desirability because even in the post-colonial world people still tend to internalize colonial categories of difference. Nonetheless, race is marked differently in different cultural locations, and, depending on the geographical location of the observer, it is sometimes, as Edward Said has shown in his book *Orientalism* (1978),[11] intertwined with a projected exoticism. The effect does not lead to a positive experience of the racial minority in East Asia. Bulgarian-French feminist Julia Kristeva describes her experience of being othered while visiting the village of Huxian in her *Des Chinoises*: "The villagers stare at the white visitors fixedly, as if they are discovering strange or funny animals that are harmless." The animals are so strange that they do not make sense. Kristeva notes that "I don't feel like a foreigner ... I feel like an ape, a martian, an other."[12] The villagers' curiosity does not derive from the European visitors' skin color alone. What Kristeva experienced was a post-revolutionary Chinese response to the Caucasian presence in the context of a general Chinese communist censorship of the democratic West. The villagers showed genuine curiosity towards white foreigners. The story would have been quite different in pre-revolutionary China. Since the late nineteenth century, the unfolding of Western exoticism in modern Chinese culture was linked to the presence of Chinese intellectuals returning from abroad and the rise of Western enclaves in Chinese urban centers. In

Republican China during the early twentieth century, dogs and Chinese were regularly banned in semi-colonial enclaves ruled by various European countries in Shanghai.[13] Thus, the Chinese interest in exotic commodities was fraught with ambivalence, and race in this context is associated more with exotic objects and wealth than with lineage.[14] For the European powers in Shanghai, the Chinese alterity posed a threat. Genuine self-reflection is an important moment for members of otherwise dominant social groups. We are not aware of the category of "race" until we are confronted with otherness, with alterity and with the gaze of others.

Furthermore, location matters in our historical understanding of racial formations. First, our understanding is skewed by our own dominant cultural locations and biases. Second, notions of race themselves are inflected by political locations. As we showed in Chapter 1, two of the predominant approaches to cultural difference, historically, are (1) the geo-humoral theory which posits that a person's features and temperament are determined by geographic location as well as climate; and (2) a theory that focuses on lineage and descent, which draws on a notion of biologically fixed racial lines of difference. Rooted in Hippocrates' and Galen's works, the humoral theory holds that a balance of bodily humors leads to healthy individuals. Climate was thought to be connected to the overall composition of individuals' humors. People living around the Mediterranean were thought to have the most harmonious balance of humors due to the region's moderate climate, while black Africans were believed to be disadvantaged by extreme heat because they lived closer to the Equator; their excess of black bile produced a friendly demeanor, but also cowardice. It was also believed that moving between different climate zones could lead to changes in complexion and physiology.[15] Geo-humoral theory seems to posit that race is impermanent, while the theory of lineage is fixated upon heritability, as manifested in the Nazi era's fixation upon the relative merits and weaknesses of the German "Aryan" race and marginalized others such as Jews, gypsies, and homosexuals.

From our own historical and political vantage points, these approaches are no longer credible or creditable. They do, however, remind us that we should be wary of "positing a simple opposition between nature and culture, or suggesting that a 'cultural' understanding of race is somehow benign or flexible [because] what we call 'race' and what we call 'culture' cannot be readily separated."[16] That said, the cultural relativism that has sometimes been posited is not without its own difficulties. Adopting a discursive notion of race does not obscure embodied, lived experiences of difference, nor does it relegate differences to the realm of abstraction. As UK-based Jamaican-born cultural theorist Stuart Hall (1932–2014) cogently argues, "what matters are the systems we use to make human societies intelligible."[17] Instead of focusing on a tree, even if it is Sethe's chokecherry tree (an individual's experience), and missing the forest (a society's attitude towards race), we should pay attention to the social infrastructures in place to mark and regulate racialized experiences.

A recent example of how narratives can move beyond both biology and heritage is the Oscar-winning film *Twelve Years a Slave* (dir. Steve McQueen, 2013) which focuses on Solomon Northup (Chiwetel Ejiofor) who is kidnapped from New York and sold into slavery in Louisiana. While race and negritude determines one's social position in the film's universe, the film examines race without routing the concept through biology. Instead, the film critiques capitalism and slavery. It also draws attention to the interconnected histories of people of African descent's movement across national borders. Racial identities are thus framed by local markers that are fluid and not biologically determined. However, such high-profile films inevitably draw attention to the identity of its creators. During a press conference at the Toronto International Film Festival, McQueen was asked that if he was an African-American, rather than a black British, director, would the film be different. He responded by emphasizing the collective history of slavery: "It's not about me being British. It's about me being part of that history [of people of African descent in the black diaspora]." He pointed out his own Grenadian descent, and the diasporic backgrounds of the film's actors: Chiwetel is British Nigerian and Lupita Nyong'o (Patsey) is Mexican Kenyan. While the question from the journalist was a well-intended and valid one, it reveals a limiting, philosophical investment in the alignment of one's racial identity and work, as if an African-American director would necessarily tell a better story of slavery. By the same token, as we pointed out in Chapter 5, cultural location matters more than racial and ethnic coordinates. Similar to the journalist's unspoken assumption, the Anglophone academy often assumes that scholars located in, for example, Asia, or who are of Asian descent, would necessarily be better equipped to understand Asian cultures regardless of their academic training. One's blood relations should not have any bearing on the scientific and intellectual inquiry into any particular culture.

Disowning race

If race is a central part of human identity, can one own or disown one's race? To which community would a multiracial person, immigrant, or diasporic subject belong? We would like to offer three cases with open-ended questions to conclude the present study.

In her 1893 short story, "Désirée's Baby," American writer Kate Chopin thinks this complex question through fiction. An adopted child with unknown parentage, Désirée, grows up to marry Armand. Their baby, as it turns out, is part black, which is seen as scandalous in antebellum Louisiana. Infuriated and assuming that Désirée is the culprit, Armand sends his wife and the baby away, going so far as to burn the cradle. It is revealed at the end that in fact Armand is the one who is part black. The moral seems ambiguous. One may ask: is this instance driven by Armand's refusal to recognize his own racial identity, or the fear of being othered—hence his need to cast Désirée as the deceiver? Multiracial subjects are often suspect because of their assumed multiple allegiances to different and even opposing communities.

More recently, in 2015, Rachel Dolezal, the head of the Spokane, Washington, chapter of the U.S. National Association for the Advancement of Colored People (NAACP), has been exposed by news media as having misrepresented herself as African-American when her lineage seems to be Czech, Swedish, and German. Notably Dolezal does not align herself with white supremacist ideologies, and, based on what we know so far, she has not done the NAACP any harm. The incident raised a storm over social media and major news outlets in the United States, initiating debates about the notion of passing and racial and cultural authenticity.[18] In *Passing and the Fictions of Identity*, Elaine Ginsberg offers a social theory of the phenomenon of a mixed-race or biracial person identifying as, or being seen as, members of different racial groups.[19] Light-skinned African-Americans during periods of racial segregation "passed" for white as a strategy of survival. Members of a minority group may adopt a new accent, grooming habits, and names to blend in with members of a privileged, majority group. While it is often a form of self-preservation, the notion of passing as members of a different race, gender, class, and even dis/ability status is problematic in that it pitches presumably essential, innate, authentic identities against identities in borrowed robes. The notion presupposes that some identities are more authentic than others.

Such cases prompt the question: is there any substance to racial identity or does it depend upon the capacity to perform it? The public anxiety surrounding this case shows that race is often, if not exclusively, defined in relation to an other. If Dolezal can be black, what is black, and who is white? As Mark Orbe argues, this case reveals "implicit ways in which social constructions of race are not natural, logical, or irrefutable."[20] Race is not intelligible when it is not visible or exhibited in some palpable form of cultural practice. In Elaine Ginsberg's words, the Dolezal incident exposes a "category crisis" that "destabilizes the grounds of privilege founded on racial identity."[21] In a broader context, the Dolezal incident reveals deep-seated anxieties about the diaspora, immigration, cultural appropriation, and passing—circumstances in which one's heritage is not readily visible or legible. As an identity marker, race is seen by many as proprietary. It is personal and cannot be appropriated, nor can it simply be adopted by performative gestures.

Last, but not least, if race is understood in popular culture in terms of both cultural practice and genetic expression, what future is there for race as a viable analytical concept? Might race become a broader or narrower category of genetic difference and class? Andrew Niccol's 1997 sci-fi dystopian film *Gattaca* imagines a post-racial scenario, one that goes beyond eugenics. Vincent Freeman (Ethan Hawke), a genetically inferior man—one of the few who are born naturally—takes on the identity of a genetically designed man born in the laboratory as most humans are in the film. Freeman has been categorized as a member of an underclass suitable only for menial jobs due to his inferior genetic make-up. Aspiring to travel to space, Freeman takes on a form of racial passing by assuming the identity of Jerome Morrow. The film portrays discrimination against the "genetically unenhanced" as similar to racism and classism in our times; after all, the underclass is labeled by such derogatory names as "in-valids," "faith births," and "defectives." As critic David Kirby observes, "rather than leading to the racial utopia as depicted in *Gattaca*, the acceptance of a genetic basis of race will only further segregate society."[22] *Gattaca* turns the premise of a utopian "post-racial" society on its head and shows the dystopian tendency of a biology-driven understanding of race.[23] The vocabulary of race matters, because the vocabulary at one's disposal determines the nature and quality of the inquiry.

Race, like many identity markers, is social shorthand for articulating differences.[24] Race is as personal as it is political. People feel a sense of possession over their race, and can be offended by any act of appropriation. As shown throughout this book, which focuses largely but not exclusively on race in the Anglo-European West, projects to conceptualize race are complicated by a symbiotic relation between definition and self-fulfilling prophecy, between typology and racism. Thinking through race estranges what is taken for granted. The construction of race is a process that emphasizes subjection and responsiveness to the demands of others. We study race historically not only to find roots of modern racism, but also to discover other views that may have been obscured by more dominant ideologies such as colonialism. Literary and historical texts contain traces of these alternative perspectives and past debates. Reading histories of race may be a passive act, but if it leads to recognition of one's self in others, then our job as critical analysts is done.

Notes

1 Raphael Holinshed, *Chronicles*, 1587, 14: 1088.
2 Ben Jonson, *Masque of Blackness*, 1605, 2.81–2.82.
3 William Shakespeare, *Winter's Tale*, 4.3.46. All quotations from Shakespeare are taken from William Shakespeare, *The Riverside Shakespeare*, Second Edition, ed., G. Blakemore Evans, New York: Houghton Mifflin, 1996.
4 Jason Demeter and Ayanna Thompson, "Shakespeare and Early Modern Race Studies: An Overview of the Field," in Jill L Levenson and Robert Ormsby, eds., *The Shakespearean World*, New York: Routledge, 2017, 574–589, 581.

5 Kim Hall, *Things of Darkness: Economies of Race and Gender in Early Modern England*, Ithaca: Cornell University Press, 1995, 6.

6 Ben Carson: "Many of his formative years were spent in Indonesia. So, for him to, you know, claim that, you know, he identifies with the experience of black Americans, I think, is a bit of a stretch." Jonathan Capehart, "Ben Carson and Cornel West actually Agree: Obama's 'Not Black Enough'," *Washington Post*, February 23, 2016, www.washingtonpost.com/blogs/post-partisan/wp/2016/02/23/ben-carson-and-cornel-west-actually-agree-obamas-not-black-enough/?utm_term=.98cbdbd1ffc4, accessed July 20, 2017.

7 Dympna Callaghan, *Shakespeare Without Women: Representing Gender and Race on the Renaissance Stage*, New York: Routledge, 2000, 75–96.

8 Toni Morrison, *Beloved*, New York: Plume Fiction, 1988, 15.

9 Morrison, *Beloved*, 79.

10 Toni Morrison, *The Bluest Eye*, New York: Alfred A. Knopf, 1994 (1970).

11 Edward W. Said, *Orientalism*, New York: Vintage, 1978.

12 "Comme s'ils découvraient des animaux bizarres et drôles, inoffensifs mais insensés [...] Je me sens singe, martienne, autre." Julia Kristeva, *Des Chinoises*, Paris: Pauvert/Fayard, 2001, 26.

13 For an informative account of expatriate life in the treaty ports, see Frances Wood, *Nog Dogs and Not Many Chinese*, London: John Murray, 2000. For an analysis, see Julia Lovell, *The Opium War: Drugs, Dreams, and the Making of Modern China*, London: Picador, 2011.

14 Frank Dikötter, *Exotic Commodities: Modern Objects and Everyday Life in China*, New York: Columbia University Press, 2007, 2–3. On how Chinese discourses of race emerged at the end of the nineteenth century under the guise of science, see Dikötter, *The Discourse of Race in Modern China*, London: C. Hurst & Co., 1992, xiii.

15 Jean E. Feerick, *Strangers in Blood: Relocating Race in the Renaissance*, Toronto: University of Toronto Press, 2010, 110.

16 Ania Loomba, *Shakespeare, Race, and Colonialism*, Oxford: Oxford University Press, 2002, 38.

17 Stuart Hall, ed., *Representation: Cultural Representations and Signifying Practices*, London: Sage Publications and the Open University, 1997, 10.

18 Among those who support "transracialism" is Rebecca Tuvel. See Rebecca Tuvel, *Hypatia*, 32:2, Spring 2017, 263–278.

19 Elaine Ginsberg, *Passing and the Fictions of Identity*, Durham: Duke University Press, 1996.

20 Mark P. Orbe, "The Rhetoric of Race, Culture, and Identity: Rachel

Dolezal as Co-Cultural Group Member," *Journal of Contemporary Rhetoric*, 6:1/2, 2016, 23–35.

21 Elaine K. Ginsberg, "Introduction," in Elaine K. Ginsberg, ed., *Passing and the Fictions of Identity*, Durham: Duke University Press, 1996, 8.

22 David A. Kirby, "Extrapolating Race in *Gattaca*: Genetic Passing, Identity, and the Science of Race," *Literature and Medicine*, 23:1, Spring 2004, 184–200, 198; and David A. Kirby, "The New Eugenics in Cinema: Genetic Determinism and Gene Therapy in *Gattaca*," *Science Fiction Studies*, 81:27, July 2000, 193–215.

23 David Theo Goldberg posits that the fantasy of post-raciality is structured around the ability to live "outside of debilitating racial difference." A post-racial society, by definition, would not allow "the key conditions of social life" to be predicated on "racial preferences" (*Are We All Postracial Yet?* Cambridge: Polity Press, 2015, 2).

24 The term social shorthand comes from Terence Hawkes, *Meaning by Shakespeare*, London: Routledge, 2012, 4.

GLOSSARY

Analytical category   an imagined analytical tool used to construct the conceptual basis of social relations.

Anthropological   the study of human beings held to be similar to or to diverge from animals.

Apartheid   a South African policy of segregation on grounds of race.

Authentication   the process or action of proving or showing something to be true, genuine, or valid.

Barbarism   a foreign state or condition imagined as uncivilized in comparison with familiar social culture and practice.

Binary assumptions   classification into two distinct, opposite but mutually constitutive forms.

Biological essence   assertion of physiological qualities (distinguished as real essence); that quality which constitutes or marks the allegedly true nature of anything.

Causal mechanisms   the processes or pathways through which an outcome is brought into being.

Civilized   marked by familiar laws and rules about how people behave with each other.

Classification   a particular way of ordering representations of what is perceived as reality.

Colonization   the action or process of settling among and establishing control over the indigenous people of an area.

Color   a visual marker of imagined characteristics.

Construction   the imagined structures underlying social existence.

Continuum   a continuous sequence in which adjacent elements are not perceptibly different from each other, although the extremes are quite distinct.

Contradiction   a combination of statements, ideas, or features of a situation that are opposed to one another.

Counter-identification   identification with the other in a way that transfers negative associations onto the subject in question.

Cultural diversity   differences such as those in particular cultural or economic or gender practices.

Culture   the sum total of ways of living practiced by a group of human beings and reiterated in time.

Deconstruction   analysis of underlying structures determining identity.

Diaspora or exile forced or voluntary movement across geopolitical borders, sometimes to escape undesirable ideologies.

Difference a point or way in which imagined people or things are not the same.

Discourse a way of arguing or writing existence into being.

Doubleness ambiguities in the perception of identity.

Environmental imagining the human world and the impact of human activity on its condition.

Ethnicity a social group that shares a common and distinctive culture, religion, language, or the like.

Eurocentrism viewing the world from the perspective of Europe.

Fixed not subject to change or fluctuation.

Great chain of being strict hierarchical structure of all matter and life, thought in medieval Christianity to have been decreed by God, and stretching from heaven to earth.

Hierarchies a system or organization in which people or groups are ranked one above the other according to status or authority.

Hybridity a cross between two cultures, plants, or languages.

Iconography traditions of visual representation.

Identity the fact of being who or what a person or thing is imagined to be.

Ideology a system of ideas and ideals, especially one which forms the basis of economic or political theory and policy.

Judicial structures alleged to be representative of inherent justice.

Knowledge production differences treated as factual.

Legislative structured according to particular legal systems.

Marginalization representing the subject matter as insignificant.

Marking investing particular subjects with particular characteristics.

Material conditions underlying economic features and physical structures that are imagined to determine social being.

Metaphorical representation referring to one thing by mentioning another.

Metonymic a figure of speech consisting of the use of the name of one thing for that of another.

Miscegenation a term applied negatively to marriage or cohabitation between people from different racial groups.

Misogyny hatred, demeaning, and discrimination of women.

Monogenesis the emergence from a single cause.

Mythological tradition familiar ways of telling stories, usually associated with folk traditions and myths.

National the construction of an imagined community of particular groups, often based on shared language, understood as primary.

Nationalism   a feeling of superiority exerted by one cultural and language group over other countries and/or groups thought to be inferior.

Naturalized traits   any trait of human activity acquired in social life and transmitted by communication.

Negritude   the affirmation or consciousness of the value of black or African culture, heritage, and identity.

Occlusion   obscuring or deleting.

Orientalism   traits imagined by the West in the representation of Asia, especially the Middle East, in a stereotyped way that is regarded as embodying a colonialist attitude.

Origins   the point or place where something is said to have begun.

Patristic traditions   patriarchal ways of telling stories, with an emphasis upon masculine narratives.

Personhood   imagined qualities assigned to particular individuals.

Phenotypic   observable physical characteristics determined by both genetic make-up and environmental influences.

Phrenology   study of the shape and size of the cranium as a supposed indication of character and mental abilities.

Polygenism   the theory that the human race has descended from two or more ancestral types.

Projection   humans defending themselves against their own unconscious impulses or qualities (both positive and negative) by denying their existence in themselves while attributing them to others.

Proto-scientific   an imagined order.

Pseudo sciences   a collection of beliefs or practices mistakenly regarded as being based on scientific method.

Race   an imagined construction of alleged traits also alleged to be the characteristics of particular economic or socially different groups.

Racial nationalisms   seeks to preserve a given race through policies such as banning race mixing and the immigration of other races.

Reiteration   characters or historical events that, by some association, have come to stand for a certain thing or an idea.

Representation   the description or portrayal of someone or something in a particular way or as being of a certain nature.

Ritual   repetitive social practice.

Savage   a member of a people regarded as primitive and uncivilized in comparison with the social practice of a particular community.

Selfhood   imagined identity—the quality that constitutes one's individuality.

Slavery   the system by which people are owned by other people as slaves.

Social evolution   the gradual development of society and social forms, institutions, etc., usually through a series of imagined stages.

The Monstrous a person or an action inhumanly or outrageously evil or wrong.

The Other that which lies outside shared conventional knowledge or cultural practice.

Theorizing a particular way of conceptualizing and ordering representations of what is perceived as reality.

Theoretical principles the ideas and abstract principles that relate to a particular subject.

Unrealizability the real and the unreal suggested within the same word.

Xenophobia intense or irrational dislike or fear of people from other countries.

INDEX

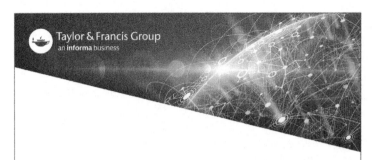

Made in the USA
Coppell, TX
10 June 2023

17919713R00144